Teaching Business Education 14–19

Martin Jephcote • Ian Abbott

 David Fulton Publishers

This edition reprinted 2008 by Routledge
2 Park Square, Milton Park, Abingdon, Oxon OX14 4RN
Simultaneously published in the USA and Canada
270 Madison Avenue, New York, NY10016

First published in Great Britain by David Fulton Publishers 2005
Transferred to digital printing

British Library Cataloguing in Publication Data
A catalogue record for this book is available from the British Library.

ISBN 1 84312 254 5

Typeset by FiSH Books, London
Printed and bound in the UK by Ashford Colour Press Ltd, Gosport, Hants.

100 Multiple Choice Questions and Answers for A Level Economics

These are organised in topics and are excellent for review purposes and a particular aid to candidates studying for AQA AS Economics, which has a multiple choice paper. The more past papers which become available, probably the less need for an alternative supply, you might think; however, this does save the teacher the tedious task of collecting past questions and organising them into topics to be useful at the appropriate points in a course, a not inconsiderable benefit.

15 Data Response Questions for AS and A Level Economics

These questions are particularly geared towards giving students practice in examination skills such as data-handling and interpretation, application, analysis and evaluation. The writer points out common errors made by candidates with suggestions for extending answers. The suggested answers might also make this a useful resource for the purposes of formative assessment.

Index

Teaching
Business Education
14–19

Also available

Teaching 14–19
Everything you need to know about learning and teaching across the phases
Gina Donovan
1-84312-342-8

Teaching in Post-Compulsory Education
Policy, practice and values
Anthony Coles
1-84312-233-2

In at the Deep End
A survival guide for teachers in post-compulsory education
Jim Crawley
1-84312-253-7

Becoming a Secondary School Teacher
How to make a success of your initial teacher training
Peter Fleming
1-84312-103-4

Contents

Preface

Teaching Business Education 14–19 is a new contribution to the literature designed to meet the needs of beginning and experienced teachers. It has evolved out of a long-standing relationship between the publishing community and the Economics and Business Education Association going back over a number of years. The major departure in this book is the shift in emphasis from economics to business education, and this reflects the trends in course development, examination entries and assessment that are prevalent in schools and colleges. The subject area has continued to grow in schools, colleges and universities, but this growth has been primarily in business studies. The content of the book is, therefore, a response to the changes that have taken place over a period of time. It seeks to capture what is currently important to teachers of business education subjects, but also indicates key areas in which developments are taking place.

One of the major differences between this and the previous books borne out of this relationship is the rapidly changing external context in which education is constructed and enacted. Devolved governance means increasingly that educational policy is being written and implemented in different arenas and gives rise to different sorts of curriculum structures. Currently external examinations provide a more-or-less common framework within which the subject area operates. However, proposed changes to post-14 education are likely to have a significant impact on the way in which business education is taught and assessed. This book attempts to begin to address some of these issues. However, the focus on learning and teaching and the common interest in the students we teach continues and will remain to provide a common focus and be the basis for ongoing dialogue.

This book, therefore, provides both theoretical perspectives and practical insights into the evolving nature of business education and draws from a wide range of contributors including those in higher education, classroom teachers, consultants and examiners. The editors wish to express their thanks to all contributors to the book who have given generously of their time. As part of the editing process the editors have sought to assemble and give direction to these separate contributions that together provide a contemporary account and critique of business education today.

The book is split into four parts, each reflecting important aspects of business education. Part 1 focuses on the major policy developments that have taken place in education and training and how these impact on the subject area. Part 2 is largely written by practising teachers and considers a range of teaching and learning issues and strategies. Part 3 is devoted to staff development and the continuing professional development of teachers. The final part contains a teacher-reviewed resource guide to a range of text- and web-based resources for business education.

About the contributors

Ian Abbott is Deputy Director of the Institute of Education at the University of Warwick. He was formerly co-ordinator of the PGCE in Business and Economics and he has taught on a number of teacher education courses.

Andrew Ashwin is an experienced teacher of business and economics and currently works as a content developer for Biz/ed. Andrew is also an experienced examiner and moderator and is the Chief Examiner for the Nuffield Business and Economics GCSE.

Paul Clarke trains business and economics teachers at the University College Worcester. He is also involved in Citizenship support networks and acts as a consultant to QCA.

Charlotte Davies is a freelance consultant in business and enterprise education working mainly with the EBEA, Young Enterprise and the Specialist Schools Trust.

Margaret Drew was head of business and office studies at a large London college and is now a freelance Chief Examiner for and consultant to QCA.

Glynis Frater has worked in the field of business and vocational education for many years. Her work includes training on management and quality issues, teaching and learning strategies and assessment as well as writing a number of publications to support vocational qualifications.

Andrew Hammond is Head of Business at Darrick Wood School, Orpington. He is senior examiner for a major examining board, an established author, and editor of the 'Business in the Classroom' section of the EBEA journal.

Cedric Humphries is Director of Business and Enterprise at Higham Lane School, Nuneaton. He has taught GCSE and A level business studies for a number of years.

Martin Jephcote is a lecturer and researcher at Cardiff University School of Social Sciences. Formerly head of the PGCE (Further Education) programme, his research interests are in post-14 education and training and he is currently engaged in projects on learning and working in further education.

Stuart Langworthy is a former head of business studies and is now Assistant Head of Enterprise at Brockworth Enterprise School, Gloucester, and business education subject co-ordinator for the University of Gloucester.

Vivianne Lawson worked in FE before entering full-time teaching. She is now based at a large Leicestershire upper school, where she has responsibility for Enterprise activities, and teaches on several business and vocational courses.

Ian Marcouse was a chief examiner of the AQA. He is a widely published author, founding editor of *Business Review* and runs an independent teacher training company.

John McAfee was a mature student who undertook his PGCE after a career in management consultancy. He currently works at a large Leicestershire upper school where he teaches business studies and manages Key Stage 4 Health and Social Care.

Brian Sanderson was formerly head of the Business Education faculty and is now an Advanced Skills Teacher at a large 14–19 comprehensive school. In 2003 he was seconded to the University of Warwick and is course co-ordinator of the PGCE in Business and Economics.

Michael Simpson is Head of Economics and Business Education at The Royal Latin School, Buckingham, and a senior examiner and moderator.

Sue Turner is a school teacher and the resource reviews editor for the EBEA's journal *Teaching Business and Economics.*

Lech Wersocki is a former teacher and head of department who now works in teacher training and assessment in North London.

Paul Widdowson is Head of Business Studies at Leiston High School and is a graduate of the Institute of Education, University of London.

PART 1

Business and Economics in a Changing World

The changing curriculum: the interaction of policy and practice

Martin Jephcote and Ian Abbott

Introduction

For teachers in schools and colleges there is a sense in which new demands are always being placed on them, and to a degree these require changes in the curriculum in terms of what is taught and how it is assessed. Indeed, the history of education in the past thirty years gives witness to how the curriculum has been used to promote one agenda or another; for example, to promote equality of opportunity, to respond to rising youth unemployment and growing disaffection, to combat crime, and to enable Britain to compete in the global knowledge-based economy. Schools and colleges have been faced with endless initiatives, with one arriving so soon after the other that they begin to be counter-productive. This works to leave the impression that educational policy-making is piecemeal and nothing more than a response to the latest panic. It might also leave teachers feeling swamped and exhausted by the constant pressure for change. What is certain is that the autonomy which teachers once thought they had has been lost because of the ways in which central government has taken more control, not just in shaping the curriculum but also through the coercive mechanisms of assessment and external quality control.

For teachers of business and related subjects the last thirty years has been a particularly turbulent time. Economics was an established A level subject and enjoyed record numbers of examination entries. Economics teachers were so confident about their subject and its base in schools that they wanted to expand to reach lower-aged pupils, and some wanted to ensure that a basic understanding of economics was a curriculum entitlement for everyone. As early as 1973 Christie believed that all pupils in secondary schools should be given some form of economics education and Holley (1973), while against proselytising the subject, was in favour of developing skills and abilities for a changing world. The idea that the Economics Association should establish an Economics Education 14–16 Project was first conceived in the early 1970s but did not get under way until 1976, making its first-phase formal report in 1980. In the period 1980 to 1983 the emphasis of the second phase of the Project was to develop exemplar materials to be used in economics, commerce and multidisciplinary social subjects. The third phase of the Project, started in 1985, was a wider dissemination phase which was directed at spearheading the spread of economic literacy through the in-service training of teachers; and in 1985 the revised exemplar materials were published in three volumes called *Young Person as Consumer*, *Young Person as Citizen* and *Young Person as Producer*. An objective of the materials was what Ryba (1984) called 'personalising' economics and was based on his view that courses in economic understanding should be available to all pupils regardless of ability. The publication of the materials was timely in a number of respects. First, they provided a concrete example of how LEAs and schools might respond to the DES consultation document *The School Curriculum* (1985), credited by Ryba and Hodkinson (1985) as the most important document to date in terms of the future of economics in the 14–16 curriculum because of its references to the needs of the economy and establishing links between schools and industry. Second, the materials informed the development of a teacher's guide for the introduction of the General Certificate of Secondary Education which in 1986 replaced the O level and Certificate of Secondary Education (CSE) and introduced the materials to a wide school and college audience.

Thirty years ago a business studies department was probably separate from the higher-status economics department. Typically, a business studies department comprised a permutation of office skills, typewriting, shorthand, commercial English, and commerce. A level business studies was first introduced in 1967 as an outcome of the pioneering work of John Dancy, the Master of Marlborough College, with financial support from the Wolfson Foundation and in collaboration with a small number of schools and the Cambridge Local Examinations Syndicate. By 1975, 50 centres entered 400 candidates (Barker 1974) and over the same period business education developed and expanded as a vocational course in further education. More than 75,000 students were enrolled on either a Certificate in Office Studies, an Ordinary National Certificate or Diploma, or a Higher National Certificate or Diploma. Dyer (1979), the then Director of the A level Business Studies Project, sought to dispel any thought that it was vocationally oriented. His predecessor, however, recognised the inherent relationships between business studies and delivering what industry wanted, that was, he suggested, to provide information on how the nation earns its living and develop an appreciation of the role of industry and commerce in this process (Clifford 1978).

Today economics stands at the margin of the curriculum whereas business enjoys the 'high ground'. Indeed, as the title of this book suggests, economics in schools and colleges is, arguably, pretty much subsumed within the broad business education framework. Lines (1988) had warned that action was needed to revitalise and renew the study of economics and Livesey (1986) and Levacic (1987) foreshadowed the likely effect of the continued adherence to an outdated economic and pedagogic paradigm on the numbers taking A level. There was also a growing perception on the part of teachers and students that it was both easier to pass and get higher grades in business than in economics.

At times, there have been opportunities for activists, such as members of the Economics Association/EBEA to be proactive, to set the agenda and work at bringing about change. At other times, they have been forced into a reactive mode, having to respond to external agendas and to changing conditions, and often this has seemed like a fight for survival. For example, in response to the rejection of the recommendations made by the Higginson Committee (1988) for the reform of A level, the Secondary Examinations and Assessment Council promoted its own review. An outcome was the development of principles to cover all AS and A level syllabuses which supported the 'twin-track' approach dividing academic and vocational qualifications. In response, in 1989 the Association undertook a major review of the post-16 economics curriculum and formally launched its Economics Education 16–19 Project in 1991. Among other things, the intentions of the Project were to stimulate a review of the nature of economics thinking in both academic and vocational contexts and consider the implications for teaching, learning and assessment strategies. It sought to address the gap between the sorts of abstract economics now so widely criticised and the interests and understanding of professional economists. It did not set out to produce a new examination syllabus but sought to clarify the nature of learning economics and provide an antidote to the existing theory-first approach.

The fact was, however, that against a background of increased staying-on rates in post-16 education, in the period 1990 to 1996 the numbers taking economics halved whereas those taking business doubled. This 'turn around' is well illustrated through the recent history of the Economics and Business Education Association (EBEA). For example, in his report to the 1990 Annual General Meeting, the Chair of the Association indicated that extending services to members who taught business studies was a priority and he reaffirmed a commitment to forging an effective partnership with the National Association of Advisers and Inspectors in Business and Economics Education (NAAIBEE) and the Society of Teachers of Business Education (STBE) (Hodkinson 1991). It was not however until 2003 that a Joint Policy Forum for Business Education succeeded in getting the EBEA, NAAIBEE, STBE and the National Association for Business Education (NABSE) into meaningful negotiations (see Wall 2004). A more immediate response to the growth of business was when, in 1993, the then Economics Association transmuted into the EBEA and its journal, once called *Teaching Economics* changed its title, first to *Economics and Business Education*, and in 1997 to *Teaching Business and Economics*. These changes reflected the decline in economics and the rise of business at GCSE and A level and as a popular General National Vocational Qualification (GNVQ) introduced in 1993.

Business and economics in the curriculum

Even though individual subjects might seem impervious to change they are not monolithic but evolve over time. It would be wrong to think that changes necessarily come about as a result of a 'grand plan' or from the deliberate workings of an identifiable pressure group, but instead changes are often the result of the complex interplay of people and events. Over time there is an ongoing contest within and between subjects over matters such as their definition, content and pedagogic practices and between subjects and subject factions over status. New generations of teachers and others within subject communities engage in a process of thinking about the purposes of the subjects they teach and in the ways in which they seek to make changes. Moreover, engagement in this evolutionary process is important if as Kirk *et al.* (1997) asserted, courses that fail to reinvent themselves in the face of new circumstances are liable to decline or disappear. Indeed, as this and other chapters illustrate, these matters are particularly pertinent to the development of business and economics education in the UK.

A starting-point is to ask what are the purposes of business and economics in the curriculum and for individual teachers to be clear about why they teach their subject. Looking at curriculum provision today we might express some dissatisfaction with existing arrangements and argue for a curriculum more suited to those culturally and socially deprived young people who form the bulk of the lower achievers. Instead of attaching so much importance to an academic curriculum we might also argue that it should be pitched at a level of practical common life experiences, rather than at the level of abstraction, which is generally considered to be more appropriate for those culturally and socially advantaged higher achievers. We might think of education as essentially preparatory for life ahead and to ensure that young people can cope with the circumstances they are likely to encounter throughout their lives. If so, then perhaps emphasis should be placed on methods of enquiry rather than on an accumulation of facts and less emphasis be given to external testing. The fact is that these sorts of concerns are not new but were raised more than thirty years ago by educationalists such as Bantock (1971) and Musgrave (1968), but continue to be recurring themes.

As early as 1974 Raynor (1974: 9) had noted the tensions and 'contradictory forces' pulling the curriculum in opposite directions. He asked:

● Should schools meet the needs of the individual child or meet the needs of society and the economy?

● Are schools to be used as a means of changing society or preserving the existing social order?

● Should schools be a vehicle to transmit traditional moral values even though these may be regularly breached in the wider society?

These are not easy questions to answer. For example, on the one hand, employers may emphasise the need to prepare young people for the world of work. Politicians may assert the need for schools to contribute to an efficient and competitive economy. Parents and pupils may be most concerned about finding jobs and providing for a secure future. Taking these together we might, without getting into issues of either defining society or specifying its systematic requirements, suggest that a key role of schooling could be to provide young people with the appropriate general and vocational knowledge and understanding, skills and attitudes that made them better prepared for changing patterns of work. A role for schooling could be seen as to induct prospective workers, managers, consumers and citizens into their more or less predetermined roles in the culture of a democratic industrialised society. This would be achieved by providing pupils with the necessary knowledge and understanding and engendering values, attitudes and beliefs which enabled them to transfer easily from school to their adult roles as effective managers, workers, consumers and citizens.

On the other hand, it could be argued that the role of schooling is not to facilitate passage into the prevailing or taken-for-granted 'norms' and structures of society. A purpose of education could be to question the future direction of society. Rather than regard existing school–society relationships as self-perpetuating, education could be seen as an opportunity to change society for the better, that is, education would be a powerful instrument for reconstruction. Education would, in this argument, not be regarded as an induction into the predetermined roles of manager, worker, consumer or citizen, but schools would provide an opportunity for pupils to question these roles and the relationships, rights and responsibilities between individuals (managers, workers, consumers and citizens), groups (firms, associations and communities) and institutions (industry and government). The processes of education would not be concerned solely with transmitting knowledge and inculcating 'appropriate' values, attitudes and beliefs but would also be concerned with questioning their bases.

Teachers of business and economics have to ask themselves how they view their role with regard to educating young people. Is it to serve the prescribed needs of an industrialised society? That is, is it about passing on knowledge and attitudes about business, industry and the economy and the development of work-related skills? Or is it about focusing on the needs of individuals and their roles in shaping society, that is, about giving insights into business, industry, the economy and the community and analysing and questioning the relationships between them?

Clearly, we have to acknowledge the realities of living, growing up and being educated in a society divided by inequality of income and wealth, dominated by a class system and unequal educational opportunity, differentiated individual expectations and future life chances. We also have to acknowledge the real school and classroom problems of trying to provide an education based on a curriculum designed to motivate and engage the interests of all learners. However, whereas in these respects education can be a powerful force for change it is not a palliative for every economic and social problem.

Lawton (1989) pointed to reconstructionism, that is, a synthesis of progressivism and classical humanism, as a means to improve society. In this, the curriculum is designed to give support to social values and those experiences which develop citizens and social co-operation within a democratic society. Knowledge is only important in the ways that it helps to develop an understanding of society.

For Lawton, (1983: 25) education was '... concerned with making available to the next generation what we regard as the most important aspects of culture' and, in the limited time available, the curriculum should be planned to ensure an appropriate selection. The term 'cultural analysis' was used to describe the process on which the principles for this selection were derived and justified. In proposing an eclectic system of cultural analysis, he drew on both classificatory and interpretative methods of looking at culture as a whole. This is about asking these kinds of questions:

(a) What kind of society already exists?

(b) In what ways is the society developing?

(c) How do its members appear to want it to develop?

(d) What kind of values and principles will be involved in deciding on this
    'development', as well as on the educational means of achieving it? (Lawton 1996: 9).

He suggested that eight subsystems, or aspects of culture, were necessary requirements for a balanced curriculum and that curriculum-planning should begin by considering to what extent these were covered by existing subjects, followed by an evaluation of the quality of that coverage. The systems are: social; economic; communication; rationality; technological; moral; belief; and aesthetic. Each was 'indispensable', and improving the curriculum required gaps to be identified and filled.

Changing priorities

The development of business and economics in the curriculum has to be seen against broader economic, social and educational change and the opportunities and constraints which they presented. For example, a key focus of the educational debate in the 1960s was on the raising of the school leaving age, where it was argued that, given the expansion in knowledge and the need for a 'better' educated workforce, the school leaving age should be raised to 16. In turn, this gave rise to a heightened awareness of and further debate over the inadequacies of the secondary school curriculum and was met by attempts in the 1980s to vocationalise the post-14 curriculum. The Job Creation Programme of 1974, and the Youth Opportunities Programme (YOP) started in 1977 and later replaced in 1983 by the Youth Training Scheme (YTS), were designed to structure the experiences of young people's transition from school to work but turned into the means of dealing with mass unemployment and keeping thousands out of the dole queues (Finn 1985). The introduction of other employment programmes and legislative changes, for example the progressive erosion of benefit entitlements from 1980 to 1991, sought to reduce what was described as a 'dependency culture' and to remove the 'option' of youth unemployment (Roberts 1995: 15).

Growing concerns about the lack of articulation between schools and the world of work were brought to a head by James Callaghan in his now famous 1976 Ruskin College Speech. The introduction of comprehensive schools had put issues such as streaming versus mixed-ability teaching, the supposed adoption of progressive teaching methods and falling standards under the spotlight. Furthermore, the world economic recession of the mid-1970s made education an easy target for politicians who sought to transfer blame. A rising population meant that education was an increasingly heavy financial burden, so that once the 'favoured child of the Welfare State' there was now growing pessimism about what a 'good' education does and at what cost (Kogan 1978: 46). In initiating the 'Great Debate', Callaghan took the opportunity to express his own concerns about falling standards and his speech marked a turning-point in government thinking towards the curriculum, especially in the linking of education to the 'needs of industry'.

Among other things, Callaghan's speech worked to accelerate the shift towards central control of education and the curriculum. The 1960s and 1970s are generally characterised as a period of consensus in education when control over the curriculum was in the hands of teachers and local education authorities (LEAs). However, moves towards central government intervention and control rapidly gained momentum during the 1980s and worked to marginalise the role of teachers and their professional associations. In a number of respects, the centralising tendencies apparent in education were at odds with the general thrust to deregulation and privatisation experienced elsewhere in the public sector. Moreover, moves towards the local management of schools, 'opting out', and other aspects of so-called deregulation, which appeared to decentralise control, were, in fact, elements of a centralised model.

Following the 'Great Debate' the 'burgeoning procession' of documents from central government agencies developed a 'state conception of how the curriculum should be organised and taught' (Salter and Tapper 1981: 1). Those interested in promoting business and economics education exploited what small concessions were made and, overall, those interested in expanding economics education had to look for linkages with other parts of the curriculum. They took advantage of statements about the need to help pupils 'acquire knowledge and skills relevant to adult life and employment' and 'understand the world in which they live' (DES, *A Framework for the School Curriculum*, 1980) and to look for opportunities 'across the curriculum' (DES, *The School Curriculum*, 1981). By 1985 there was an optimistic mood. The DES had sought the views of the Economics Association on the principle of equipping all pupils by the age of 16 with some economic awareness and understanding. At about the same time HMI had undertaken an investigation of the teaching of economic understanding in schools (HMI 1987). In papers presented to an Economics Association seminar in July 1985 it was stated that interest in the development of economics education had never been higher (Hodkinson 1986). But as Hodkinson went on to point out, earlier expectations about the expansion of economics as a separate examination subject had not come about. Instead, the opportunity to provide an economics education for all was coming via the Technical Vocational Education Initiative (TVEI).

Launched in 1983, the TVEI marked a particular shift away from local to central control in the ways in which funding was 'earmarked' to promote vocational education and not passed directly to LEAs to do with as they wished. The thrust of both the TVEI and its predecessor, the Certificate of Pre-vocational Education (CPVE), was towards new patterns of curriculum, teaching and assessment. It was an attempt to shift styles of teaching and learning from didactic methods more associated with academic subjects to learner-centred, problem-solving and participatory approaches, thought to be a better preparation for the world of work. Within the TVEI both economic understanding and business were given some prominence, the latter partly because of its promise to deliver information technology. In 1986 the Manpower Services Commission published a report of its TVEI-related in-service training activities in which the focus was on 'economic awareness'. This put the emphasis on the need to understand and evaluate the implications of individual and group decision-making with respect to the use of resources and to explore these idea within the existing curriculum.

With the introduction of the National Curriculum in the period 1988–94 the reforms associated with the TVEI were short-lived and the mood became more pessimistic. The contents of those subjects chosen for inclusion were defined and prescribed in their associated attainment targets and programmes of study. Paradoxically, given all those earlier attempts to vocationalise the curriculum, neither business nor economics was included and the return to a subject-based curriculum illustrated all too vividly the contradictions between the economic and political within state policy-making (Ball 1994). Apart from 'lip-service' to cross-curricular themes, there was virtually no provision in a crowded curriculum for the preparation of young people for the world of work. During the early stages of the introduction of the National Curriculum, Economic and Industrial Understanding (EIU) became a focus for activity. Of the five cross-curricular themes this 'benefited' from the financial and practical support made available by a number of sponsors and agencies. However, in time there opened up a schism between competing factions interested in promoting differing definitions and versions of economic understanding. In particular, some wanted to give emphasis to the economics agenda whereas others were more interested in the schools industry agenda. Although it was the case that these differences could not be resolved, events were taken over by the rolling out of the National Curriculum so that all cross-curricular themes were marginalised (see Jephcote and Davies 2004).

Initially the introduction of the National Curriculum caused major concerns for the subject area and there were fears that business and economics might disappear at Key Stage 4 (Davies 1994). In practice the subject area has thrived and prospered as an option choice at GCSE, but as we have already noted there has been a significant shift from economics to business studies. Pupils have voted with their feet and opted to take business studies in large numbers at GCSE. At GCSE level, in 1992, 20,472 studied economics; by 2003 this figure had fallen below 7,000. In 1992 business studies attracted 119,989 entries, there was a slight increase by 2003 with 125,000 entries. At GCSE-level business studies remains a major option choice for a significant number of students, and is one of the most successful subjects outside the compulsory subjects laid down by the National Curriculum. Certainly reform of the National Curriculum, which has provided a greater amount of choice at Key Stage 4, has helped business studies to remain popular, but students and parents also view the subject as relevant and interesting.

The last 15 years have seen continuing development within the subject area as a number of new courses have been introduced. Business and economics have remained as popular academic subjects, with GCSE and Advanced level continuing to be viewed as valuable qualifications, especially for entrance to higher education. However, economics has declined in popularity as business studies has continued to attract increased numbers. In 2003 32,253 students took A-level business studies, making it one of the top ten A level subjects. These areas have not been resistant to change and there has been a limited revision of content and continued reform of assessment methods. In particular, modular programmes have been introduced and greater emphasis has been placed on coursework at the expense of examinations.

Of greater significance has been the large increase in the range of vocationally related courses being offered by business and economics departments. This has coincided with an increase in participation rates post-16 as successive governments have attempted to encourage more young people to stay in education and training. In some comprehensive schools the move away from the traditional emphasis on academic subjects for an increasing number of post-16 students has led many business departments to offer an ever increasing range of courses which were deemed to be more relevant to young people. These courses were more closely related to the world of work and offered an alternative route for entry into Higher Education or the labour market. Within schools the business and economics department has been at the forefront of these developments, with many departments taking the lead for vocational initiatives across the school. This has led to areas such as health and social care and leisure and tourism coming under the control of economics and business departments.

By far the most important vocationally related programme to be introduced was the General National Vocational Qualification (GNVQ). GNVQ was piloted in 1992 and fully implemented in 1993 and was seen as part of the overall process aimed at increasing the skills and flexibility of young people who enter the labour force (ED/DES 1991). According to Jessop (1993: 133) a major objective of GNVQs 'was to encourage a far higher proportion of young people to stay in full-time education beyond the end of compulsory schooling at age 16 than hitherto'. GNVQs were intended to be equivalent to the 'gold standard' of A level, but with the added bonus of a strong vocational emphasis.

This programme significantly extended the opportunities for work in vocational areas and moved the subject area away from the academic route offered by the traditional A levels in Economics and Business Studies. This development provided opportunities for significant growth in the subject area. Advanced Business GNVQ was intended to have equal status to A level, but teaching methods and assessment procedures were significantly different with a strong emphasis on coursework and greater student participation.

However, the introduction of GNVQ was not straightforward and there were a number of criticisms relating to assessment and course structure (see for example Smithers 1993 and Ofsted 1994). A major review of GNVQ was undertaken and the programme became a popular choice for many young people post-16 (Capey 1996). However, GNVQ still had many critics and suffered in comparison with A level. As a consequence GNVQ was perceived to be an easier option than A level and despite the many changes to GNVQ it was often referred to as a second-class route.

The review of 16–19 education, that resulted in the implementation of Curriculum 2000 (QCA 1999, 2001), saw the conversion of Advanced GNVQ into the Advanced Vocational Certificate of Education (AVCE). This involved less emphasis on coursework and the development of a more 'academic approach'. A common format with AS and A2 level was introduced with 6 units of study.

Curriculum 2000 also saw some alterations in the assessment and content of both A-level business and economics. We will return to look at this in more detail in Chapter 3, but the outcome for the subject area is dual qualifications in business studies: AS, A2 level and AVCE, alongside economics at AS and A2. Despite the changes the subject area remains popular with post-16 students and this is a major area of work for business and economics teachers. Currently approximately one in four post-16 students takes a business-related course.

There have also been a number of developments within economics and business studies at Key Stage 4. However, GCSE remains the major area of work for teachers of business and economics. The vast majority of comprehensive schools offer GCSE business as an option choice for pupils 14–16. GCSE economics is only available in a limited number of schools, and it is difficult to imagine that this situation will change in the foreseeable future. Despite a number of changes to the National Curriculum over the past 15 years business and economics has remained outside the core of compulsory subjects. However, the changes to the National Curriculum have allowed greater choice at Key Stage 4 and a number of previously compulsory subjects are now only available as option choices. As a popular option with pupils and parents business studies has benefited from this development. Having to compete for space in the curriculum is nothing new for business and economics teachers and they feel more confident about retaining a significant role at Key Stage 4. Business, which was once considered to be a marginal subject at Key Stage 4, is now more secure as the pattern of provision starts to fragment.

As a whole the GCSE has remained relatively unchanged since it was introduced in 1986. There has been reform of assessment and some updating of content with new subject criteria, but the overall structure remains broadly the same. There is a mixture of coursework and end of course examinations, and GCSE business remains a popular option for many Year 10 pupils.

At Key Stage 4 the introduction, in September 2002, of a new range of GCSE programmes, now referred to as the Applied GCSE, was a significant development. Applied Business was one of the eight areas introduced to replace the previous GNVQ Part One qualifications. This qualification is intended to provide a vocational context for the study of business. Links with business are an integral part of the course and project work has to draw on real and relevant business scenarios. Students are encouraged to make use of extended work experience to gain practical experience of the vocational sector, and greater emphasis is placed on coursework.

The introduction of the Applied GCSE provides another opportunity for development within the subject area. However, the impact this programme will have on the 'traditional' GCSE remains to be seen. It seems ironic that a course called Applied GCSE Business has been introduced, because it is difficult to imagine a business course that isn't in some way applied. Perhaps this tells us something about the way in which the existing GCSE business has been taught? It also raises a number of issues about the academic and vocational nature of the subject area. Economics has clearly been seen as an academic subject, which might be one of the reasons for the decline in student numbers. On the other hand business is more obviously a vocational subject, so why do we need another business course?

Despite these questions and an ongoing debate about the nature of the subject area, teachers have to get on with the realities of introducing new courses. For a detailed analysis of the practical implications arising from the introduction of applied business see Chapter 7.

From September 2002 all school pupils have to be taught Citizenship as part of the National Curriculum. In many areas the introduction of Citizenship mirrors the problems associated with the implementation of Economic and Industrial Understanding. There is a clear issue around ownership of the subject and who will actually be responsible for delivery. The reality in many schools is that business and economics departments have been heavily involved in the implementation of Citizenship (see, for example, Stoney 2004). Significant parts of the content of Citizenship, especially at Key Stage 4, comprise elements of business and economic understanding. For example:

- How the economy functions, including the role of business and financial services;
- The rights and responsibilities of consumers, employers and employees;
- The wider issues of global interdependence and responsibility, including sustainable development;
- The United Kingdom's relations in Europe, including the European Union. (QCA 2002)

Whatever the arguments surrounding the introduction of Citizenship it clearly offers the opportunity to make elements of business and economics available to all school pupils, and we will return to this in more detail in Chapter 4. If this is done properly by staff who understand the concepts involved it should increase interest in business and economics and lead to increased numbers of students opting to take courses in the subject area. In addition the Government continues to recognise the significant role business and economics education can play in the creation and maintenance of a successful economy. A significant part of the Government's strategy to raise standards in schools is the creation of specialist schools. The number of specialist schools is being increased and schools can now apply for Business and Enterprise status. These schools have to secure some funding from the private sector, but they also receive a capital payment of £100,000 and additional funding for each pupil (DfES 2002). A full explanation of the application process is contained in Chapter 20. However, allowing schools to acquire specialist business and enterprise status can only raise the profile and status of the subject area. Business and economics is now able to compete on more equal terms with subjects such as technology, maths and modern foreign languages. In addition the current Labour Government has a strong commitment to the development of enterprise education in schools. There will be £60 million available to develop enterprise capability (Davies 2002). This is likely to contribute to further growth in the subject area as business and economics teachers take the lead in developing enterprise education.

Summary

Taken together, the ongoing restriction of the autonomy of LEAs, institutions and teachers have all contributed to increasing deprofessionalisation and worked to decrease the role of teachers and others in subject communities with respect to subject definition, content and pedagogic practices. The curriculum and the individual subjects it is comprised of are an outcome of both its social and political construction. In other words, although we can recognise increasing political control through policy-making and its implementation, at the same time the ongoing social interaction of teachers and others has an important bearing on the outcome.

Moreover, an end to this process of change has not been reached, but what we are witnessing is the evolutionary nature of 'school' subjects. Concerns about the UK economy, especially in light of the impacts of globalisation, have become a key driver for current educational reform and provide a rationale for the current policy-making emphasis on preparing young people for the world of work, and this is explored in Chapter 2. This provides another set of challenges and opportunities for business and we might do well to think that those subjects that are able to reinvent themselves are not only those more likely to survive but are also those likely to offer a more relevant curriculum to learners.

Certainly business and economics departments have attempted to provide a more relevant curriculum for learners. It is often business and economics that has been involved in pioneering considerable curriculum change. Business and economics departments have been at the forefront of developments relating to vocational education and to the introduction of programmes of study which develop new approaches to teaching, learning, and assessment. In particular, the subject area has made extensive use of ICT to support learning, and developed less didactic ways of teaching. Coursework and the use of portfolio evidence have also been encouraged. Links with a number of outside agencies have been fostered, and many business and economics departments have developed extensive contacts with business. Given the successful track record the subject area has enjoyed it seems well placed to take advantage of further changes that are likely to occur in the foreseeable future. However, we cannot afford to become complacent, and business and economics teachers will have to continue to innovate and be prepared to take a lead in curriculum development as new initiatives are implemented.

The next 'big thing' which may have a major impact on the subject area in England could be the implementation of the proposals for the reform of the 14–19 curriculum and qualifications framework, as proposed in the White Paper *14–19 Education and Skills* (DfES 2005). We will return in the next chapter to look in more detail at these proposals and the other policy developments in the rest of the United Kingdom and how they might impact on business and economics. There is no guarantee that the recommendations contained in the White Paper will actually be implemented. If a number of the proposals are introduced it will have a significant impact on all post-14 institutions and teachers in addition to the particular effect on the work of business and economics teachers.

At this stage business and economics are well-established subjects in the post-14 curriculum. The whole of the education system has gone through a series of changes in the last 25 years. Business and economics has been at the forefront of many of the initiatives that have been introduced. As a result of this process a range of academic and vocational courses and programmes are being made available to learners in schools and colleges. Teaching staff from business and economics are heavily involved in a number of local and national initiatives. The sections and chapters of this book will illustrate the stage the development of business education – business and economics – has reached and the possibilities for further development. In particular each section will deal with a range of issues:

- Part 1 will focus on the key changes within education and training and how they impact on the business and economics curriculum.

- Part 2 will look at teaching and learning in the business and economics classroom from a practitioner's perspective.

- Part 3 will concentrate on the issues relating to initial and continuing teacher development.

- Part 4 provides details of a range of text- and web-based resources for business and economics.

References

Ball, S. J. (1994) *Education Reform: A Critical and Post-structuralist Approach.* Buckingham: Open University Press.

Bantock, G. H. (1971) 'Towards a theory of popular education', in R. Hooper (ed.), *The Curriculum: Context, Design and Development.* Edinburgh: Oliver & Boyd, pp. 251–64.

Barker, R. (1974) 'Lessons from the A level Business Studies Project', in D. Whitehead (ed.), *Curriculum Development in Economics.* London: Heinemann Educational Books, pp. 179–95.

Capey, J. C. (1996) *Review of GNVQ Assessment.* London: NCVQ.

Christie, D. (1973) 'Economics in the early stages of the secondary school', in D. Whitehead (ed.), *Curriculum Development in Economics.* London: Heinemann Educational Books, pp. 105–17.

Clifford, J. (1978) 'From school to work: an O level pilot scheme', *Economics,* XIV, **4**(64), 123–6.

Davies, P. (1994) 'Pressures and opportunities in Key Stage 4', *Economics and Business Education,* **2**(1:5), 38–43.

Davies, H. (2002) *A Review of Enterprise and the Economy in Education.* Norwich: HMSO.

DfES (2002) *Schools Achieving Success.* London: DfES.

DfES (2005) *14–19 Education and Skills.* London: HMSO.

Dyer, D. (1979) 'Business studies: school and community – links with industry', *Economics,* XV, **4**(68), 121–4.

Employment Department/Department of Education and Science (1991) *Education and Training for the 21st Century.* London: HMSO.

Finn, D. (1985) 'The Manpower Services Commission and the Youth Training Scheme: a permanent bridge to work?', in R. Dale (ed.), *Education, Training and Employment:*

Towards a New Vocationalism? Oxford: Pergamon Press, pp. 111–26.

Higginson Committee (1988) *Advancing A Levels: Report of a Committee Appointed by the Secretary of State for Education.* London: HMSO.

Hodkinson, S. (1986) 'Introduction', in S. Hodkinson and D. Whitehead (eds), *Economics Education: Research and Development Issues.* London: Longman, pp. 1–5.

Hodkinson, S. (1991) 'Report of the Chair of the Economics Association to the AGM, 1990: forward into a new decade', *Economics* XXVII, 2, (114), 70–1.

HMI (1987) *Economic Understanding in the School Curriculum.* Stanmore: DES.

Holley, B. (1973) 'The place of economics in the secondary school curriculum', in D. Whitehead (ed.), *Curriculum Development in Economics.* London: Heinemann Educational Books, pp. 85–92.

Jephcote, M., and Davies, B. (2004) 'Recontextualising discourse: an exploration of the workings of the meso level', *Journal of Education Policy*, 19(5), 547–63.

Jessop, G. (1993) 'Emerging framework B: towards a coherent post-16 qualifications framework: the role of GNVQs', in W. Richardson, J. Woolhouse and D. Finegold (eds), *The Reform of Post-16 Education and Training in England and Wales.* Harlow: Longman.

Kirk, D., Macdonald, D. and Tinning, R. (1997) 'The social construction of pedagogic discourse in physical teacher education in Australia', *The Curriculum Journal*, 8(2), 271–98.

Kogan, M. (1978) *The Politics of Educational Change.* Glasgow: Fontana.

Lawton, D. (1983) *Curriculum Studies and Educational Planning.* London: Hodder & Stoughton.

Lawton, D. (1988) *The National Curriculum*, Bedford Way Papers 33. London: Institute of Education.

Lawton, D. (1989) *Education, Culture and the National Curriculum.* London: Hodder & Stoughton.

Lawton, D. (1996). 'The changing context: the National Curriculum', in S. Hodkinson and M. Jephcote (eds), *Teaching Economics and Business.* Oxford: Heinemann, pp. 7–24.

Levacic, R. (1987) 'What changes should be made to the "A" level Economics Syllabus for the 1990s?' *Economics* XXIV, 4(100), 100–5.

Lines, D. (1988) 'The future directions of advanced level economics', *Economics* XXIV, 2(102), 71–8.

Livesey, F. (1986) 'Whatever happened to economics?' *Economics*, XXIII, 2(94), 54–8.

Musgrave, P. (1968) *Society and Education in England Since 1800.* London: Methuen.

Office for Standards in Education (1994) *GNVQs in Schools: Quality and Standards of General National Qualifications.* London: HMSO.

Qualifications and Curriculum Authority (1999) *Qualifications 16–19: A Guide to the Changes Resulting from the Qualifying for Success Consultation.* London: QCA.

Qualifications and Curriculum Authority (2001) *Review of Curriculum 2000: QCAs Report on Phase One.* London: QCA.

Qualifications and Curriculum Authority (2002) *Citizenship Orders*. London: QCA.

Raynor, J. (1974) *The Curriculum in England*. Milton Keynes: Open University Press.

Roberts, K. (1995) *Youth and Employment in Modern Britain*. Oxford: Oxford University Press.

Ryba, R. (1984) 'The economics education 14–16 project, Phase 2: the creation of the project's exemplar materials', *Economics* xx, 4(88), 141–7.

Ryba, R., and Hodkinson, S. (1985) 'Economics for the 14–16 year old', in G. B. R. Atkinson (ed.) *Teaching Economics*, 3rd edn. London: Heinemann, pp. 110–29.

Salter, B., and Tapper, T. (1981) *Education, Politics and the State*. London: Grant McIntyre.

Smithers, A. (1993) *All Our Futures: Britain's Education Revolution*. Dispatches Report of Education. Channel 4 Television.

Stoney, J. (2004) 'Using discussion to develop students' economic thinking in citizenship lessons', *Teaching Business and Economics* 8(3), 33–9.

Wall, N. (2004) 'Responses to the DfES regarding the consultation document subject specialism', *Teaching Business and Economics* 8(1), 3–5.

The reform of 14–19 education and training: the emerging work-related curriculum

Martin Jephcote and Ian Abbott

Introduction

The construction of the school curriculum and the process of schooling can be used to contribute to the types of knowledge needed to maintain or promote dominant economic, political and cultural arrangements. Indeed, over the last thirty years education has become the focus for intense debate between politicians, industrialists and academics, and the supposed relationship between educational provision and economic performance has increasingly underpinned educational policy-making.

The longer-term perspective

We need to realise, however, that these debates are rooted in a complex past of competing ideologies, loyalties and traditions. Some writers (for example, Weiner 1981; Finn 1985; Barnett 1986; Elbaum and Lazonick 1986; Marquand 1987; Gamble 1990; Prais 1993) have sought to examine and explain Britain's relative economic decline as compared with major international competitors and to indicate the past and future role of education. Their analyses suggest that, for many years, inappropriate educational provision has been a contributory cause of Britain's relatively poor economic performance. In the 1997 White Paper *Excellence in Schools* (DfEE), the Government stated:

> by comparison with other industrialised countries, achievement by the average student is just not good enough. These problems have deep and historic roots. We failed to lay the foundations of a mass education system at the end of the 19th century as our competitors – France, Germany and the USA – were doing...mass education was neglected, and governments were content to rely on private schools to provide the elite entry to universities and the professions. (p. 10)

As early as 1851 the Great Exhibition showed that European competitors were fast catching up with British industry and, in response, in 1853 the Department of Science and Art was set up. Official reports showed that the rapid progress of German industry was the result of an organised system of state elementary schools. Furthermore, the relatively poor showing made by British exhibitors at the 1867 Paris Exhibition reflected '…inadequate technical training of the industrial classes', and there was evidence of American engineering products penetrating colonial markets (Armytage 1964: 111). As the nineteenth century drew to a close changes in employment patterns were also apparent and the move to new processes of production created an increasing demand for technical labour; and the design and wider use of complex machinery created a demand for skilled mechanics and engineers. The move to larger business organisations created a demand for better-trained managers and clerks, and specialisation in financial services increased the need for administrators. The rate of innovation required that a wide range of workers should be flexible in their approach to work, possess fuller knowledge and more specialised skill, and develop the qualities of judgement and responsibility. Taken together, this would require a systematic provision of education for all (Ashworth 1960).

What evolved, however, was far from a co-ordinated educational system, and at the start of the twentieth century signs of strain began to show, especially because of a growing threat from foreign competition (Musgrave 1968). What carried forward from the nineteenth century was the prevailing view that equated respectability with a white collar job. This attitude was hardened by economic uncertainty where, for many, academic success was regarded as a passport to a job in the expanding army of clerks demanded by the expansion of the financial services sector. Moreover, whereas clerical skills were general and more easily transferred from one employer or from one sector to another, industrial training was more job-specific, and industrial employment was dependent on growth and more susceptible to short-term economic change.

Although there was a succession of committees of enquiry and reports, little changed and, as the twentieth century moved on, why, asked Barnett (1986: 209) was it that Britain was 'on the eve of the Second World War still without an education and training system worthy of a first-class technological power'? He asserted that, in part, the answer lay in the legacy of the industrial revolution which left Britain's post-war economy dependent on the 'intelligence, energy, zeal and adaptability of the mass of her industrial population' (p.187). However, these qualities, he claimed, were lacking because of the handicap of a workforce 'composed of coolies, with the psychology and primitive culture to be expected of coolies' (p.187). An unwillingness to change and an attitude towards production which was about getting the most pay for the least amount of work were, according to Barnett (1986), ingrained and lasting characteristics. This, he suggested, accounted for the fact that, even after the Second World War, workers refused to look beyond their own job and their own wage to the larger interests of industry and the economy. He also pointed to the difficulties emanating from the education of the privileged classes in which the public schools offered a liberal education dominated by the classics and religion and were concerned primarily with the formation of character.

By the 1960s policy-makers had seen:

> a direct and indisputable correlation between educational reform and economic prosperity: a skilled and educated workforce would facilitate economic growth which would, in turn, constitute a firm base for continuing educational expansion.
>
> (Chitty 1987: 12)

However, although time had moved on, Britain's legacy of the past left teachers and students, employers and employees and policy-makers with dominant values and attitudes towards industry, work and enterprise and, in particular, to the role of education in bringing about economic recovery. Mathieson and Bernbaum (1991: 5) suggested that the state's failure to introduce effective reform in the past stood as a 'monument to the outstanding successes of the British education system in embodying and perpetuating the values of society's dominant elites'. And Ahier (1991) argued that Britain suffered because of the prevalence of an 'anti-industrial culture' and from the 'persistent characteristics of British society', including a lack of enthusiasm and preparation for the worlds of industry and commerce.

Paradoxically, it was Callaghan's Ruskin College speech in 1976 (see Chapter 1) that resulted in the attempt by the Right to bring the enterprise culture into schools and colleges and which coincided with a programme of economic and institutional reform involving the privatisation and deregulation of publicly provided goods and services and the promotion of free market ideologies (Keat 1991). However, the idea that the cause of youth unemployment was a lack of skills and poor attitudes became less convincing as it became clearer that traditional routes into employment, especially manufacturing, were diminishing. The new focus on enterprise turned attention away from other shortcomings and transferred responsibility for economic decline away from government and onto individuals. Thus, enterprise education was promoted as a means to bring about economic recovery and was part of a broader project which promoted individualism, individual responsibility and choice. The 'marketisation' of education was not only included in the programme of widespread reform of the public sector but was also used to promote enterprising qualities in individuals, such as initiative, self-reliance, responsibility and a willingness to take risks, all necessary to overcome the so-called 'dependency culture'.

As Esland (1990) pointed out, a major focus of political discourse over the last 25 years has been the intractability of poor economic performance, despite various attempts designed to change the structure of education and training. It is the case that many of the problems to do with education and training and economic performance at the time of Callaghan's speech remain unsolved. So, even though post-16 staying-on rates have more than doubled, we still hear of the problems of low skills, skills shortages, skills gaps and mismatches between the supply of and demand for labour with appropriate knowledge and skills. It was, of course, the service sector which saw the biggest increases in employment opportunities, with the numbers growing by about 2.7

million in the period 1983 to 1990 (Employment Department 1990) whereas, over a similar period, the numbers of 17-year-olds in full-time work fell from 29 to 13 per cent (Roberts 1995).

Equipping young people for working life: the reform of 14–19 education and training

In recent years, improving educational provision in general and the introduction of more widespread vocational education have been brought to the fore of policy debates. Consequently, investment in education and training has become synonymous with investment in human capital. It might be the case, however, that new solutions are needed for what we have seen to be long-established problems.

Too many young people left school with low qualifications, low levels of literacy and numeracy and negative attitudes towards industry and were 'effectively immunised against further education or training' (Raggatt and Unwin 1991: xiii). There was, in response, a plethora of initiatives, many supported by the TVEI, including the expansion of work experience, the introduction of Young Enterprise and Mini-Enterprise in school projects and the promotion of economic awareness in secondary and further education. The different reforms were designed to raise the status of vocational education.

However, with the introduction of the General Certificate of Secondary Education (GCSE) and, even more, the subject-based National Curriculum, the advancement of almost any form of specific vocational preparation was all but abandoned in pre-16 education, accentuating the academic–vocational divide and fostering its continuance.

Consequently, during the 1990s, the link between education and the economy was focused on post-16 education and, heralding the 1990s as 'the Skills Decade', the Secretary of State for Employment stated:

> Britain is faced with an unprecedented challenge to its international competitiveness. Our future economic growth and well-being depend on our ability to overcome it.
>
> (Employment Department 1990)

Investment in human capital, the primacy of economic goals and the need for an appropriate system of education and training continued as recurring themes. As Brown and Lauder (1996) pointed out, the need was for Western governments to look to their own social institutions and human resources to meet the challenge of globalisation and to win a competitive advantage in the global economy. This advantage was seen to depend on raising the quality and productivity of human capital where 'knowledge, learning, information and technical competence are the new raw materials of international commerce' (p. 4). In turn, the assumed importance of 'knowledge' began to drive systems of education and training in the belief that better quality would determine national prosperity and, even though the importance of knowledge was exaggerated, nation-states were forced to invest in the knowledge-based economy and compete in the 'global knowledge wars' (Brown and Lauder 1996). An answer, at least in the policy rhetoric, seemed to be in the creation of a 'learning society'. In *Learning Pays* (1991) the Royal Society for the Encouragement of Arts, Manufactures and Commerce (RSA) asserted that education was the best investment available to individuals, companies and nations and found evidence to suggest that those nations who failed to invest suffered decline. In *Profitable Learning* (1992) the RSA saw a need to change the existing system and to offer financial incentives as a means of breaking the cycle between low expectations, low levels of motivation and lack of opportunities to learn. They drew up a ten-point plan to help create a 'learning society' and, like the Confederation of British Industry (CBI) in its report *World Class Targets* (1991), they set out national learning targets. They required that by 2002 everyone would continue in formal learning at least to age 18 and achieve at least an NVQ Level 3, or GCE A level or equivalent and, by the year 2012, all would continue in formal learning until age 21 and achieve an NVQ Level 4 during the course of their lives. Although the 'learning society' continues to be a contested concept encompassing the economic imperative, greater inclusivity and the liberal tradition (Gorard *et al.* 1998), there is, however, some consensus in which it is recognised that, because of globalisation and the requirement of increased competitiveness, individuals need to be committed to lifelong learning and there needs to be improved education and training (Ainley 1998; Cooke *et al.* 2000).

The 1991 White Paper *Education and Training for the 21st Century* (DES/Welsh Office) signalled the need for a framework of vocational qualifications 'relevant to the needs of the economy' and based on equal esteem with academic qualifications. The introduction in 1993 of college-based General National Vocational Qualifications (GNVQs) gave 'the appearance of a political solution' aimed at satisfying the differing demands of employers and post-compulsory education (Gleeson and Hodkinson 1999: 159). However, John Major's insistence on the maintenance of A levels as 'the benchmark of academic excellence' did nothing to advance the introduction of GNVQs. Again, the need to break down the academic–vocational divide and the need for education and training to be more responsive to the needs of industry was apparent in the 1994 White Paper *Competitiveness: Helping Business to Win*, which stated:

> Hard working people with high skills, and the knowledge and understanding to use them to the full, are the lifeblood of a modern internationally competitive economy. While we are second to none in securing results from those in our society who choose the most academic options we need to raise further the attainment of those, whatever their age, who choose vocational education and training. (p. 30)

The Dearing Review (*Review of Qualifications for 16–19 Year Olds*, SCAA, 1996) also identified a need for more breadth together with the modification of syllabuses to include core skills, that is, those skills now deemed necessary both to enter the world of work and to remain flexible within it. However, the reluctance to introduce radical change and abandon the 'gold standard' of A levels was underlined in the recommendations made by Dearing. Perhaps from a fear of offending opposition from within the Conservative Party, he also adhered to the primacy of the 'rigour' of A levels and the separation of academic and vocational routes (Halsall 1996). The ongoing refusal to consider seriously a unified system in preference to a multi-track approach made impossible the closing of the academic–vocational divide. Moreover, it maintained barriers to access and progression which ran counter to those visions of a learning society which promoted social equality and personal fulfilment (Spours *et al.* 2000). So, even though GNVQs might widen participation, they continued to attract criticism for concentrating on the accreditation of low-level skills and for their reliance on a competency-based system of assessment. Like so many initiatives, GNVQs and the TVEI before it were an attempt to introduce a vocational route but, as we well know, in English society relatively few aspire to the technical route, seen by many to be suited to other people's children and other schools (Gleeson and Hodkinson 1999). Moreover, GNVQs have continued to experience low status because of the accumulated negative perception which young people and their families have of the succession of post-16 schemes from the late 1970s onwards (Ahier and Esland 1999).

In the concluding stages of the last Conservative Government's period in office the first ever White Paper on the education and training of 14–19-year-olds in England was published: (*Learning to Compete: Education and Training for 14–19 Year Olds*, (1996). This drew on widespread consultation concerning the DfEE's *Equipping Young People for Working Life: A Consultative Document on Improving Employability through the 14–16 Curriculum* (1996), which, among other things, highlighted the need for more opportunities within the National Curriculum to prepare 14–16-year-olds for working and adult life and for the development of vocational options at 14+. This was a response to what it saw as the 'unprecedented' social and economic challenges to be faced in the twenty-first century and its belief that the UK was, at Levels 2 and 3, behind Germany and France but broadly comparable to the USA and Singapore in skills attainment. These challenges were supposedly to be met by equipping young people with the ability to adapt and respond to rapid change and to prepare them for the transition from school to work, with a particular emphasis on the development of communication skills and application of number.

In the Green Paper *Schools: Building on Success* (DfEE 2001), the Government set out its strategy to transform secondary education aimed at raising further levels of pupil achievement and reducing levels of complete drop-out. 'This historic poor performance was', the Green Paper suggested, 'rooted in society and the economy' (p. 4) and there was now the opportunity to see education

> not only as the key to developing equality of opportunity, but also to enabling the nation to prepare for the emergence of the new economy and its increased demands for skills and human capital. (p. 8)

In a letter circulated with the Green Paper, the Secretary of State for Education and Employment added:

The links between excellent education provision and future economic prosperity have never been clearer. The need to create an education system that prepares children for a rapidly-changing world is crucial.

In education change is ongoing and, despite the introduction of Curriculum 2000, new proposals continued to be put forward by the Government. As we noted in the previous chapter the Applied GCSE was introduced in 2002. In *Work-Related Learning for All at Key Stage 4* (2003) the QCA reaffirmed its commitment, stating that from September 2004, there is a statutory requirement that all young people should experience some work-related learning. Schools should ensure that all students can learn through work such as work experience or part-time work, learn about work through vocational courses and careers education and learn for work by developing skills for enterprise and employability.

The former Secretary of State for Education and Employment had vowed 'to make vocational education as much a part of everyday school life for pupils over fourteen who want to follow that route as academic study is today' (DfEE press release, 24 January 2001). The intention of this proposal was to enable young people to develop technical skills for work in engineering and computing, and traditional craft skills to enable them to work as plumbers, gas fitters and engineers. The development of new vocational school-based GCSE programmes, available to all 14–16-year-olds, would, the Minister suggested, overcome 'the neglect of vocational and technical education… a British disease'. A range of initiatives have been implemented by successive governments in an attempt to:

- achieve parity of esteem between vocational and academic qualifications;
- provide a framework which incorporates the general (academic), vocationally related, and occupational pathways and make connections between them;
- develop a flexible system which allows learners to combine academic and vocational routes and to switch pathways if necessary;
- move towards an integrated 14–19 system allowing learners to progress at their own rate and to opt out of some subjects;
- provide opportunities for more young people to remain in education and training.

Learning pathways

From 1997, the Labour Government's attention turned to a national strategy to raise standards, increase employability skills and improve Britain's economic performance. However, according to Marples (2000), what followed was unlikely to change the status quo, symptomatic of a backward-looking approach and a 'piling on of yet more qualifications, within a divided and incoherent system' (p.135). So, although September 2000 saw the introduction of Advanced Subsidiary levels, the extent to which students mix between A level and vocational subjects remains limited.

In all phases of education, raising standards became the Labour Government's key agendum and was seen as the key to success for individuals and the economy. Initially the Government focused on the primary phase and on the early years of secondary schooling. Examples of policy intervention include the National Literacy and Numeracy Strategies. In pre-16 education, the National Curriculum had already detailed Programmes of Study which set out subject by subject what pupils should be taught and the Attainment Targets which set out the expected standards of pupils' performance. Over time, the emphasis was to be less on the running of schools and more on intervention and support. Many of the New Labour Government's intentions were signalled in their first White Paper, *Excellence in Schools* (1997), in which the 'new approach' was to be 'Education, Education and Education' and was, according to the Prime Minister, the best economic policy that Britain had. The White Paper saw knowledge and skill acquisition as the key to success, with Britain's economic prosperity and social cohesion dependent on a society in which everyone was 'well-educated' and able to learn throughout life (p. 9). This was to counter putative historic levels of pupil underachievement, failing schools and underperformance compared with other industrialised countries.

The Labour Government believes that education and training has a key role in any attempt to deal with social and economic problems. The Government would argue that it is essential that Britain has a well-educated and trained workforce to compete with other industrialised and developed nations. The Government's economic argument for improving school standards is fairly straightforward:

1 In order for Britain to survive as a prosperous nation we must be able to compete in world markets.

2 Success in this enterprise depends upon having a highly numerate and literate workforce.

3 However, standards in our schools are not rising fast enough, and in this respect Britain compares unfavourably with many countries, especially those in the Pacific Rim.

4 The Government must therefore raise expectations among teachers by setting challenging targets for pupils' achievements.

5 In order that these targets might be realised in a few years, the Government needs to shake up school pedagogy through initiatives that ensure everyday classroom practice is in line with the best methods available and that ineffective strategies are discarded.
(Docking 2000: 3)

As we have seen earlier in secondary schools, the Education Act 1996 had already made provision for the disapplication of some National Curriculum subjects. The revised National Curriculum, implemented in August 2000, gave emphasis to inclusion aimed at securing learners' participation and to ensuring that there were appropriate opportunities for them to achieve. The regulations permitted disapplication of some subjects to allow pupils to participate in extended work-related learning. In particular the proposals for the continuing reform of the National Curriculum in England include:

- A statutory requirement for all schools to provide access to a minimum of one course leading to a qualification in each of the entitlement areas – the arts, humanities, design and technology, and modern foreign languages, with the expectation that schools should offer at least two courses in each entitlement area.

- Further changes to the disapplication regulations, thus allowing schools to disapply certain National Curriculum subjects for two purposes: to undertake extended work-related learning; for any reason provided it educationally benefits the pupil.

- A new statutory requirement and framework for work-related learning.

- Greater development of ICT skills through other subjects and additional ways to accredit ICT capability of pupils who do not follow discrete ICT courses (for example through the use of Key Skills qualifications).

- Changes to the science programme of study (for example, increased emphasis on practical applications).
  (QCA/NFER 2003)

From 2004, disapplication was no longer considered exceptional and to be available to any student who would benefit (QCA 2004).

Curriculum 2000

What is commonly referred to as 'Curriculum 2000' was broadly supported in both England and Wales. Curriculum 2000 was based upon the acknowledgement that academic provision post-16 was too narrow and that vocational courses were considered to have less status than their academic counterparts:

> For too long, vocational studies and qualifications have been undervalued. This must change – we must introduce qualifications and pathways that are of an excellent standard, that deserve and are accorded high status.
>
> (DfES 2002: 1)

As a result of Curriculum 2000 a common format was introduced with six modules making up a full A2 qualification. This initiative split the A level into two parts: A/S and A2. Students normally take the A/S examination at the end of their first year of post-16 study and they can then choose if they wish to carry on with the remaining three modules to obtain the A2 qualification. As we noted in the previous chapter, Curriculum 2000 led to the replacement of GNVQ with the Advanced Vocational Certificate of Education (AVCE). There were also changes in the method of assessment with less emphasis on coursework. This qualification had a similar structure with six modules, but it was not split into two parts. From September 2005 this will be replaced by a new qualification Advanced Applied Business which will adopt the same levels and standards as the A/S and A2 qualifications. However, it is expected that the assessment procedures will more closely resemble GNVQ rather than AVCE.

One of the major factors underpinning Curriculum 2000 was to give learners greater choice and flexibility. In particular, learners should be able to have a greater choice between and be able to mix academic and vocational programmes. This was to be supported by a programme of Key Skills (Communication, Application of Number, ICT, Improving Own Learning and Performance, Working with Others, and Problem Solving) for all post-16 programmes.

In practice the outcomes of the significant changes associated with the introduction of Curriculum 2000 have been rather disappointing:

> Curriculum 2000, was introduced with what has now been recognized as 'undue haste' and produced considerable upheaval in post-16 education. Young people had previously studied perhaps three subjects, often over two years at A level, were faced with the burden of 4 or 5 subjects to be assessed at AS level followed by three A2 units. . . . The post-16 curriculum was further overloaded by the Key Skills qualifications. The former GNVQ had been transformed into an AVCE and was looking more and more like an academic A level. Teachers felt that the lead-time for introducing such far-reaching reforms had been too short.
>
> (Abbott and Huddleston 2004: 251)

Another outcome of the implementation of Curriculum 2000 was the replacement of GNVQ at Foundation and Intermediate levels. Pre-16 this is not a significant issue given the introduction of applied GCSE. However, post-16 it might cause problems because the GNVQ programmes were popular with learners who wanted to make a new start in a different environment. Certainly GNVQ courses at Foundation and Intermediate levels provided opportunities for learners to re-engage with education. It remains to be seen if the new Applied GCSE programmes can be as successful as GNVQ in fostering positive attitudes to learning. The last assessment date for Foundation and Intermediate business is summer 2007. Apart from the increased workload for learners, following the introduction of Curriculum 2000, teachers and lecturers certainly reported additional demands on their time. According to Savory (2002) subject teachers in business education faced a considerable increase in their workload.

Prospecting the future

Constitutional reform has resulted in education and training policy being devolved to different bodies in the separate parts of the United Kingdom. Wales now has a National Assembly, Northern Ireland devolved powers and Scotland a separate Parliament. For a number of years Scotland has had a separate and established education system and distinct policies have been developed. In England, Wales and Northern Ireland education and training policy continues to be, to some extent, a development of a collective past, but with widening and more disparate aspirations for the future. In England, the raising of standards continues to be a dominant theme and is to be achieved by greater choice and flexibility, and, as in Wales and Northern Ireland, it appears there will be a greater 'tailoring' of the 14–19 curriculum to meet the needs of individual learners.

In the 2003 White Paper *14–19: Opportunity and Excellence* (DfES), the need for greater co-operation between schools and colleges to remedy 'the weaknesses of our vocational offer' (p. 4) was signalled. This is to be based on greater flexibility and choice, including new applied options and for programmes to be tailored to individual needs and aptitudes. Science is to be compulsory for all and all students are to learn about work and enterprise. Greater co-operation between schools and colleges has been the major feature of the Increased Flexibility Programme (IFP) which has been in operation since September 2002. The IFP programme is designed to

- Raise the attainment in national qualifications of participating pupils
- Increase their skills and knowledge
- Improve social learning and development
- Increase retention in education and training after 16.
  (DfES 2002)

Under this programme Key Stage 4 learners are allowed to spend part of their time in different learning environments. This is usually the local further education college, although it could also be a local employer. The learners, who have been disapplied from parts of the National Curriculum, can follow vocationally related programmes such as the applied GCSE or take vocational awards such as National Vocational Qualifications (NVQ). Targets have been set to measure the success of this programme; for example 75 per cent of the learners should remain in education or training post 16. Staff who are working in further education, across all subject areas, are now being asked to teach 14–16-year-olds as partnerships developed between different educational institutions.

In 14–19 education and training we have seen a huge number of initiatives and policy documents. In Wales, the Qualifications, Curriculum and Assessment Authority (ACCAC) set out its plans in *A Framework for Work-Related Education for 14–19 Year Olds in Wales* (2000). In this, it saw work-related education as a central preparation for adult and working life: it should include the opportunity to learn directly in the workplace, and also experience of an enterprise activity and/or inputs from employers into the curriculum. The Welsh Assembly government set out its intentions for education in *The Learning Country* (2001) and took forward its ideas in *The Learning Country: Learning Pathways 14–19* (2002) and in its subsequent *Action Plan* (2003). This was to begin a move towards individually tailored learning pathways encompassing a wide choice of courses and other experiences. Key elements include a work-focused experience, community and voluntary experience and personalised learning support. This is supplemented with detailed guidance in *Learning Pathways 14–19 Guidance* (2004), which makes clear that science remains an essential element of the curriculum at Key Stage 4 and that young people should have an understanding of Wales, Europe and the world. The Welsh Assembly government is committed to transforming 14–19 provision and wants 95 per cent of people by the age of 25 to be ready for high-skilled employment. A learning core should run through 14–19 education and training and should meet the needs of each learner, and offer choice and flexibility, impartial careers advice, and access to personal support including a learning coach.

In Northern Ireland, proposals for changes to the curriculum framework were set out by the Council for the Curriculum, Examinations and Assessment (CCEA) in its *Phase 1 Consultation* (2000). Its general aims proposed that young people should have learning opportunities that develop them as an individual, as a contributor to society and as a contributor to the economy and the environment. And by way of improving relevance and enjoyment of the curriculum it proposed that personal education, citizenship and employability should be a statutory entitlement. Following consultation, advice to the minister in 2003 recommended the inclusion of learning for life and work, comprising personal, social and health education, local and global citizenship and education for employability.

In England the culmination of this process has been the 14–19 Education and Skills White Paper. The Tomlinson Review identified a series of common problems that have affected education and training over many years. Reflecting the issues that we have already outlined, earlier in this chapter, the Tomlinson Report sets out why reform, despite all the recent policy initiatives, is still needed:

- **Raise participation and achievement.** For participation at 17, 2002 data rank the UK 24th out of 28 OECD countries with a participation rate of 76 per cent. More than 5 per cent of young people reach the end of compulsory schooling with no qualifications. Particular care will be needed to ensure that we raise the disproportionately low participation and attainment of some minority ethnic groups.

- **Get the core right.** The literacy and numeracy and Key Stage 3 strategies are improving basic skills among our young people, but there is still more to do to ensure that all young people have the skills needed to succeed in higher education (HE) and the workplace.

- **Strengthen vocational routes.** The existing patchwork of vocational qualifications fails to provide coherence and progression for learners. Too many are of uncertain quality and fail to provide clear progression routes to further learning and/or employment.

- **Provide greater stretch and challenge.** This year, 22.4 per cent of A level entries achieved an A grade. Higher education admissions officers and employers complain they are finding it increasingly difficult to distinguish between top-flight candidates, and learners themselves are being held back by the lack of opportunity to demonstrate their full potential.

- **Reduce the assessment burden.** Excluding the National Curriculum and vocational qualifications other than GNVQs and VCEs, there were around 7.5 million subject entries in 2004, with 57,000 examiners. The sheer volume of assessment creates a formidable burden at all levels of the system and is only partially offset by the benefits derived from assessment.

- **Make the system more transparent and easier to understand for learners, universities and employers.** Too many learners lack a clear route map through the system, and end-users are often unclear about the relevance and value of qualifications which young people hold.
(DfES 2004: 18)

The Tomlinson Report attempts to cover all aspects of education and training 14–19. As a consequence it is a huge document and there are a large number of recommendations. However, the major proposal contained in the report is the replacement of the existing system of 14–19 qualifications with a framework of diplomas at different levels. The diploma would be made up of core and main learning. The core would include areas such as ICT, literacy, numeracy, an extended project, common skills including personal awareness, and a recognition of wider activities undertaken by learners. The main learning would refer to the broad academic and vocational area studied by the learner. It is envisaged there will be up to twenty 'lines of learning' which will make up the main learning areas. The outline diploma framework is shown in Table 2.1.

Table 2.1 Proposed 14–19 qualification framework (DfES 2004: 7)

	Diplomas	*Current qualifications*
Advanced	Core Main Learning	*Level 3*: Advanced Extension Award; GCE and VCE AS and A level; Level 3 NVQ; equivalent qualifications
Intermediate	Core Main Learning	*Level 2*: GCSE grades at A*–C; Intermediate GNVQ; Level 2 NVQ; equivalent qualifications
Foundation	Core Main Learning	*Level 1*: GCSE grades D–G; Foundation GNVQ; Level 2 NVQ; equivalent qualifications
Entry	Core Main Learning	*Entry*: Entry-level certificates and other work below Level 1

If the diploma framework is implemented it should lead to an integrated 14–19 curriculum. Learners should be able to work their own way through the diploma depending on their own skills and interests. At last full recognition will be given to a range of extra-curricular activities undertaken by learners, such as young enterprise, work experience and community service. According to Tomlinson there is a need to improve the status of vocational qualifications. Therefore it is envisaged that in addition to the introduction of an overarching diploma, vocational qualifications will be strengthened by:

- **Better vocational programmes** of sufficient value to combine core learning (including basic and employability skills) with a specialised vocational curriculum and assessment and relevant work placement. Vocational programmes would be designed with the involvement of employers and should be delivered only in institutions which are suitably equipped.

- **Rationalised vocational pathways** capable of providing progression within the diploma framework to Advanced level and beyond, and linked, where appropriate, to National Occupational Standards in order to provide avenues to employment.

- **A series of vocational options** which can be combined with general and academic subjects in mixed programmes.

- **Better work-based learning** through the integration of apprenticeships and the proposed diploma framework.

- **Stronger incentives to take vocational programmes,** as the common requirements for content, volume and level of study mean that all diplomas have general currency while also signifying relevant attainment within a particular vocational area.
(DfES 2004: 8)

The Tomlinson Report outlines proposals for long-term reform which could take up to ten years to implement. This is one of the lessons learnt from the implementation of Curriculum 2000, which was introduced without due consultation or sufficient lead-time. The result was chaos and severe damage to the credibility of the system. The recommendations contained in the Tomlinson Report are clearly designed to address many of the issues which have created problems in the 14–19 curriculum over many years.

However, the publication of the White Paper (DfES 2005) not only rejected much of what Tomlinson recommended, but also reinforced the separation of academic from vocational education. The proposals are for an education system based on choice and designed to meet individual needs. The overall intentions are to:

- Tackle our low post-16 participation – we want participation at age 17 to increase from 75% to 90% over the next 10 years;

- Ensure that every young person has a sound grounding in the basics of English and maths and the skills they need for employment;

- Provide better vocational routes which equip young people with the knowledge and skills they need for further learning and employment;

- Stretch all young people; and
- Re-engage the disaffected. (DfES, p. 4)

The White Paper recommends that the GCSE and A level are retained at the heart of the system with a strong emphasis on the acquisition of functional skills in English and maths. The number of A level modules will be reduced from 6 to 4 and harder examination questions will be introduced. Diplomas at foundation, level 2 (GCSE) and level 3 (A level) will be available in 14 vocational areas including business administration and finance. To achieve a diploma young people will need to achieve appropriate standards in English and maths, specialised material, relevant GCSEs and A levels and have work experience. The diplomas will be developed by sector skills councils (SSCs) and specialist schools will be awarded extra income to become centres of excellence in vocational education. It is difficult to see how these proposals, which are significantly different from those put forward by Tomlinson, will solve the problems we have outlined in this chapter. It seems the government's decision not to introduce a coherent system, reform assessment or introduce a unified qualifications framework may mean that another opportunity has been missed.

Summary

Attempts to make the school and college curriculum more suited to the needs of industry and the economy are not new. There still seems to be a reluctance to address the need for wholesale reform. The removal of the distinction between 'academic' and 'vocational' subjects seems to be an essential step in any reform. In England and Wales future reform tends towards the need for an overarching framework, tailored to the needs of individuals, and allows a greater mixing of different sorts of courses than is now the case. Certainly there is a great emphasis on the importance of designing a curriculum that is appropriate for individual needs.

However, there are still many who oppose radical change, see for example Smithers (2004). Only time will tell if the sort of changes now being implemented and those at their early stage of development will have the desired impacts for individuals, for employers and for the economy. It does, however, seem that developments continue to be incremental and, moreover, are so complex in their structure that they are likely to give rise to confusion. We have seen in the past that the piecemeal introduction of policies has failed to have the desired effect. A number of vested interest groups will try to sideline change. If we are to address some of the issues that have plagued education and training for the past 150 years, perhaps now is the time for a radical solution to the problems facing 14–19 education and training. If not we are likely to continue to repeat the mistakes of the past and the problems encountered in 1851 will still be with us in 2051.

References

Abbott, I., and Huddleston, P. (2004) 'The curriculum: 14–19', in V. Brooks, I. Abbott and L. Bills (eds), *Preparing to Teach in Secondary Schools*. Maidenhead: Open University Press, pp. 241–54.

Ahier, J. (1991) 'Explaining economic decline and teaching children about industry', in R. Moore and J. Ozga (eds), *Curriculum Policy*. Oxford: Pergamon Press, pp. 123–46.

Ahier, J., and Esland, G. (1999) 'Introduction', in J. Ahier and G. Essland (eds), *Education, Training and the Future of Work 1: Social, Political and Economic Contexts of Policy Development*. London: Routledge, pp. 1–13.

Ainley, P. (1998) 'Towards a learning or a certified society? Contradictions in the New Labour modernization of lifelong learning', *Journal of Education Policy*, 13(4), 559–73.

Armytage, W. (1964) *Four Hundred Years of English Education*. Cambridge: Cambridge University Press.

Ashworth, W. (1960) *An Economic History of England 1870–1939*. London: Methuen.

Barnett, C. (1986) *The Audit of War: The Illusion and Reality of Britain as a Great Nation*. London: Papermac (Macmillan).

Brown, P., and Lauder, H. (1996) 'Education, globalization and economic development', *Journal of Educational Policy*, 2(1), 1–25.

CBI (1998) *Greater Expectations: Priorities for the Future Curriculum*. Confederation of British Industry, Human Resources Brief, April 1998.

Chitty, C. (1987) 'The comprehensive principle under retreat', in C. Chitty (ed.), *Redefining the Comprehensive Experience*, Bedford Way Papers 32. London: Institute of Education, pp. 6–27.

Cooke, P., Cockrill, A., Scott, P., Fitz, J. and Davies, B. (2000) 'Working and learning in Britain and Germany: findings of a regional study', in F. Coffield (ed.), *Differing Visions of a Learning Society: Research Findings*, vol. 1. Bristol: Policy Press, pp. 199–230.

DfEE (1996) *Learning to Compete: Education and Training for 14–19 year olds*, Cm. 3486, December 1996. London: HMSO.

DfES (2001) *Schools: Building on Success, Raising Standards, Promoting Diversity, Achieving Results*. London: HMSO.

DfES (2002) *Extending Opportunities: Raising Standards*. London: DfES.

DfES (2004) *14–19 Curriculum and Qualifications Reform. Final Report of the Working Group on 14–19 Reform*. London: DfES.

DfES (2005) *14–19 Education and Skills*, Cm. 6476. London: HMSO.

Docking, J. (2000) *New Labour's Policies*. London: David Fulton.

Elbaum, B. and Lazonick, W. (1986) 'An institutional perspective on British decline', in B. Elbaum and W. Lazowick (eds), *The Decline of the British Economy*. Oxford: Oxford University Press, pp. 1–19.

Employment Department (1990) *The Skills Decade*. Sheffield: Employment Department.

Esland, G. (1990) 'Introduction', in G. Esland (ed.), *Education, Training and Employment, 1: Educated Labour, the Changing Basis of Industrial Demand*. Wokingham: Addison Wesley, pp. x–xv.

Finn, D. (1985) 'The Manpower Services Commission and the Youth Training Scheme: a permanent bridge to work?', in R. Dale (ed.), *Education, Training and Employment: Towards a New Vocationalism?* Oxford: Pergamon Press, pp. 111–26.

Gamble, A. (1990) *Britain in Decline*, 3rd edn. Basingstoke: Macmillan.

Gleeson, G. and Hodkinson, P. (1999) 'Ideology and curriculum policy', in M. Flude and S. Sieminski (eds), *Education, Training and the Future of Work*, vol. 2. London: Routledge, pp. 158–76.

Gorard, S., Rees, G., Fevre, R. and Furlong, J. (1998) 'Learning trajectories: travelling towards a learning society', *International Journal of Lifelong Education* **17**(6), 400–10.

Halsall, R. (1996) 'Core skills: the continuing debate', in R. Hassall and M. Cockett (eds), *Education and Training 14–19: Chaos or Coherence?* London: David Fulton, pp. 73–88.

Keat, R. (1991) 'Starship Britain or universal enterprise?', in R. Keat and N. Abercrombie (eds), *Enterprise Culture*. London: Routledge, pp. 1–17.

Marples, R. (2000) '14–19 lifelong learning', in J. Docking (ed.), *New Labour's Policies for Schools: Raising the Standard?* London: Kogan Page, pp. 119–38.

Marquand, J. (1987) 'Education and the economy: a view from the MSc', in H. Thomas and T. Simkins (eds), *Economics and the Management of Education: Emerging Themes*. London: Falmer Press, pp. 85–93.

Mathieson, M., and Bernbaum, G. (1991) 'The British disease: a British tradition?', in R. Moore and J. Ozga (eds), *Curriculum Policy*. Oxford: Pergamon Press, pp. 55–64.

Musgrave, P. (1968) *Society and Education in England since 1800*. London: Methuen.

Prais, S. J. (1993) *Economic Performance and Education: The Nature of Britain's Deficiencies*. London: NIESR.

QCA/NFER (2003) *Consultation on Proposed Changes to the Key Stage 4 Curriculum*. Slough: NFER.

QCA (2004) Disapplication of the National Curriculum subjects at Key Stage 4 (www.gca.org.uk/14-19).

Raggat, P. and Unwin, L. (eds) (1991) *Change and Intervention: Vocational Education and Training*. London: Falmer Press.

Roberts, K. (1995) *Youth and Employment in Modern Britain*. Oxford: Oxford University Press.

RSA (1991) *Learning Pays*.

RSA (1992) *Profitable Learning*.

Savory, C. (2002) 'Teaching Economics and Business Studies after Curriculum 2000: the teacher's voice'. *Teaching Business and Economics*, **6**(3), 39–41.

Smithers, A. (2004) 'Diploma in demolition', *Guardian*, 18 October.

Spours, K., Young, M., Howieson, C. and Raffs, D. (2000) 'Unifying acedemic and vocational learning in England, Wales and Scotland', in F. Coffield (ed.), *Differing visions of a Learning Society: research findings, volume 1*. Bristol: The Policy Press, pp. 71–104.

Weiner, M. J. (1981) *English Culture and the Decline of the Industrial Spirit 1850–1980*. London: Penguin.

E-learning in business and economics

Andrew Ashwin

Introduction

E-learning has been part of the education scene for many years. In some respects it was the fortunate few who had the resources, the technology and the confidence to use these tools in the classroom. Now it is often seen as a panacea to all manner of problems facing schools and colleges, and the term is not always used with precision. The 'e' implies some form of electronic and, therefore, technological input and the 'learning' part suggests that students will 'learn' as a result of this interface. It is pertinent, therefore, to start off with a definition of what we mean by 'e-learning'.

In its *Towards a Unified E learning Strategy* interim report the Department for Education and Skills (DfES 2003: 4) stated:

> If someone is learning in a way that uses information and communication technologies (ICTs) they are using e learning. They could be a pre-school child playing an interactive game; they could be a group of pupils collaborating on a history project with pupils in another country via the Internet; they could be geography students watching an animated diagram of a volcanic eruption their lecturer has just downloaded; they could be a nurse taking her driving theory test online with a reading aid to help her dyslexia – it all counts as e learning.

By implication it seems that e-learning somehow involves some form of computer-based technology. However, although watching a video in the classroom could be classed as e-learning, the definition seems to accept that a machine that codes information and presents it in a variety of formats is what we really mean by e-learning. It does, however, suggest that e-learning is somehow a tool rather than a set of processes to do with extracting and organising information. This chapter argues that e-learning is much more than just a tool and that it contributes to the complex process we know learning to be and can contribute in an important manner.

The use of computers allows students to do any or all of the following:

- Access information from a variety of sources from around the globe at any time;
- Format the information collected and present it in a variety of ways;
- Use images and video clips to highlight and demonstrate models, scenarios and events;
- Generate links with other schools, colleges and centres of education to build collaborative learning;
- Access a greater variety and scope of methods of assessment.

It is important to stress that e-learning is a complement to other forms of learning and not a replacement. It should form part of an articulated approach to learning that helps students to access their different learning styles more appropriately.

One key feature for business education students is the opportunity of getting up-to-date and relevant information quickly. While the textbook, by comparison, is out of date before it is even published, online resources can be updated and refreshed at speed to provide 'real time' learning opportunities. Such speedy access to information does highlight, however, the need for students to have the skills to know what to access, what to use and what not to use. So, as well as practising the use of applications it is imperative to inculcate in learners a set of information literacy skills to do with the careful selection, analysis and application of information.

What does the 'learning' part of e-learning mean?

Learning is as much about the process as the outcomes, and in the knowledge-driven economy, learning skills have been brought to the fore. Learning is about conflict, change, confusion, making mistakes and ultimately challenging preconceptions. This might involve any or all of the following:

- An ability to confront and cope with change with confidence;
- The ability to be creative in thought and in problem-solving;
- The ability to make connections between unrelated information and to be able to draw conclusions;
- Evidence of changed perceptions and thinking in relation to the subject matter as a result of the acquisition of new information.

E-learning must both complement and facilitate these characteristics.

The problems in business education

Students come to business education classrooms with a wealth of accumulated experience but with limited formal understanding and perhaps a rather naive view of what the subjects might offer them. Studying business or economics is not, in itself, going to make the student more able to start up and run a business, nor is it necessarily going to lead to greater earnings potential. Moreover, because of the dynamic nature of these subjects there are particular challenges in relation to making connections and coping with and confronting change confidently. So let us look at the current state of e-learning with regard to business education subjects.

Information and aids to learning are available in a variety of forms.

1. The internet

- Company websites
- News items from the BBC, *The Guardian*, Ananova, *Financial Times*, *The Economist*, and so on.
- Financial information – Bloomberg.com
- Colleges and universities throughout the world
- Online journal articles
- Government statistical data – ONS and Treasury
- Specialist subject-based sites – National Learning Network (NLN), Biz/ed, etc.
- WinEcon
- Exam board websites that provide information on specifications, subject reports, sample papers, past papers and possibly online assessment and inset.

2. School/college intranet sites

- Providing notes
- Course programmes
- Information
- Exam details
- Tests and quizzes
- Homework tracking
- External links
- Assessment monitoring

3. Presentation facilities

- *PowerPoint* and *Macromedia Flash*-based presentations

4. Managed learning environments

- 'used to include the whole range of information systems and processes of an educational institution (including its VLE if it has one) that contribute directly, or indirectly, to learning and the management of that learning' (www.jisc.ac.uk/).

5. Virtual learning environments

Systems developed to facilitate the interaction and exchange of information between students and teachers/lecturers in an educational institution; for example:

- *Blackboard*
- *WebCT*

6. Video conferencing, customised learning programmes

Triple A, Tutor 2U CD-ROMs, CD-ROM material, provision of animations, games and simulations, digital video-streaming and student ownership and access to PCs, laptops and hand-held devices, for example personal digital assistants (PDAs) or pocket computers.

Problems facing the development of e-learning

A DfES (2003) report identified that e-learning is not embedded into teaching and learning at all levels. It recognised that there are piecemeal developments in e-learning that are of high quality but not available to all learners, that there are funding problems for developing e-learning environments and that e-learning needs to better provide for individual learning needs.

A problem inherent in the development of any e-learning programme is the need to develop materials of the highest quality. This does not just mean ensuring spelling and punctuation are correct but also concerns the accuracy and integrity of the content and the necessity of complying with accessibility and usability standards. The main pieces of legislation and regulation relevant here are the Disability and Discrimination Act (1995) and the Special Education Needs and Disability Act (SENDA) (2001). The inclusion of all manner of coding into e-learning resources, such as the inclusion of *Macromedia Flash* animations and the use of Java script, may provide many opportunities to develop and make interesting learning materials but they can be seriously detrimental to many learners who may not have access to the technology or who have other special needs not catered for by the animation or resultant program. The key to quality provision is in ensuring that materials are available and accessible for every learner irrespective of their situation, ability or need. Most quality resources meeting such standards will have accessibility statements clearly identified within their materials.

The current resource availability

Let us focus on the types of material that are available to be used by students and teachers. Specialist subject area providers currently include the various BBC sites devoted to revision help www.bbc.co.uk/schools/16/business.shtml, www.bbc.co.uk/schools/gcsebitesize/business/ and SOS Teacher www.bbc.co.uk/schools/sosteacher; Revision Guru www.revisionguru.co.uk/; the LTSN sites for business and economics (now under the auspices of the Higher Education Academy), www.economics.ltsn.ac.uk/teaching/interactive.htm and www.business.ltsn.ac.uk/; S-Cool www.s-cool.co.uk; Tutor 2U www.tutor2u.com/; Triple A Learning www.triplealearning.co.uk/index.html; and Biz/ed www.bized.ac.uk/.

These are perhaps the sites that most students and teachers will be familiar with in relation to content material. They provide a wealth of quality information presented in different ways with different aims. In terms of revision, the BBC sites, Tutor 2U and S-Cool provide the student with a wide range of valuable information which could, in most cases, be used as an alternative to a textbook. These sites also provide useful hints and tips for students on examination-related techniques, discussions about pre-released case studies and so on.

Most of the above are free to users but some are subscription-based (Triple A Learning) or have parts of their content on a subscription base or available to purchase as CD-ROMs (Tutor 2U). The sites tend to have a slightly different focus within the framework of economics and business education. Some are focused on revision while others provide a broader range of resources.

Triple A Learning, for example, aims to provide a customised package for the delivery, monitoring and evaluation of business and economics courses tailored to the needs of particular institutions, while Biz/ed is seeking to provide resources that can be used as part of lesson development and planning and major online gaming and simulation environments.

With all this information comes some element of responsibility. There are increasingly cases where students are exploiting this wealth of information, copying material directly from the internet and passing it off as their own. The existence of essay bank sites provides students with the opportunity of getting their work done for them or straightforward opportunities to copy large amounts of information. This situation is also occurring in the use of coursework submissions. Large tracts of materials taken directly from company websites and so on are now regular features of such work, and the opportunity for the teacher to be able to identify where this is occurring are becoming increasingly difficult.

As teachers, therefore, we have a responsibility to educate students in the appropriate use of such materials. The practice of 'lifting' such material is unlikely to contribute much to the development of e-learning, nor will it help develop a student's understanding of the subject matter and appropriate ways to develop effective learning strategies. Teachers and students, therefore, have to recognise that the ideas and information on the internet are not theirs to own but to use, and as such should be credited in the normal way. To combat this there are plagiarism detectors being launched that allow teachers and lecturers to be able to scan student submissions and to identify instances of plagiarism, and such devices are likely to become more widespread in the future.

The current scene therefore boasts much in terms of the availability of supporting materials for use in the classroom. Part of the problem lies in knowing what is available, checking through that material and building it into schemes of work and planning programmes. In many respects there is almost too much information and the fear is that we may be missing something that is all-important to our teaching and learning. It is important therefore to maintain a degree of discipline in the use of such materials; to base planning on variety and richness of resource to ensure that students' individual learning styles are met and that all assessment objectives are covered.

The future

The future promises much more flexibility in the curriculum, offering students the possibility to mix courses or units from full courses in completion of a diploma-style award. E-learning will be an important part of this flexible approach. At its heart will be the need for subject boundaries to be less rigid than they currently are. Students building diplomas in the way suggested will have to be far more aware of the impact of elements of their learning on other disciplines. For example, work done in a psychology unit may have direct relevance to work covered in a marketing unit of a business-related course; students doing maths and statistics courses may be able to apply their theoretical knowledge to economics and business studies courses in a far more obvious way than is currently the case.

A role for e-learning in this process is significant and in its broadest sense provides greater opportunity for students to be able to collaborate and for cross-curricular themes to be explored and developed. The use of email-based systems, virtual learning environments and forums allows students to be able to access information from tutors and each other at any time of the day. Such environments could allow students to follow a course remotely to a considerable extent, while still being required to attend certain parts of the course in a traditional manner. Some schools and colleges in the UK are already experimenting with 'e-learning' days where the students follow structured work away from the school or college.

Students can access course notes and presentations, activities and case studies and get access to financial information of all types through the VLE. They will be able to get access to their past work history, and to previously submitted work, to submit work online, get it assessed online and sit exams online while the teacher will be able to manage assessment online, get rich data to inform them of progress and check for plagiarism.

Other potential developments include the expanded use of PDAs (Personal Digital Assistants). Such devices may offer students and teachers a range of possibilities for making computing truly mobile and represent a cost-effective approach in comparison to laptops and further investment in PCs.

'Best practice'

To help generate this flexibility and cross-curricular approach, resources will need to be developed that meet course needs but give the broader view that students will need. Biz/ed (www.bized.ac.uk) produces a series of mini-research projects aimed at students in the 16–19 bracket. These projects are designed to encourage students to take a topical issue and to explore the issue in more detail. It seeks to help students to focus on research techniques and find out where to access relevant information. There is an element therefore of educating students in the appropriate use of the e-learning environment and especially the efficient use of the Web. To this end, how to search effectively, how to skim-read articles, and how to select information are important parts of that process.

Biz/ed incorporates an Internet Resources Catalogue. This catalogue contains links to material that has been quality-checked prior to inclusion and is focused on key areas of business- and economics-related subject areas. For example, if a student wants information on management theories, there are resources available relevant to this theme, from a Spotlight on Sir John Harvey Jones through relevant journals and to the Erasmus Research Institute of Management!

Organisation of resources to allow students to access what they need rather than wasting time searching for the information is an important part of the e-learning infrastructure, whether it is part of the institutions intranet, VLE or a national initiative, it is important that we are able to manage the flow of information that e-learning makes use of and depends on, but which can obfuscate the learning process.

The future development that is likely to impact most on the quality of the e-learning experience is in the development of games and simulations. The necessity of students engaging with and interacting with their learning experience has been recognised and is a major part of the normal teaching and learning environment in the classroom. Technology has developed sufficiently to enable more dynamic processes to be incorporated, which are more accessible to all. The use of technologies such as

Macromedia Flash and Scalable Vector Graphics (SVG) will allow animations and graphics to be far more targeted and useful in helping explain processes. The further development of games and simulations will enable students to recognise and cope with the impact of changes that they make and to build in more real-world consequences enabling them to better understand the consequences of decision-making. The collaborative learning aspect can be further developed through the use of video-conferencing and video-streaming.

The development of the Virtual Football Club at Biz/ed is one such example. The VFC seeks to give students the opportunity of understanding the business and financial pressures of running a football club. It is not about managing the team but about managing the financial survival of the club. By running clubs from different leagues students get an understanding of the different financial pressures that clubs face in different sections of the football league and non-league structure. They can play the game individually in a short period of time, as a group-based activity in the classroom, between different groups within the same institution or between institutions. The latter can be supplemented by discussions and debates via video-conferencing links. The aim of such resources is to build in flexibility of study and encourage a greater degree of interactivity in the learning process. By involving students in this way teachers are able to mix traditional teaching with 'real life' examples provided by e-learning.

Summary

The value of e-learning is in its flexibility and in the ways that it brings a sense of realism to the classroom that engages learners in the learning process. Although such developments can be time-consuming, costly and technically sophisticated, the existence of a wide variety of resources enables teachers and students to concentrate on the learning process while a team of technical and educational professionals does the development work. It is in such a division of labour that e-learning will really fulfil the potential it has promised for the last 20 years.

Reference

DfES (2003) *Towards a Unified E Learning Strategy: Interim Report.* Nottingham: DfES.

CHAPTER 4

Citizenship and business education

Martin Jephcote

Introduction

In England, from September 2002 citizenship was made part of the non-statutory framework for personal, social and health education and is a new statutory foundation subject at Key Stages 3 and 4. The programmes of study and an attainment target are based on three elements:

- Knowledge and understanding about becoming informed citizens;
- Developing skills of enquiry and approach;
- Developing skills of participation and responsible action.

For 16–19-year-olds there is no statutory requirement but an expectation for citizenship education to extend into this phase.

In Wales, the Qualifications, Curriculum and Assessment Authority for Wales (ACCAC) took a different approach by linking citizenship education to its promotion of a Curriculum Cymreig and to the promotion of education for sustainable development and global citizenship (ACCAC 2002). It is not an additional requirement but is regarded as part of the existing school curriculum and of school life with learning opportunities to be found in existing subjects and in personal, social and health education (PSHE). Education for global citizenship

> enables people to understand the global forces which shape their lives and to acquire the knowledge, skills and values that will equip them to participate in decision making, both locally and globally, which promotes a more equitable and sustainable world.
>
> (ACCAC 2002: 6)

In Northern Ireland, 'Learning for Life and Work' has been introduced at Key Stages 3 and 4 and includes local and global citizenship, which becomes a statutory requirement by 2006. The broad aim of education for citizenship is 'to develop the capacity of young people to participate in a fair and inclusive society throughout their lifetime' (www.CCEA.org.uk).

Background

The link between citizenship and business education is not new. Indeed, the early expansion of economics as a school subject was given support by the Association for Education in Citizenship, which linked the study of economics to its promotion of positive citizenship when throughout Europe democracy was under threat (Szreter 1967). Nor is the attempt to bring to the fore the promotion of active citizenship alien to the business and economics teacher in more recent times. For example, the Economics Association (now the EBEA) published *Understanding Economics: Young Person as Citizen*, along with *Young Person as Consumer* and *Young Person as Producer* (Economics Association 1985). Indeed, in different ways and at different times importance has been attached to the notion of citizen as 'worker' or 'consumer' and has worked to position people not as citizens but as individuals in an industrialised capitalist economy (Hall *et al.* 1998).

At the time of the introduction of the National Curriculum in 1988 and through the following years citizenship was given some prominence. In the 1990s the 'New Right' began to equate citizenship with 'active citizenship' and to solving problems such as crime and deviancy. Implicitly there was an attempt to define what it was to be a 'good citizen'. It is, however, with the coming to power of the Labour Government in 1997 and, in particular, the interest of David Blunkett the then Secretary of State for Education that has given citizenship education a new lease of life.

Citizenship is not, however, without its problems but remains contested in its definition and in its practical expression in schools. The remainder of this chapter will explore these issues and propose a way forward for business education teachers.

What is citizenship?

A problem with trying to define citizenship is that, in the main, people in the UK do not think of themselves as citizens. To do so is not part of our culture and history. So, unlike the USA where there is a written constitution and citizens swear their allegiance to the flag, in Britain there is an evolving legal and constitutional framework which is the outcome of ongoing social interactions.

Perhaps what we might readily agree is that in the UK the concept of citizenship is both legal and sociological embodying a two-way relationship encompassing both rights and responsibilities:

> Citizenship can be described as both a set of practices (cultural, symbolic and economic) and a bundle of rights and duties (civil, political and social) that define an individual's membership in a polity.
>
> (Isin and Wood 1999: 4)

There is a real sense in which the boundaries and meaning of citizenship are constantly being challenged as a result of transformations in economy, culture and society. For example, membership of the European Union, mass economic migration and an increasingly multicultural world are all factors which ought to challenge us to reconsider what we mean by citizenship. Similarly, we need to recognise the impact of globalisation and the information age (see Chapter 1). At the same time, we have to cope with the apparent paradox of these sorts of transformations and the rise of nationalism, and recognise the threats to political sovereignty as well as the advantages and disadvantages it brings to individuals. In such periods of transformation citizenship becomes a 'field of contest', that is, in the fields of political and social power and in the field of theory and ideas.

Heater (1990) cited in Davies *et al.* (1999) provided five key perspectives on citizenship:

Table 4.1 Key perspectives on citizenship

Identity	A sense of belonging
Civil citizenship	Legal rights and responsibilities
Political citizenship	As a member of a democratic society
Social citizenship	(Equal) access to health, education and a reasonable standard of living
Civic virtue	Giving something back to society (in kind)
And to these we might add:	
Economic citizenship	Contributes to wealth creation (through work)

For teachers there is a need to consider if the school curriculum should be used to promote any or all of these aspects of citizenship and for teachers of business education to consider their role and that of the subject.

What is citizenship education?

Like the definition of citizenship, citizenship education is also a contested term.

David Blunkett called on his former university tutor, Bernard Crick, to chair a working party on behalf of the Qualifications and Curriculum Authority (QCA). In their *Final Report* the Advisory Group on Education for Citizenship and the Teaching of Democracy in Schools (QCA 1998) identified three strands which, they suggested, should run through all citizenship education:

1. Social and moral responsibility. Children learning from the very beginning self-confidence and socially and morally responsible behaviour both in and beyond the classroom, both towards those in authority and towards each other.

2. Community involvement. Learning about and becoming helpfully involved in the life and concerns of their neighbourhood and communities, including learning through community involvement and service to the community.

3. Political literacy. Pupils learning about the institutions, problems and practices of our democracy and how to make themselves effective in the life of the nation, locally, regionally and nationally through skills and values as well as knowledge – this can be termed *political literacy*, seeking for a term wider than political knowledge alone.

The report went on to suggest the benefits of citizenship education:

For pupils: an entitlement in schools that will empower them to participate in society effectively as active, informed, critical and responsible citizens of our democracy and of the wider world.

For society: an active and politically literate citizenry convinced that they can influence government and community affairs at all levels.

This agenda arose out of ongoing moral panics about the need to reduce crime, to instil 'traditional' family values and to get young voters along to the ballot box! The school, it appeared, was to be the place to inculcate these values. According to Hall *et al.* (1998) citizenship appeared in the curriculum because of concerns about the economy, unemployment and income disparity and was regarded as a means of promoting greater social inclusion.

Citizenship education and the school curriculum

For citizenship education the contest for definition and inclusion takes place in the arena of the school curriculum. A problem for citizenship education is that its claim for inclusion makes a territorial claim and challenges the established status and hierarchy of school subjects and subject knowledge. This is true of any new subject or theme or when a popular subject wants to expand. New and expanding subjects require a place in the curriculum; they require time and resources which, in the main, can only be found if they are taken from elsewhere. Moreover, for those who propose the introduction or expansion of subjects there is the real or perceived promise of enhanced career opportunities in the form of better promotion prospects, and an expanding role in the school which might bring greater security, power and status. At the same time, this poses a threat to the established order and there is evidence to show how at the school level interested parties seek to defend their ground and resist invaders. Subject communities work to protect their own interests and to promote their own subject pedagogies, and school subject histories provide an all too vivid account of how this works (see, for example, Goodson 1983, 1988, 1991; Jephcote 2004).

Bernstein (1996) usefully helps us to understand how these processes work using the term 'classification' to describe how subjects insulate themselves from each other and 'framing' to describe the relationships between them. Drawing on these ideas, Whitty *et al.* (1994a, 1994b) sought to explain the poor fortune of cross-curricular themes at the time of the introduction of the National Curriculum. They proposed that themes such as Economic and Industrial Understanding were 'invisible' and lacked the characteristics of real subjects including discrete allocation of time, setting of homework, and formal examinations. As such, they are regarded by pupils as 'non-subjects' and the 'everyday' knowledge they seek to impart is regarded as inferior (Paechter 1998). This is not to say that the knowledge that these themes or citizenship education seek to impart are any less important than other established subjects but that the micro-politics of schools works to marginalise them.

Before the QCA made its proposals citizenship education was rarely regarded as a subject but usually 'nested' in other areas. For example, it was integral to integrated humanities, delivered through themes such as peace studies and equality, and many modern foreign languages teachers have sought to use the subject to promote cultural diversity and understanding. Many schools operate extra-curricular activities such as shadow elections, or deal with citizenship education issues through cross-curricular dimensions such as anti-sexism and anti-racism. In the main, these concessions posed little threat to the status quo. However, the intention of the QCA was that in England citizenship education should be more than a theme and in its original proposal suggested that it should occupy at least 5 per cent of curriculum time and be established as a subject in its own right. This created a different set of conditions for contest.

What are the prospects for citizenship education?

If nothing else, it is as Hall *et al.* (1998) suggested, that in the more widespread promotion of citizenship education what schools already did is now opened up to debate, contestation and critical analysis. Halliday (1999) applauded the renewed emphasis on citizenship and was attracted to social and political concepts that enable participation in a liberal democracy. However, he was sceptical about the framework proposed by the QCA and the likelihood of bringing about changes in the political culture of the country. His proposal was for even more compulsion and prescription given that if schools are free to choose what aspects to emphasise, they are likely to play on what they already do, such as PSHE, which emphasises morals and values. Moreover, if it is left to teachers, they are likely to pander to pupils' interests and concentrate on values. This not only begs the question as to what values but also suggests there is no hope of reaching a consensus on content! Halliday's solution was not to focus on getting agreement about a common set of values but to focus on the resolution of disputes and conflicts and to give pupils the problem-solving skills they need

Frazer (2000) drew attention to the general opposition to the introduction of citizenship education in schools. Because of the lack of consensus, there were no established traditions and no well-articulated dominant account of the nature of politics, civil life or the constitution. She drew on evidence to claim that a number of forces were working against the introduction of citizenship education:

- Some suspect citizenship education as an attempt to promote middle-class stereotypes of the 'good citizen'.
- The promotion of 'traditional British values' gives rise to fears about nationalism, and to more division than consensus.
- Cynical attitudes about politics and politicians – and an apathy if not antipathy.
- Citizenship undermines the traditional constitutional relationship of 'ruler' and 'ruled'.
- The tendency in schools to steer clear of political education in order to remain balanced and unbiased.
- Emphasis given to moral values and human rights rather than political values, relationships and processes.
- Growing resentment and antipathy towards government interference in education.

Frazer's conclusion was that citizenship education is a fragile coalition of interest groups whose educational aims cannot all be realised.

The fact is that in England, Wales and Northern Ireland citizenship education is being delivered in a variety of ways. A DfES sponsored study (Kerr *et al.* 2003) found that in England two-thirds of school leaders had an exiting strategy for teaching citizenship and that 90 per cent was delivered through citizenship-related modules in personal, social and health education (PSHE). Other opportunities were provided through schools councils and clubs but with a take-up rate of only 10 per cent. In the main, planning for citizenship education seemed to have been undertaken by head teachers with little or no consultation with teachers or students, and 75 per cent of schools have appointed a co-ordinator with a view to using existing staff to deliver citizenship education through existing subjects and other curriculum provision.

Citizenship and business education

The foregoing account should raise some concerns in the minds of any teacher of business education interested in the linking of their subject to citizenship education. Notwithstanding the issues of definition and purpose, business education teachers might be well placed to either 'host' some aspects of citizenship education in their own subjects or act as a catalyst across the school. But do so with some caution, especially in consideration of the sorts of criticism wielded by Chris Woodhead:

> In principle, it sounds fine…Tackled sensibly this would be a sensible agenda. But in fact, the subject is set to become an educational nightmare: ludicrously grandiose in its aspirations, shot through with political correctness and based upon the discredited progressive thinking that has damaged the lives of so many children…If the government really wanted to do something about citizenship it would tackle illiteracy and ignorance…
>
> (*The Sunday Times*, 21 April 2002)

As Davies (2004: 26) asked, 'Why should teachers of economics and business devote any of their precious time to fishing in these murky waters?' First, he drew attention to the need to protect the subjects' interests and by remaining interested in citizenship avoid the threat of cut-backs. Second, he saw direct links to GCSE syllabus revisions such as 'to appreciate the perspectives of a range of stakeholders in relation to the environment, individuals, government and enterprise' and to the citizenship requirement for pupils to know 'how the economy functions'. This presents economics and business teachers with a range of choices. Not least, he suggested, is the need to remain interested and involved in both planning and practice or face exclusion.

Given the advance of the global economy and concerns for 'citizens' to be aware of democratic processes there seems to be a case for economics and business teachers to make a contribution. So, whereas it seems like good sense to suggest that young people should understand something about how the economy works and is managed – not least so that they can then make informed decisions – deciding what to teach, when to teach and how to teach it is not so clear. Schools are so different in terms of curriculum provision, management styles and the people who work in them that there is no point in even trying to provide a panacea. Individual teachers, if they are so predisposed, will have to find ways of promoting change within their own institutions mindful of the need to steer a course which does not bring them into conflict with others. Teachers of economics and business might choose, therefore, either to advance citizenship education in their own classroom or to act as a catalyst for curriculum change.

A particular contribution that teachers of economics and business might make is to bring to bear their skills in getting pupils to consider matters from a range of perspectives. This is about exploring alternative perspectives and solutions, being aware of the implications of one choice over another and the consequential impacts of decision-making on people, communities, the economy and the environment. Moreover, these are the sorts of skills which young people need when they move through their lives so that they can assess the effects of government policy, and on which ultimately they will base their decision in elections. This is close to the rationale expressed by the Curriculum and Assessment Authority for Wales (ACCAC 2002: 6), which suggests that education for sustainable development and global citizenship is about

- the links between society, economy and environment and between our own lives and those of people throughout the world;
- the needs and rights of both present and future generations;
- the relationships between power, resources and human rights;
- the local and global implications of everything we do.

A problem which teachers of economics and business must address is the place and emphasis they want to give to economic and business theory. Outside the economics and business classroom a theory-first approach is unlikely to be helpful, although this is not to say that some theory is not a good idea. However, outside the specialist classroom it is probably better that the approaches and analytical frameworks, the 'ways of working' and ways of thinking that economics and business offers, are given prominence. Indeed, economics and business teachers are well used to getting their pupils to engage in argument and critical thinking, to identify strengths and weaknesses, to consider the alternatives, to look at costs and benefits from the point of view of individuals, local communities, the national economy and beyond.

This requires a structured and incremental approach to learning. This starts with teachers providing relevant tasks with the appropriate support, but it also allows an important role for pupils to develop their own line of thinking and own line of enquiry. How to find information, how to make judgements about the quality of the information, and how to analyse it and synthesise it into an argument, are all important abilities. 'Listening' to the views and arguments of others is another essential ingredient and this involves in different ways taking 'on board' other people's points of view, assimilating new information and, if appropriate, modifying one's own opinion. Crucially, it is about having an open mind but, at the same time, being able to use available evidence to recommend a solution to a problem. In this way, the contribution from economics and business is to challenge what is often taken for granted, and this helps to ensure that citizenship is not a place to rehearse and develop entrenched and dogmatic positions. Citizenship ought to be about promoting fairness, tolerance and mutual respect and, as the Northern Ireland Council for Curriculum, Assessment and Examinations (www.CCEA.org.uk) stated, should provide pupils with opportunities to engage in democratic processes that foster

- the right to be heard and the responsibility to listen to others;
- the right to be treated fairly and the responsibility to treat others in a similar fashion;
- an understanding of the consequences of individual and collective decisions and subsequent actions.

Perhaps what we ought to accept is that outside specialist economics classrooms, or even within them, the case made by Davies (2002) for an economic element in citizenship education is, to say the least, very challenging. For example, developing what he called an economic understanding of matters – such as the imposition of stealth taxes; the power of large corporations over small firms, individuals and governments; the importance of asset values; or the long-term implications of economic policy – are indeed important matters, but they cannot be reduced to a set of handy hints delivered via a worksheet in PSHE. Indeed, as he pointed out, these are difficult concepts to inculcate and it is unlikely that schools will take the 'maximalist' approach that he suggests is necessary.

Summary

It is clear that citizenship education offers opportunities for teachers of business education to become involved in its planning and/or delivery if they so choose. Although it remains a contested area both in its definition and for space in the school curriculum, this does mean that there is scope for teachers to shape its form and content, and in so doing they can draw on the advice from the various curriculum bodies. In terms of economic understanding contributing to citizenship education, specialist economics and business teachers would regard Davies' (2002) proposals as a sound basis but might wonder if head teachers would allocate the necessary resources to this.

End note

Citizenship is also offered as a specialist subject. 'Citizenship Studies' is offered as a GCSE short course and 'Social Science: Citizenship' as an AS level.

For further information see:

www.accac.org.uk
www.qca.org.uk
www.dfes.gov.uk
www.ccea.org.uk

References

ACCAC (2002) *Education for Sustainable Development and Global Citizenship.* Cardiff: QCA for Wales (www.accac.org.uk).

Bernstein, B. (1996) *Pedagogy, Symbolic Control and Identity: Theory, Research, Critique.* London: Taylor and Francis.

Davies, I., Gregory, I. and Riley, S. (1999) *Good Citizenship and Educational Provision.* London: Falmer Press.

Davies, P. (2002) *Educating Citizens for Changing Economics*. Institute for Education Policy Research, Staffordshire University, Working Paper 2.

Davies, P. (2004) 'Contributing to citizenship education by improving the quality of students' arguments', *Teaching Economics and Business* 8(2), 26–30.

Economics Association (1985) *Understanding Economics: Young Person as Citizen*. Harlow: Longman.

Frazer, E. (2000) 'Citizenship education: anti-political culture and political education in Britain', *Political Studies* **48**, 88–103.

Goodson, I. F. (1983) *School Subjects and Curriculum Change*. Beckenham, Kent: Croom Helm.

Goodson, I. F. (1988) *The Making of Curriculum: Collected Essays*. London: Falmer Press.

Goodson, I. F. (1991) 'Studying curriculum: a social constructionist perspective', in I. F. Goodson and R. Walker (eds), *Biography, Identity and Sociology*. Basingstoke: Falmer Press, pp. 168–81.

Hall, T., Williamson, H. and Coffey, A. (1998) 'Conceptualizing citizenship: young people and the transition to adulthood', *Journal of Education Policy*, **13**(3), 301–15.

Hall, T., Coffey, A. and Williamson, H. (1999) 'Self, space and place: youth identities and citizenship', *British Journal of Sociology of Education* **20**(4), 501–13.

Halliday, J. (1999) 'Political liberalism and citizenship education: towards curriculum reform', *British Journal of Educational Studies* **47**(1), 43–55.

Isin, E. F., and Wood, P. K. (1999) *Citizenship and Identity*. London: Sage.

Jephcote, M. (2004) 'Economics in the school curriculum: its origins, and reflections on the workings of a subject community', *Teaching Business and Economics* 8(1), 13–19.

Kerr, D., Cleaver, E., Ireland, E. and Blenkinsop, S. (2003) *Citizenship Education Longitudinal Study: First Cross-Sectional Survey 2001–2002*, DfES Research Report 416. London: DfES.

Paechter, C. F. (1998) 'Schooling and the ownership of knowledge', *Curriculum Studies* 6(2), 161–76.

Qualifications and Curriculum Authority (1998) *Final Report of the Advisory Group on Education for Citizenship and the Teaching of Democracy in Schools*. London: QCA.

Szreter, R. (1967) 'Economics in secondary education', in N. Lee (ed.), *Teaching Economics*. Sutton: Economics Association, pp. 13–23.

Whitty, G., Rowe, G. and Aggleston, P. (1994a) 'Discourse in cross-curricular contexts: limits to empowerment', *International Studies in Sociology of Education* **4**(1), 25–42.

Whitty, G., Rowe, G. and Aggleston, P. (1994b) 'Subjects and themes in the secondary-school curriculum', *Research Papers in Education, Policy and Practice* **9**(2), 159–82.

PART 2

Teaching and Learning

Teaching, learning and assessment in business education

Martin Jephcote and Ian Abbott

Introduction

This section of the book includes chapters which explore the different ways in which teaching, learning and assessment takes place in business education classrooms and reflects some of the approaches commonly employed. It also reflects some of the contexts in which teaching and learning in business education takes place, such as applied business or enterprise. Overall, the purpose of this chapter and those that follow is not to attempt to provide a theoretical understanding of learning processes but to give insights into what teachers and learners do in the contexts in which teaching and learning takes place.

The politics of teaching, learning and assessment

It is something of an understatement to suggest that the 14–19 phase marks a critical stage in young people's lives. For many, however, we know that the transition into adult life and employment is not a smooth process. Many lose interest in learning before the age of 16 and so many others never realise their full potential. For a minority, disaffection becomes part of a cycle of low expectations, disengagement and poor achievement. This not only leads to poor life chances for individuals but also undermines the goal of economic growth. As the era of information, knowledge and global competition unfolds, familiar and old ways of doing things quickly disappear and so too the types of jobs and the skills they need. Those teaching business education subjects have long recognised the contribution they can make in providing an education that better prepares young people for the challenges of living and working in a fast-changing society. We need, however, to do more than provide the key skills needed by employers but also construct a society which builds on and extends the wider capacities and talents of individuals.

What is clear from other chapters in this book is that central government has recognised not just the link between education and economic performance but also, in turn, the need for greater control over curriculum content and assessment. So, for example, the Qualifications and Curriculum Authority (QCA) provides definitions of subjects, their aims, contents and assessment objectives and dictates the types of assessment and the balance between them. According to the QCA:

- Business studies concerns the business aspects of organisations within their economic, political and social contexts. Business studies involves the investigation of how enterprise adds value by organising the production of goods and services. The performance of business is studied from a range of perspectives. Economics is one of several disciplines which contributes to the understanding and analysis of business behaviour.

- Economics is concerned with the interdependent behaviour of consumers, producers and governments as they allocate and distribute scarce resources. Economics involves the investigation of the allocation of scarce resources to the production and distribution of income and wealth. Business provides an important context in which economists study resource allocation.

At A/AS level, the QCA business studies criteria state that students should be encouraged to

- develop a critical understanding of organisations, the markets they serve and the process of adding value. This should involve consideration of the internal workings and management of organisations and, in particular, the process of decision-making in a dynamic external environment;

- be aware that business behaviour can be studied from the perspectives of a range of stakeholders including customer, manager, creditor, owner/shareholder and employee. In addition, students should be aware of the economic, environmental, ethical, governmental, legal, social and technological issues associated with business activity. Students should understand that Business Studies draws on a variety of disciplines and that these perspectives and disciplines are interrelated;

- acquire a range of skills including decision-making and problem-solving in the light of evaluation and, where appropriate, the quantification and management of information.

The criteria further state that students should acquire a critical understanding of businesses and the environment within which they work and be able to evaluate material and information as presented in a range of formats so as to distinguish between fact and opinion in order to make informed judgements. Business studies should provide opportunities for developing and generating evidence for assessing the Key Skills:

- Communication
- Information Technology

- Application of Number
- Improving Own Learning and Performance
- Working with Others
- Problem-Solving

The 'learning trilogy'

From behaviourist psychology it is perhaps Bloom's taxonomy of educational objectives which continues to have a significant impact on teaching, learning and assessment. In its most simple form Bloom categorised learning as a hierarchy (see Table 5.1).

Table 5.1 Bloom's taxonomy of educational objectives

Knowledge	Define / name / recognise / recall
Comprehension	Identify / illustrate / explain
Application	Select / predict / use / demonstrate
Analysis	Compare / contrast / criticise / differentiate
Synthesis	Discuss / argue / relate / summarise
Evaluation	Judge / determine / defend

A reading of many business and economics syllabuses, examination board assessment criteria and the chapters in this book written by teachers and examiners give witness to the pervasiveness of this taxonomy. For example, see Table 5.2 for the assessment objectives (AO) prescribed by the Assessment and Qualifications Alliance (AQA) for A/AS level Business Studies.

Table 5.2 The AQA assessment objectives for A /AS level Business Studies

	Assessment Objectives	*Weighting*		
		AS	*A2*	*A level*
AO1	Demonstrate knowledge and understanding of the specified content	25–35%	15–25%	20–30%
AO2	Apply knowledge and critical understanding to problems and issues arising from both familiar and unfamiliar situations	20–30%	20–30%	20–30%
AO3	Analyse problems, issues and situations	20–30%	20–30%	20–30%
AO4	Evaluate, distinguish between fact and opinion, and assess information from a variety of sources	15–25%	25–35%	20–30%

Like it or not, Bloom's taxonomy continues to provide a specification for learning and the design of modes of assessment and, all too often, also provides a rationale for the selection of the strategies and approaches for teaching and learning. Where teachers view the success of their students in terms of grades achieved in external examinations, the need for a close articulation of this learning trilogy – between learning objectives, approaches to teaching and learning and modes of assessment – is all too apparent. At worst, this leads to a curriculum content which does not stray from the published syllabus, where teacher exposition and directed activities crowd out any room for learners' inquisitiveness and classroom assessment strategies are only those used by the examination board.

Of course, there does need to be an articulation between objectives, strategies and assessment. So, for example, if importance is attached to the acquisition of a set of facts then a straightforward transmission mode of teaching and a multiple choice test will suffice. If, however, importance is attached to making an evaluative judgement, it would seem to be more important to give learners access to a range of information and ask them to engage in an analysis of it. In this case an essay or a presentation to a critical audience will be a more appropriate form of assessment. However, again the AQA set out a framework which specifies the balance of internal and external assessment and the type and range of synoptic testing to be employed. A level specifications in business studies may have a maximum internal assessment weighting of 30 per cent. All specifications should include a minimum of 20 per cent synoptic assessment, and all synoptic assessment units should be taken at the end of the course and be externally assessed. Ways in which synoptic assessment might be conducted include

- decision-making/problem-solving exercises, requiring candidates to draw together knowledge, understanding and skills learned throughout the course to tackle a decision, problem or issue that is new to them;
- a case study within which specific questions require candidates to apply knowledge, understanding and skills learned throughout the course;
- internal assessment requiring candidates to apply knowledge, understanding and skills learned in other parts of the course, e.g. a project based on experience of work;
- preparing a business plan.

At what is often regarded as the end-stage, the AQA also determine the overall grade criteria. Its grade descriptions indicate the level of attainment characteristic of the given grade at A level and give a general indication of the required learning outcomes at each specified grade. The grade awarded will depend in practice upon the extent to which the candidate has met the assessment objectives overall. Shortcomings in some aspects of the examination may be balanced by better performances in others.

Grade A

Candidates will demonstrate in-depth knowledge and critical understanding of a wide range of business theory and concepts. They will apply this knowledge and understanding to analyse familiar and unfamiliar situations, problems and issues, using appropriate numerical and non-numerical techniques accurately. They will effectively evaluate evidence and arguments, making reasoned judgements to present appropriate and supported conclusions.

Grade C

Candidates will demonstrate knowledge and understanding of a range of business theory and concepts. They will apply this knowledge and understanding to analyse familiar and unfamiliar situations, problems and issues. They will use both numerical and non-numerical techniques. They will evaluate evidence and arguments to present reasoned conclusions.

Grade E

Candidates will demonstrate knowledge and understanding of a limited range of business theory and concepts. They will show some ability to use this knowledge and understanding in order to analyse familiar and unfamiliar situations, problems and issues. They will make some use of both numerical and non-numerical techniques. Candidates' evaluation of evidence and arguments will be limited.

From teaching to learning

The terms 'teaching and learning' and perhaps more often 'learning and teaching' are now a part of the common language of the teacher. This language reflects a desire to close the gap between, on the one hand, teachers and teaching and, on the other, learners and learning. This might appear to be a play on words, but it is more than that. The new language signifies both a shift, or at least the desire for a shift, in the relationship between teachers and learners and the ways in which teaching and learning and its assessment is transacted. It represents an attempt to move from the teacher-led transmission mode of didactic teaching to a student-centred, interactive and participatory style of learning and to a more inclusive notion of assessment.

In the teacher-led approach, historically associated with behavioural psychology, the starting-point is the formulation of objectives, that is, statements about what the teacher decides is important to be learned. Knowledge is 'owned' by the teacher and, more or less, teaching is about passing on this knowledge, and the teaching styles adopted ensure that learners acquire an indisputable body of facts. In its narrowest conception, this behaviourist approach is an ends–means model of learning with teachers acting in the role of instructor, employing a limited range of testing strategies. In contrast, experiential learning gives emphasis to 'learning-by-doing', in which the teacher adopts the role of facilitator of learning. In its extreme, students take control of their own learning, are encouraged to engage in open-ended reflection and self-evaluation and might even have a hand in the design of their own assessment. Knowledge is regarded as tentative, open to challenge, and recognises the importance of learners' prior experiences and 'everyday' knowledge.

Moreover, we live in a world where learners are no longer prepared to be treated as passive recipients. As teachers we know that successful learning is underpinned by 'tapping-into' learners' own interests and by motivating learners through interesting, challenging and relevant activities. All too often, however, an emphasis on testing can have a negative impact on motivation and on learners' future learning. Moreover, low achievers are doubly disadvantaged by tests in the way that being labelled as a failure impacts on their ability to learn and further lowers their self-esteem and the chance of future effort and success (Assessment Reform Group 2002a).

There are a wide variety of strategies and resources to draw on, as shown in Table 5.3.

Table 5.3 Strategies and resources

Strategies	Resources
Teacher exposition	Handouts / worksheets
Class discussion	Newspapers
Group work	Photographs
Role play	Books
Visits / fieldwork	Databases
Debates	Internet
Games / simulations	TV / video
Visitors	CD-ROM
E-learning	Case studies
Projects	

The relationship between teacher and learner might be seen in terms of it being 'closed' or 'open'. The difference is to do with the ownership of the task, how the classroom is organised to promote learning and, ultimately, the extent to which a learner will engage in what they think is an abstract or an irrelevant issue.

Table 5.4 Relationships between teachers and learners

	Closed	Open
Context	Controlled by the teacher, not negotiable. Over-adherence to the examination syllabus.	Framed by the teacher, but with room for negotiation. Goes beyond the confines of the examination syllabus.
Origin and frame	Teacher sets the problem. Objectives are tightly specified. Questions and answers are predetermined.	Teacher maps the problem but allows students a role in setting the parameters. Objectives enable exploration, enquiry and risk.
Focus/key concepts	Knowledge is 'fixed', questions are met with 'right' answers. Little or no room for value judgements.	Knowledge is tentative, limitations are recognised, questions are explored. Value judgements are expressed and explored.
Tasks	Hypotheses are given. Arguments are staged; pre-set and routine tasks lead to a well-rehearsed solution to a bounded problem.	Students make or contribute to formulation of hypotheses, and generate their own arguments. Problem-solving tasks are open-ended, require investigation and can result in alternative solutions.
Methods/ Strategies	Criteria for judging the solution to a problem are given. Methods are chosen to underpin the right answer and accepted solution. An emphasis on note-taking and routine activities.	Criteria for judging a solution to a problem are open to discussion. Investigations, discussion and presentation allow for an expression of value judgements, and evaluation of alternative solutions.
Students' role	Students employ routine methods. Discussion is limited, superficial and in search of predetermined answers. Students passively accept foregone conclusions, there is little or no time for personal reflection.	Students select methods best suited to an investigation. Group work and discussion are central. Students are encouraged to come to their own conclusions and support these with accumulated evidence. Students are encouraged to reflect on their own interpretations.
Accounts	Students reproduce textbook accounts and conclusions. By and large accounts are 'stylised', accepting of theory and are uncritical.	Students recognise complexity, and can evaluate alternative solutions to problems.

The setting of objectives, and the choice of strategies and resources, must satisfy the test of 'fitness for purpose' and should not be used for the sake of it. Thought should be given to the different preferences and learning styles that learners exhibit. As a 'rule-ofthumb' it is perhaps better to employ a variety of strategies and resources so as to appeal to a range of learning styles and to be more motivational.

Supporting learning

In its extreme version, student-centred 'learning-by-doing' teachers abdicate their responsibilities and leave learners stranded. There are, therefore, important roles for the teacher in supporting students' learning. Some of these are shown in Table 5.5.

Table 5.5 Supporting students' learning

Planning	Turns the syllabus into a scheme of work, plans lessons, prepares resources
Framing	Whether open or closed, teacher frames the learning
Asking questions	Probes learners' understanding, challenges ideas
Monitoring	Maintains overall direction
Supporting	Provides encouragement and gives access to information
Checking	Evaluates progress, attends to individuals
Provide feedback	Encourages and supports future learning
Reflecting	Engages in self-review and encourages learners to review their own learning

This sort of structured approach might too easily lend itself to tight teacher control and prescription where an overall purpose is to get learners to come to a common understanding. If so, this is likely to ignore the ways in which learners make sense of the world around them and the ways in which they bring to and use their everyday knowledge in the classroom. An important stage of learning, therefore, is to get learners to reflect on the differences between what they know and believe and what the teacher or other students know and believe. In this way, they are not led to believe that their own 'knowledge' is necessarily right but are encouraged to reassess its basis.

Assessment

An important part of the role of any teacher will be the assessment of their learners. Assessment has been the focus of increased interest, and indeed reform, since the introduction of the National Curriculum in 1988. The changes that have been introduced have placed increased emphasis on assessment at each Key Stage and particularly within the 14–19 age group.

A number of issues arise in relation to assessment. In particular concerns are raised over the assessment of those skills which are said to be naturally occurring, such as taking part in discussions or listening and responding appropriately. Clearly these are very different from assessing if a learner has totalled a column of figures correctly.

At the heart of this dilemma is the need to provide accountability across a wide range of learning experiences and programmes of study, to confirm learning, to measure standards and effectiveness as well as to contribute to the personal development of learners. It is clear from this that assessment performs a range of functions:

> For now, it is important to note that learning is not simply a cognitive (thinking) activity. There are equally important emotional and social dimensions to learning. One's beliefs about one's own capacity to learn are shaped by previous experience of learning which translates into positive or negative motivation and poor or high self-esteem. Social pressures from the peer group, school and family also play a part in enhancing or inhibiting one's capacity to learn. Well judged feedback and feedforward attend therefore, not only to the cognitive aspects of learning but also to those more elusive social and emotional elements.
>
> (Brooks 2002: 21)

Formative and summative assessment

Formative assessment provides a continuous process which charts achievement, identifies areas for development and indicates next steps. It can be both formal and informal. Action planning may be part of the formative assessment process in that students should be asked to consider what they need to do next in order to move their learning on. Formative assessment will be part of the overall process of teaching and it enables teachers to intervene in the learning process which is used to influence future teaching and learning. A teacher can use formative assessment even before any teaching has taken place because teachers should identify the starting-point of learners. It is important for teachers to know what learners in their class know, and in some cases what they don't know. This information can then be used to develop strategies to improve teaching and learning. The crucial aspect of this process is feedback, which should be of benefit to teachers and learners. Feedback should influence the design and delivery of future lessons and it should guide and motivate learners.

Summative assessment is used to judge if the aims of the course have been achieved, for example through the setting of a final examination. It usually results in the award of a mark, grade or level. With competence-based qualifications, summative assessment is used to ensure all units have been covered and that evidence has been provided to confirm it. However, it is important to remember that summative assessment can be used in a formative way because examination or test results can be used to influence future learning. The key aspect is not the timing or the type of assessment, rather the purpose (Wiliam and Black 1996). If assessment is used to provide feedback to improve teaching and learning, then it is formative. If learners are given a written task in a business education lesson and the teacher just gives a series of ticks and records marks that would be summative assessment. It only becomes formative when the information is used to alter future teaching or to give feedback to learners.

Providing appropriate feedback is an essential part of the teacher's job, but there is a common misconception that feedback will automatically lead to improved learner performance:

> Even when teachers' comments on work are thorough and point the way to improvement, pupils often do not engage with or respond to them. Corrections are frequently not made. Inadequate work is seldom improved. Even when pupils attempt to respond to comments, teachers do not sufficiently acknowledge this when next marking their books. The full potential of marking to support progress is rarely capitalised on.
>
> (Ofsted 1998: 93)

Teachers therefore have to provide feedback to learners, and this can be a difficult process. It is important that teachers develop the skills of providing effective feedback to learners. Details of effective and less successful approaches to feedback are given in Table 5.6.

Assessment for learning

Assessment then is not simply seen as something which is used for grading work, it is recognised as part of the overall learning process. Assessment *of* learning is usually something done to pupils and is usually associated with external assessment and awards. Assessment *for* learning is about classroom assessment that is used to improve learning and raise standards. To this end the Assessment Reform Group (2002b) drew on widespread research to propose the use of ten guiding principles (see Table 5.7):

> Assessment for learning is the process of seeking and interpreting evidence for use by learners and their teachers to decide where the learners are in their learning, where they need to go and how best to get there.

Assessment for learning is important within business education, and successful adoption of this approach will clearly lead to improved performance in external examinations for learners. Within the subject area there is a great deal of attention paid to preparing learners for public examinations. The contents of the EBEA journal, *Teaching Business and Economics*, testifies to the importance of this. In any edition there will usually be at least one article devoted to dealing with assessment issues in the subject area. The proliferation of coursework and the variety of different types of examination have been a major cause of concern for subject teachers. However, this advice on how best to prepare learners for end-of-course or module assessments is no substitute for effective teaching:

> How best to tackle an examination paper is an important skill for students to acquire, but it is best seen as a complement to good teaching and not a substitute for it. It is a route towards more efficient performance in examinations, in that it serves to enable students to make the

most of what they know and can do. How much they know and can do, however, is determined by the quality of their teaching and learning experience during the whole of their time on the course, and that in turn is very much a function of your skill not only in teaching but also in compiling a coherent programme for the course you offer.

(Phillips and Unwin 2001: 29)

Table 5.6 Providing Feedback (adapted from Brooks 2004: 120)

Constructive	Counterproductive
Prompt feedback (The ideal is immediate feedback provided during performance so that pupils have an opportunity to implement what they have learnt before the work is completed)	*Delayed feedback* (Most likely to be ignored if pupils have already moved on to a new topic)
Written comments (When used to provide a clear explanation of ways in which work is successful and how future performance could be improved)	*Marks and grades* (A powerful form of feedback which 'overrides' comments. Encourages complacency in the able and despondency in the less able)
Task-involving feedback (Focuses on the knowledge, skills and concepts relevant to succeeding with a task)	*Ego-involving feedback* (Encourages pupils to focus on themselves, how well they are performing and comparing themselves with others)
Criterion-referenced assessment (Assessment is linked to explicit criteria which are clarified before pupils embark on a task)	*Criterion-weak assessment* (Criteria are muddled (Ofsted 1998) or tacit)
Scaffolded feedback (Creates a 'state of mindfulness' (Black and William 1990: 51) with regard to the feedback, giving pupils as much help as they need to progress but no more)	*Corrective feedback* (Least helpful where teachers correct every error so that pupils are not encouraged to think about or apply the feedback)
Balanced feedback (Strengths and achievements are set against areas for improvement without dwelling unduly on either)	*Unbalanced feedback* (Dwells on the positive or the negative without properly acknowledging the other dimension)
Positive tone (Can be created by acknowledging achievements first and treating weaknesses as targets for development)	*Negative tone* (Can be created by drawing attention to what is wrong with work first or offering critical comments with no indication of how to improve)
Feedforward present (Can be achieved by providing time for pupils to read and respond to feedback and by following up on previous feedback next time)	*Feedforward absent* (Where teachers neglect the links between feedback and future performance, pupils are encouraged to do likewise)

Table 5.7 Principles to guide assessment for learning (adapted from *Assessment for Learning: Research-Based Principles to Guide Classroom Practice*, Assessment Reform Group, 2002, www.assessment-reform-group.org.uk)

Principle 'Assessment for learning…	*Application* 'Assessment for learning should…
Is part of effective planning	Be part of effective planning of teaching and learning; learners should use information about progress to plan their own learning
Focuses on how students learn	Focus on how students learn; learners should be aware of the 'how' of learning and not just the 'what'
Is central to classroom practice	Be recognised as central to classroom practice; should be part of an ongoing dialogue between teachers and learners
Is a key professional skill	Be regarded as a key professional skill for teachers; teachers need to develop skills in observing learning, and analysing and interpreting evidence
Is sensitive and constructive	Recognise the emotional impact of assessment; assessment can have an impact on confidence and motivation
Fosters motivation	Take account of learner motivation; provide constructive feedback and emphasise progress
Promotes understanding of goals and criteria	Promote commitment to a shared understanding of the assessment criteria
Helps learners know how to improve	Provide constructive feedback to learners on how to improve; learners need to know how they can improve in their next stage of learning
Develops the capacity for self-assessment	Help learners with a capacity for self-assessment to be more reflective and self-managing
Recognises all educational achievement	Recognise the full range of learners' achievements; when learners do their best it should be recognised

Assessment reform

Assessment and, in particular, testing has become a significant feature of education in all parts of the UK. However, this is especially true in England:

Many children starting school in 2000 should expect to take some form of external test or examination every year with the sole exception of year 8, although even here some new tests are planned for the most able...England has now achieved the dubious distinction of subjecting its school pupils to more external tests than any other country in the world and spending more money on doing so.

(James 2000: 351)

A complicated system of assessment has been developed with the ultimate aim of raising standards of learner achievement. An outcome of this process is that secondary schools now have a wealth of data from National Curriculum testing which provides a set of benchmarks allowing comparisons to be made. This is obtained in a number of ways, but most significantly through the DfES Autumn Package which has information on pupil performance across England, and can be used to compare present with previous data (www.dfes.gov.uk/standards). For example 2004 Key Stage 3 results can be compared to the 2001 Key Stage 2 results. GCSE results can also be compared against levels of performance in Key Stage 3 tests. In addition many schools now buy into the Year Eleven Information System (YELLIS) and the A Level Information System (ALIS). This information allows schools to track and compare patterns of learner performance over a number of years. This system enables schools to explore patterns of good and poor performance and build this into future planning.

The wealth of assessment information available does, however, create some problems for schools and individual teachers because this has to be translated into action in relation to teaching and learning. The danger is that the data are only used to give information about what has already happened and in some cases what has gone wrong. It subsequently becomes easy to blame teachers and schools for poor performance. So the data have to be made useful to teachers and learners so that they can improve performance:

> The use of national data sets could easily promote a fatalistic approach about what might or might not be possible: a pupil with a particular input score might easily be written off given the predictions about what pupils with that input score might expect to attain by the end of their schooling...The challenge, therefore, is to use data to demonstrate to learners that if the majority of pupils with a given profile will end up with a particular outcome, then application, commitment, effort and good teaching can help them to do better than that.

(Husbands 2004: 132)

Many schools have utilised the available data by adopting target-setting for individual learners. Subject specialists working with pastoral colleagues take the data and translate this into realistic targets for learners to achieve. The success of this approach depends on the development of effective teaching strategies and positive mentoring. This is an approach commonly utilised in business education. The emphasis within the subject area on teaching groups who are going to be taking public examinations makes some form of target-setting inevitable. Teachers are judged internally by examination results.

Schools are then subjected to public scrutiny by the annual publication of examination results.

If the huge amount of data that are collected is not used to improve learner performance then there would appear to be little benefit gained from the huge amount of money and effort allocated to this process. The data can only provide so much, and while it is an important diagnostic tool it is then up to individual teachers and learners to decide how best to take this process forward.

In common with other areas of the curriculum the assessment systems in business and economics have been subject to frequent change over recent years. As we have seen the Government has placed great emphasis on assessment in the form of testing as a means of measuring rising standards. However, this might actually disguise some of the more fundamental problems, which exist:

> By requiring testing to take place, policymakers can be seen to be addressing critical reform issues. So a high stakes testing programme is often a symbolic solution to a real educational problem. It offers the appearance of a solution, and indeed, as test scores rise over time, because of teaching to the test, policymakers can point to the wisdom of their action. However, the reality is that the testing programme may not be a cure for the education problem.
>
> (Gipps 1994: 35)

The latest proposals to reform the 14–19 assessment system in England contain some interesting proposals for the reform of the assessment procedures. In particular there is a strong emphasis on giving teachers a greater role in the assessment process:

> Diplomas and components would be assessed in ways which support teaching and learning and greater intellectual and skills development, and are fit for purpose. Within open diplomas up to and including intermediate level, assessment of main learning and the extended project would be predominately teacher-led. This does not mean the end of examinations and tests. Assessment should be conducted on through a range of different styles including time limited test and examinations, set assignments, and practical and written tests and observations, some of which should be externally assessed, both to reinforce teachers' own assessments and to aid national monitoring of standards.
>
> (DfES 2004: 9)

Generally, the move to increase the involvement of teachers in the assessment process should create a range of opportunities for teachers and learners. If the proposals are implemented, this development should also enable the introduction of a more flexible system which takes more account of individual learner needs. However, there will be increased pressure on teachers if more time is required for assessment purposes. There will also be an ongoing debate about standards because teacher assessment is often deemed to be less rigorous than external examinations. It is to be hoped that learning becomes paramount with a movement away from teaching to the exam.

Summary

The emphasis placed on raising learner performance and the key role attached to assessment in this process has resulted in an ongoing debate about standards. It is too simplistic to say that education standards are rising or falling. At 14–19 level the changes that have taken place in subject content, and the structure and type of assessment, have made it difficult to compare past with present performance. Too often improvements in learner performance are greeted with claims that the assessment has become easier. What it is true to say is that the assessment process has changed. The movement away from traditional end-of-course examinations and the development of more coursework and case study material in business and economics has resulted in fundamental changes to teaching and learning. Learners are being asked to develop a different set of skills with more emphasis on research, analysis, synthesis, application and evaluation. In addition learners are required to utilise ICT and to take more responsibility for their own learning.

As a consequence of these developments there is a need for a different sort of articulation between learning, teaching and assessment. In a system driven by external assessment and subject to external control there is a need for teachers to reclaim their classrooms. Above all else, the classroom is a place where teacher and learners interact so that the setting of learning objectives, the use of teaching and learning strategies and assessment should be part of an iterative process. This implies some sort of dialogue between teachers and learners so that the process of learning is based on ongoing reflection and review. The huge amount of data available on learner performance should be used to support this process. Planning, teaching and reviewing should be part of an ongoing cycle so that teachers, and to some extent learners, are constantly asking:

- Have the learning objectives been met?
- What evidence is there that learning has taken place?
- Was there an articulation between the learning objectives, strategies and assessment?
- What can I do to improve learning and teaching?
- How can I use data to improve teacher and learner performance?
- How does assessment support the learning process?

References

Assessment Reform Group (2002a) *Testing, Motivation and Learning.* Cambridge: University of Cambridge Faculty of Education.

Assessment Reform Group (2002b) *Assessment for Learning: Research-based Principles to Guide Classroom Practice.* Assessment Reform Group.

Black, P. and Wiliam, D. (1998) 'Assessment and classroom learning', *Assessment in Education* **5**(1), 7–78.

Brooks, V. (2002) *Assessment in Secondary Schools.* Buckingham: Open University Press.

Brooks, V. (2004) 'Using assessment for formative purposes', in V. Brooks, I. Abbott and L. Bills (eds), *Preparing to Teach in Secondary Schools.* Maidenhead: Open University Press.

DfES (2004) *14–19 Curriculum and Qualifications Reform. Final Report of the Working Group on 14–19 Reform: Summary.* London: DfES.

Gipps, C. V. (1994) *Beyond Testing: Towards a Theory of Educational Assessment.* London: Falmer.

Husbands, C. (2004) 'Using assessment to support pupil achievement', in V. Brooks, I. Abbott and L. Bills (eds), *Preparing to Teach in Secondary Schools.* Maidenhead: Open University Press.

James, M. (2000) 'Measured lives: the rise of assessment as the engine of change in English schools', *The Curriculum Journal,* **11**(3), 343–64.

Ofsted (1998) *Secondary Education 1993–1997: A Review of Secondary Schools in England.* London: The Stationery Office.

Phillips, P., and Unwin, A. (2001) 'Passing the test: assessing business finance on the AVCE Business', *Teaching Business and Economics* **5**(3), 24–9.

Wiliam, D. and Black, P. (1996) 'Meanings and consequences: a basis for distinguishing formative and summative functions of assessment?' *British Educational Research Journal* **22**(5), 537–48.

Using ICT in the business education classroom

Lech Wersocki

Introduction

The aim of this chapter is to show how to use information communication technologies (ICT) to help teaching and learning in the business education classroom. It will give examples of good practice and in doing so will help teachers to develop those resources and practices to achieve subject-specific learning outcomes.

It should be remembered, however, that ICT is also taught across the curriculum and is the responsibility of all teachers. For example, as the standards for newly qualified teachers (NQTs) state, they should know how to use ICT effectively both to teach their subject and to support their wider professional role. Moreover, ICT continues to be a motivating force in learning and is a powerful tool in the repertoire of skills and resources an effective teacher brings to the process of learning.

What is effective use of ICT in business education?

According to the Teacher Training Agency (TTA 2000):

- Decisions about when, when not and how to use ICT in lessons should be based on whether the use of ICT supports good practice in teaching the subject. If it does not, it should not be used.

- In planning and in teaching, decisions about when, when not and how to use ICT in a particular lesson or sequence of lessons must be directly related to the teaching and learning objectives in hand.

- The use of ICT should either allow the trainee or the pupil to achieve something that could not be achieved without it; or allow the trainee to teach or the pupils to learn something more effectively and efficiently than they could otherwise; or both.

In practical terms, meeting the criteria set out by the TTA means that the question must always be asked. 'Will the use of ICT aid the business/economics learning objectives?' Evidence from a recent Ofsted (2004: 1) report suggests that, among schools in the UK:

> Business education departments are often at the forefront of using ICT in secondary schools, but in one school in six the use of ICT to enhance teaching and learning is unsatisfactory.

and

> Business education generally makes effective use of IT for the purposes of presentation, research and data handling. Its use beyond these areas is less well developed.

The implication of the above is that there is scope to develop good practice in using ICT to support learning but there is also room to develop the skills of information literacy. This is about:

- finding, selecting and using information appropriately;
- knowing when and why to use or not to use information;
- knowing when and how to apply that which is used in the development of an argument, in the making of a judgement or in proposing a solution to a problem.

In other words, ICT might provide access to information but individuals must develop the skills to use it.

Hardware, software and the school resources

All schools organise their ICT resources in different ways. 'The most effective use of ICT is made in those departments where teachers and pupils have immediate access to ICT' (Ofsted 2004: 5). Good access is 'most often the case where combined ICT and business education faculty have been established' (Ofsted 2004: 10).

Dual purpose ICT rooms/classrooms are very effective in allowing ICT to support business/economics learning. Such rooms allow the class teacher to choose when it is appropriate to use ICT or deskwork rather than being pressured by the constraint of booking an ICT room. It is also good practice to vary the use of the room in the course of one lesson between desk and ICT where each style of teaching supports the other. Likewise, the use of pairs in discussion at the monitor is an excellent way of supporting learning. Larger network rooms that can accommodate a full class may also be available although, as access to these rooms can be limited, preparation for the lesson at the computers is often done beforehand in a standard classroom. This practical constraint still works to separate ICT from other forms of learning and can add to its mystification.

Many schools have data projectors which can run off any computer or the network. These are not difficult to operate and the screen effectively becomes the teacher's monitor. Similarly, interactive whiteboards with their touch-screen facility bring the teacher out from behind a keyboard and can be very helpful for students also to make a point on the board or to run a demonstration.

The internet is very popular among students, but it has been found to be good teacher practice to structure search time online through short focused research activities. Studies have shown that students have wasted much time because of poor search skills or by searching for information which is otherwise easily found in textbooks. Clearly, there is a need for students to acquire and practise these skills. CD-ROMs vary a lot in quality but many still offer a lot of very useful offline data that can be made available on the school or college network or other virtual learning environment (VLE) such as *Blackboard*.

Staff and students

Although the business education department may have its own network, ICT purchasing and resourcing will usually be with the approval of the ICT co-ordinator/head of ICT. They will almost certainly be line-managing the staff who ensure maintenance and upkeep of the networks. Close relationships with these colleagues are essential, particularly if the business/economics department needs to set up files on the school network, input data or information on the school intranet or load software or data for whole-class use.

The ICT skills of students will vary from individual to individual. It would be good practice to review ICT work across the range of levels for a new intake of students at the start of a session or course. Carrying out such a needs analysis will lead to more relevant planning when writing ICT use into a scheme of work. As an alternative, a business-relevant ICT baseline skills test could be devised. An implication of this is that both skills-building and ICT use should as far as possible be differentiated.

Developing good practice

Developing good presentation skills will enhance teaching and learning; so developing Powerpoint skills will be an excellent investment of time. Whether a novice or an experienced practitioner, a very good preparation would be to review Unit 1 of the Year 7 Scheme of Work in the National Strategy, available through www.ncaction.org.uk or www.standards.dfes.gov.uk/keystage3/subjects/ict/. This excellent unit invites Year 7s to design a Powerpoint presentation about themselves. It is a useful learning experience and illustrates how such a presentation should be structured. More broadly it is an interesting insight into one aspect of what some students have already done in Key Stage 3 (and what they are capable of doing in your class) and a demonstration of how to structure teaching in an ICT room.

When putting together a presentation, thought should be given to how pictures and images can be used to reinforce the learning, that is, to make a presentation memorable! Emphasis is not on detailed text but on key terms and bullet points. An important learning aim here can be teaching students how to take notes. Each slide can be the template for a page of notes. The students can copy the heading and bullet points of each slide then add sketches and supplementary notes during explanation and discussion. Depending on the lesson aims and the skills of the class, the teacher may take in students' notes to see that they are developing their skills appropriately. Visual learners will be helped with an image that illustrates the key terms. For example, 'teamworking' can be accompanied by an iconic image of a meeting or a sports team. If teamworking has led to a fall in wastage then let an image of broken crockery fall down the screen as the bullet point appears. If profit is the next point let a currency image rise up the screen. Images can also be mnemonics.

Likewise, auditory learners can be supported too as Powerpoint can offer sound-effects. A rising sales curve can be accompanied by a crescendo. Economic collapse can be signalled by a crash. For the most ICT-literate teacher small video clips can become part of the presentation. Again, use only small memorable clips that fix an idea or concept.

Revision can be supported by lessons where the students have to team up to make a brief presentation on a particular aspect of business, economics or a particular case study. Clear rules have to be set limiting the text on-screen and ensuring a minimum number of slides. In essence, the students have to pare the topic down to its key components for it to work as a presentation, which is what they would do if they were making revision cards or highlighting key phrases. If the presentation is done on an interactive whiteboard then tactile learning can be supported by encouraging them to alter the slides on-screen by moving words and images around by hand.

Wordprocessing, as has been mentioned, is used a lot in writing up coursework but rarely for active learning. Worksheets are a key learning tool. Information, data, questions and answers are the backbone of much student-centred learning. In the 14–19 phase all too often worksheets are content-driven and inaccessible to many students. A good source of inspiration in developing worksheets are those designed for the primary phase or early secondary years; the variety and style of individual and group activities can be adapted to cover business or economic content. As an example, a lively Year 12 lesson on recruitment was concluded with a 15-minute activity in the ICT room where students accessed a word sheet from the shared drive and copied it into their own user area. The sheet contained words and phrases relevant to recruitment and a table below containing two empty columns. The students had to match the words with the phrases and drop them into the boxes in the table. Once they had done that they had to put the words and phrases into the correct order. This activity gave the students a chance to use what they had learned in their active session, it gave them a set of revision notes and it calmed them for their next lesson.

Analytical thought can be encouraged by sequencing phrases or ideas. Thus, a flow chart of empty boxes can be set up which starts with the phrase 'Interest rates rise sharply'. Students can then drag and drop a series of phrases that show the possible consequences of this: 'Higher mortgages', 'Less disposable income', 'Less spending in shops'. This sort of activity is best done in pairs to encourage discussion. If there is an interactive whiteboard students can be encouraged to use this in feeding back to the whole class. As an extension, students could write in evaluative statements to one side of the cashflow such as 'This is good for…', 'This is bad for…' and list who wins and loses as a consequence. The sequence they have built up on their worksheet can be printed off and used as the framework for an essay or similar question that they can complete for homework.

Callouts (text boxes shaped to look like talk or think bubbles) can be used to sequence an argument or to help understand the feelings of different stakeholders in given business situations. This is a powerful tool for students who can 'see' the arguments but need a framework to sequence the ideas into a linear written piece.

A final mention should be made about interactive quizzes. This is a process where a question appears on screen and the student answers it by clicking on an option which will then tell them to try again or that they are correct. With a little investment of time these can be created, for example by using hyperlinks. These are used by students in Key Stage 3 when they design web pages, so they are not as difficult as they sound! Such sheets are a handy revision tool but should only be a small part of a lesson. Likewise, crosswords and word searches, which can be created by using free software available on the net; www.theteachernet.co.uk is a useful route to many resources and links and can be a motivator for some students.

There is a huge amount of data available on the internet and on CD-ROMs. At a low level the data can be ready-processed and presented by the class teacher on a database or spreadsheet so the class can manipulate the data to develop theories and draw conclusions. This can be done with the use of sort-and-filter functions. For example, a database of countries showing a range of socio-economic factors can be sorted according to individual factors such as GDP or literacy rates to establish relationships between factors that the students can discuss. Filters can be used in the same way to isolate top or bottom countries in a range of categories or to establish patterns of economic activity according to geographic locations. Extension work for such a unit could be for students to access the internet and extract data on countries that support their conclusions.

A much more complex and open-ended project could be for students to take the role of a business person seeking to expand into the EU. As the choice will be where to expand into the EU and how to distinguish their product, much economic, commercial, social, cultural, political and geographic data will be relevant. A starting-point could be http://europa.eu.int/comm/eurostat/, www.dti.gov.uk or www.tradepartners.gov.uk, although students should be relatively free to locate their own sources. Through individual and group discussion students should develop not only their business understanding but also their information literacy skills.

Spreadsheets are rightly seen as a potentially key feature of business learning, especially in the field of finance. There are many books which include ICT activities aimed at students on vocational courses. These are very good, but it must be remembered that business/economic learning is the paramount aim and this needs to be maintained through structuring the students' time spent on the spreadsheet and balancing this with class time and time spent on paper and pencil exercises. 'The assumption that pupils busily engaged on computers are also learning something is a false one' (Ofsted 2004: 6).

As an example, a simple profit and loss account can be taught as a paper and pencil exercise. Follow-up time spent at a spreadsheet can reinforce this learning. It is important at this stage that students are instructed to create the relevant formulas using + and − only. Thus, when completing the formula for total expenses, they must write out, laboriously, the long formula (B1+B2+B3 . . .). If a student knows or discovers that he or she can use the 'Sum' function then let them, because they understand what they are doing. Others can continue, because they are reinforcing that the expenses total is all the above figures added up. For the other formulas the teacher can give instructions or let the students put in what they think is right based on their prior learning. This can be done with students in pairs at a monitor as discussion is relevant. If, during this exercise, fingers are tracing relationships between cells then it is likely that learning is taking place. The same principle applies to the creation of a cashflow, although in this instance it would be good practice, after the students have the first month column, to encourage the students to copy and paste across the screen to create the basis of the following months' columns.

Creating an accounting document enables students to develop analytical and evaluative skills by testing their document with 'what if' questions. For example, a Year 11 class that have created their own cashflows in a previous lesson are directed to a new cashflow on the shared drive and have downloaded it into their user area. (It is good practice to have a 'ready made' cashflow or other document to ensure all students start on the new activity with an accurate and correct document.) Working in pairs, students answer a series of 'what if' questions, such as, 'What will happen to the cash at end figure in April if raw material costs go up by £100 in all the months from December?' and make changes to the cashflow to answer these questions. Following these, more generic exam-style questions are asked: 'What would be the effect on cashflow of a rise in expenses?' Then analytical/evaluative questions: 'What could be done to improve cashflow?' Further extension questions invite students to make changes to the cashflow and print the results to show the best course of action regarding investment, borrowing and/or cost-cutting.

At a higher level the functions and formulas in a spreadsheet can inform issues such as ratios and can even be used by students to formulate their own models of how the economy works or how people respond to increases in wages, responsibilities or punishments. For example, students could take a 'Theory Y' perspective and create a simple model where output is increased as positive factors, such as consultation, are increased. Groups of students could discuss the exact numerical value of these factors, weighing up their relative values. Another group could come up with a 'Theory X' model with its own set of values. These activities can be fun although developing technical ICT skills must not progress at the expense of business/economic learning.

Summary

Business education lends itself to the use of ICT; however, ICT should never be an end in itself but a tool to support teaching and learning and to develop students' information literacy skills. These transferable skills can be used in a variety of contexts including further learning, work and throughout life.

References

Ofsted (2004) *ICT in Schools 2004: The Impact of Government Initiatives: Secondary Business Education*, HMI 2184. London: Ofsted. www.ofsted.gov.uk

TTA (2000) *Using ICT to Meet Teaching Objectives in Business and Economics*. London: Teacher Training Agency, Publication No. 176/11-00. www.canteach.gov.uk

CHAPTER 7

Teaching the Applied GCSE

Glynis Frater

Introduction

A good starting-point when making a decision about whether to teach business at Key Stage 4 through an applied programme rather than the standard GCSE is to ask: Why is it different and how will it benefit the pupils who learn through it and the teachers who teach it?

A review of the content of the course makes it clear that the Applied GCSE in business provides an opportunity for pupils to investigate business in a real-world context. For most making the decision to change from teaching the single-award GCSE to the double-award Applied GCSE was not a difficult one. There was a need to find a more relevant programme of study that would provide an opportunity for pupils across a wide spread of ability to learn successfully, and to remain engaged and motivated. Pupils needed to have the opportunity to work in an environment that provided a variety of different learning opportunities and to work together in a constructive and supportive way.

As the course is open to all ability ranges and is not tiered, unlike the single GCSE, there has been a need to think carefully about the nature of different cohorts and whether they could be taught in a truly mixed-ability forum.

The curriculum model

The Applied GCSE Business course has three units: two that are internally assessed and one that is externally tested.

Although the titles are the same for all the awarding bodies that offer the qualification, the content does differ slightly and there may be changes made to the content in future reviews. One of the first decisions that had to be made was choosing the awarding body and making sure that the specification being used was the one produced by that awarding body. Each unit has the same weighting of 33 per cent. Each unit is broken down into a series of themes. The content of the units is summarised in Table 7.1.

Table 7.1 Unit structure of the Applied GCSE Business

Unit 1: Investigating Business
● A review of business aims and objectives
● An investigation into different types of ownership
● The choice of location and its impact on the business activity
● The functional areas and how they interrelate
● A consideration of how effective communication is within the business
● A look at market competition, economic conditions and environmental constraints
Solely assessed through a portfolio of evidence. Weighting 33%
Unit 2: People and Business
● Identifying the stakeholders in the business and their roles and influences
● Investigating job roles and rights and responsibilities of employers and employees
● A look at the recruitment process within a business and for the individual pupil
● A review of customer service and consumer protection
● A consideration of the effects of conflict resolution and employee disputes
Solely assessed through a portfolio of evidence. Weighting 33%
Unit 3: Business Finance
● Following the sequence of financial documents in a business
● Developing an understanding of break-even, cashflow and budgetary management
● Finding out about balance sheets
● Understanding sources of finance and the importance of financial planning
Externally assessed by a 90-minute examination. Weighting 33%

There were many considerations taken into account while deciding how to teach the different units. None of the awarding bodies suggested a right way to do it; the structure of the course would differ depending on a number of factors:

● Staff availability and expertise.

● When is the best time to work towards and sit the externally assessed unit?

● How should the programme be planned to take into consideration pupils who may need to re-sit the externally assessed unit?

● How should work experience impact on the learning opportunities for pupils studying this course?

● Planning visits to business, and a programme of visiting speakers, to provide a context for learning.

- Where does the content of one unit impact on that of another?
- How much time should be spent on underpinning teaching and learning prior to the development of evidence for the portfolio or in preparation for the test?

Tables 7.2 and 7.3 show two examples of different models of delivery.

Table 7.2 Model A (term times are approximate and therefore timings may need adjustment)

Year 10 term 1 – 10 weeks	Year 10 term 2 – 10 weeks	Year 10 term 3 – 10 weeks
Induction (2 weeks) Planning a business visit (2 weeks) Activities and assignments to develop underpinning knowledge for unit 1 (6 weeks)	Assignment to develop portfolio evidence for Unit 1 Planned timetable to incorporate interim formative feedback and deadlines (10 weeks) Completion of Unit 1	Introduction to Unit 2 to develop underpinning knowledge including role play, interview practice and CV writing (6 weeks) Work experience (2 weeks) Review of work experience and careers guidance (2 weeks)
Year 11 term 1 – 10 weeks	Year 11 term 2 – 10 weeks	Year 11 term 3 – 3 weeks
Planning and executing a visit to a business to investigate job roles etc. (2 weeks) Assignment to develop portfolio evidence for Unit 2 Planned timetable to incorporate interim formative feedback and deadlines (8 weeks) Completion of Unit 2	Inviting a visiting speaker to explain the importance of prudence in business finance (1 week) Activities, worksheets, assignments, quizzes, practice tests to develop underpinning knowledge for Unit 3 – Business finance (7 weeks) Revision (2 weeks)	Revision up to the external assessment of Unit 3. (Taking into account when pupils finish for study leave)

Other possible models include:

- Teaching the externally assessed unit first but emphasising the importance of the different functional areas and good communication to develop some of the underpinning knowledge for Unit 1.
- Beginning with Unit 2 to develop an understanding of the importance of people to a business. Role-play activities to demonstrate the importance of customer service and effective recruitment can provide a platform for examining the aims and

Table 7.3 Model B

Year 10 term 1 – 10 weeks	Year 10 term 2 – 10 weeks	Year 10 term 3 – 10 weeks
Induction (2 weeks) Planning a business visit (2 weeks) Activities and assignments to develop underpinning knowledge for the first business for Unit 1 – Investigating Business (6 weeks)	Assignment to develop portfolio evidence for first business for Unit 1 Planned timetable to incorporate interim formative feedback and deadlines (10 weeks) Completion of half of Unit 1	Activities and teaching and learning of underpinning knowledge for Unit 2 drawing on some of the knowledge gained in developing knowledge for Unit 1 Using work experience as the vehicle for investigating business, gathering information and observing people at work, job roles and the recruitment process, stakeholders etc...
Year 11 term 1 – 10 weeks	Year 11 term 2 – 10 weeks	Year 11 term 3 – 3 weeks
Assignment to develop portfolio evidence for Unit 2 (6 weeks) Planned timetable to incorporate interim formative feedback and deadlines Activities, worksheets, assignments, quizzes, practice tests to develop underpinning knowledge for Unit 3 – Business finance (4 weeks)	Pupils to take the external assessment for Unit 3 in the January window (up to 3 weeks) Planning a business visit to investigate the second business for Unit 1 Assignment and teaching and learning for developing evidence for the second business for Unit 1	Revision for those pupils taking re-sits for Unit 3 Time set aside for finishing portfolios for both Units 1 and 2

objectives of business and how businesses need to satisfy their external and internal customers thus providing some of the underpinning knowledge for Unit 1.

- Teaching Units 1 and 2 simultaneously using the same business examples throughout Year 10 and concentrating on Unit 3 in Year 11 to provide two re-sit opportunities.

Timetabling the programme has required a great deal of thought. Ideally there should be twice as much time as for a single-award GCSE. It is important to make sure that there is enough time for pupils to experience business in a real-world context and to be able to demonstrate their understanding through positive independent and experiential learning opportunities. Finding the time to cover the in-depth content of this course in single time has proved difficult for those who have followed this route. Taking into account economies of scale, somewhere between one and a half time and double time might make for the right model.

Blocks of time have proved useful for visits, role play, inviting speakers into school or to provide opportunities for pupils to work together in groups or investigate a business using the internet. Getting back-to-back lessons can prove difficult, and requests need to be made to those producing the timetable. Where this is not possible some schools managed one lesson before lunch and one afterwards. A long session using back-to-back lessons can be difficult for pupils if there is nothing planned, so some planning seems essential to vary the activities for this time. Single lessons have proved useful to consolidate investigation or to review a visit.

Roles and responsibilities

As with all well-planned and structured strategies it is clear that defining who is doing what is vital to the success of a vocational programme such as this one. The commitment of senior management is essential to the process to ensure that time, resources and staffing requirements are given the same priority as any other curriculum area or subject. Where this was not immediately clear there was an ongoing battle for parity with other courses. The setting of SMART targets has proved to be an integral part of the process and in-built review has been invaluable as an essential part of effective quality assurance. In a small department the manager is the same person as the practitioner who is delivering the course. This does not appear to be a problem as long as the time and the responsibilities are clearly defined. Those delivering the programme need to plan in opportunities for developing schemes of work, assignments and lesson plans, formative feedback, tracking, assessment and internal moderation of portfolios. In most cases the pupil has a role in managing and tracking their work. Good practice suggests that the pupil takes responsibility for organising their work, planning investigations and developing evidence that meets the requirements of the course. Pupils need to have clearly defined targets set for them to ensure that they are continually striving for improvement. Setting down clearly defined ground rules for the pupil does appear to make the job of the teacher much more manageable and enjoyable.

Teaching and learning

A sound knowledge of the specification and all its different sections is clearly essential. However, it is particularly important to concentrate on the two sections of the specification that provide the information to plan a programme of teaching and learning and provide the basis of a successful course. For the portfolio-driven units these are

- What you need to learn
- What you need to produce (The Assessment Evidence Grid)

The 'What you need to learn' section explains the underpinning knowledge that is necessary in order to be able to meet the criteria laid down in the assessment evidence grid. It is a mistake to ignore the criteria in this section. A sound understanding here gives pupils the foundations upon which to develop work that will satisfy the criteria as well as providing the tools to meet the higher grades. A good example of the importance of this first section is where pupils are expected to have a sound understanding of all the different forms of business ownership but are only asked to define two forms of ownership as part of the assessment evidence grid. It is clear that where a pupil has a good understanding of all forms of ownership he or she can develop their explanation of ownership of their chosen business, first by describing its ownership and then by explaining those forms of ownership that might not be suitable; or why the business might wish to change its form of ownership in order to more readily meet its aims and objectives. It is this more in-depth understanding of ownership that will help the pupil to meet the criteria for the higher grades.

It is important to spend some time understanding clearly the requirement of the 'assessment evidence grid', which clearly lays out what evidence the pupil needs to produce to put into a portfolio. Assignments written for the pupil must allow for the evidence to be generated that meets the criteria at the different levels of response. It is important to seek the opinion of a third party to check that all the criteria are covered.

Textbooks and didactic teaching have not generally been the most successful means of making sure the pupil can produce effective evidence. Pupils work best when encouraged to find out for themselves. They can then apply that knowledge directly to the business being studied. Pupils certainly seem to learn more successfully through independent investigation using a variety of different sources, working together in groups or individually to disseminate and share knowledge and information to provide the opportunity to develop material for oral, written or visual presentations. (Table 7.4 shows some examples.) These cover part of some of the assessment evidence grid and represent lessons or groups of lessons taught. They are not examination board specific.

Unit 3 is tested through an external examination and does not have an assessment evidence grid to follow. Here it is equally important to provide examples of how finance is controlled in different kinds of businesses. Too much theory without specific examples will not provide pupils with the ability to answer the questions or interpret data in sufficient depth. One example that has worked very successfully is where the pupils developed a mini-enterprise, designing financial documents, working out how much the business would need to break even, producing cashflow forecasts and then completing profit and loss accounts and balance sheets. Pupils even talked to a bank about how they might seek sources of finance to help to finance their imaginary venture. Pupils developed a portfolio in much the same way as for Units 1 and 2 as a

Table 7.4 Examples of independent investigations

Ownership

Class divided into 6 groups. Each group investigates one form of ownership. Each group disseminates their information to the other groups. As a class the pupils discuss the reasons why different businesses locally have chosen their particular form of ownership.

Pupils investigate a business and its form of ownership.

Mark band 1 – Describe the ownership.
Mark band 2 – Explain why this form of ownership is appropriate to the business.
Mark band 3 – Discuss and evaluate the reasons why the form of ownership helps the business meet its aims and objectives, or how a different form of ownership might help the business to grow.

Stakeholders

Class discuss a current contentious local issue, new ring road or airport, mobile phone mast, business closure, etc.
Class identify who has a stake in the final decisions. A spider diagram is produced to represent the major stakeholders.
Class divided into groups and each group represents the views of the different stakeholders explaining why they believe they are the most important stakeholder and why.

Pupils identify the major stakeholders in the business they are investigating.

Mark band 1 – Describe the role of the main stakeholders and their importance to the business.
Mark band 2 – Explain in detail the role of the different stakeholders and examine why some stakeholders are more important than others.
Mark band 3 – Consider and examine how some of the stakeholders might influence business decisions and how this might impact on the business's aims and objectives.

Functional areas

Collect a number of organisation charts from company reports, from textbooks and from company websites. Divide the class into groups and give each group an organisation chart to investigate. Each group finds a definition for each of the different functions represented on the chart using textbooks and other sources. The group should then discuss how the different functional areas help each other to make sure the business runs smoothly. Each group should present their findings to the class so that the class can share all the information that has been collected.

Individual pupils find or create an organisation chart from one of the businesses they are investigating and identify the different functional areas represented on the chart. They should identify the main purpose and activities for each functional area.

Mark band 1 – Describe some of the purposes and activities of the business.
Mark band 2 – Explain the importance of each functional area to ensuring the business is successful.
Mark band 3 – Examine how effectively the functional areas work together to achieve success for the business.

Job roles

Collect a number of different job descriptions from business websites, advertisements, the local council and other sources. Divide the class into groups and give each group a job description to work with. The groups work together to examine the key roles that are described. Each group develops a presentation to explain the key roles and to examine the skills and attributes an individual would need to have to apply for that job role.

Each individual finds out about key job roles within the business they are investigating.

Mark band 1 – A description of the job roles including the activities the postholder undertakes and other details such as pay and security.
Mark band 2 – An investigation into the jobholder's key responsibilities, who they are responsible for and what authority they have to make decisions.
Mark band 3 – A clear analysis of how important the job role is in the structure of the business, with some examples of what might happen if a key postholder did not fulfil his or her responsibilities.

revision tool. Another revision or teaching aid is to provide pupils with copies of different company accounts so that they can discuss how financially healthy they are and what they might do in the future.

Staff development

Staff development has proved to be a vital component in any model for success. Especially where this is the first time the school and the staff involved have embarked on a vocational programme of study. The areas for training that have been identified are as follows:

Whole-school awareness of the vocational dimension. A vocational specialist should explain the vocational perspective to staff, and the differences in teaching and learning, pupil movement and the need for independent and experiential learning opportunities.

The management perspective. Managers need to have a clear understanding of their roles and responsibilities in terms of course-planning.

Training for practitioners. Practitioners need to have training in teaching and learning strategies, assessment, resource-building and assignment writing.

Pupils should have a comprehensive induction in order to develop an understanding of how this course differs from others they might be studying. Pupils should have an opportunity to develop study skills.

Parents need to be informed as to the value of this programme as a holistic way of learning that will provide their children with highly developed key skills alongside a sound understanding of how business operates.

Resources

It is generally agreed that this course would be very difficult to run without a base room to work from. ICT is necessary to develop high-quality portfolio evidence and to allow pupils to investigate independently. Pupils all use some kind of working folder to keep their work in progress and they also need to have a secure place to keep their growing portfolio. It does not seem to be a good idea to provide a set of textbooks. Pupils inevitably rely too much on their content and regurgitate the theory. The best advice seems to be to buy a number of different textbooks. Best practice is most definitely to have a variety of other resources available.

Quality assurance

The first and most important aspect of making sure that this course is effective is to ensure senior management commitment. Everything else will flow from this. Where this commitment is sought and made the following model seems to ensure effective quality assurance.

Planning

Timetabling, staffing, training, resource-building, schemes of work, assignment-writing, course delivery, assessment.

Delivery

Induction, developing study skills, teaching and learning, developing portfolio evidence, regular staff reviews, formative feedback for pupils, summative feedback for pupils.

Review

Verification of assignments and portfolio evidence, classroom observation, course review and revision, resource review and development.

Time is the most essential resource so that this process can take place effectively. It is vital to provide opportunities for internal verification of both assignments and portfolio evidence. Sufficient time for meetings to review progress and to track the progress of individuals and of groups of pupils is essential to the process. Formative feedback provides an excellent mechanism for pupils to improve their work and their grade. Where this is built into the development of the portfolio there is a profound improvement in the work produced and in the motivation of pupils. Classroom observation has provided teachers with a good opportunity to share good practice and reflect on effective strategies that improve pupil-centred learning.

Forging links with business and the community

The local area will provide a range of opportunities. For example, making use of a local shopping centre or an industrial estate can reveal all sorts of business activity:

- Different forms of ownership might reflect the nature of the business. The location of the business might help to develop an understanding of competition and marketing activity.

- Economic change can have an effect on the ability of different businesses to survive and can provide good opportunities for discussion.

- Environmental issues can be discussed in the light of local business activity. For example, local golf courses where farms used to flourish; large factories making way for new housing developments and light industrial estates.

Finding businesses to study has been a problem for some, especially those schools in rural locations. A good strategy is to make contact with the local Learning Skills Council,

Business Link or the Education Business Partnership. Some teachers have made good use of the Teacher Placement Scheme and have spent a week in industry developing resources and finding out how to bring business to life in the classroom.

Summary

Pupils who have successfully completed this course have gained a great deal in relation to their business knowledge as well as having developed some excellent key skills. The ability of pupils to work independently and to share experiences and ideas with others, to confidently ask questions or to listen and respond effectively are all skills that have been enhanced.

The opportunity for pupils to develop their work through the completion of a portfolio of evidence for two-thirds of the course has certainly provided a vehicle for increased motivation. As the portfolio grows the pupils are encouraged to develop increasingly high-quality work and they become very aware that this will give them more points and a passport to a higher grade.

However, the success of the programme is determined by adhering to the critical success factors that have been discussed here. The need to plan effectively at all stages is vital. In order to plan it is essential to have time and resources with which to work. None of this is possible unless there is genuine senior management commitment. The message for senior management for anyone who wishes to secure such commitment is that this course will motivate and enthuse both pupils and staff.

CHAPTER 8

Applied Business at A/AS level

Paul Widdowson

Introduction

From the late 1980s there has been renewed interest in vocational education although, as indicated in other chapters, our culture is still very resistant. There continues to be a need to expand vocational education as a means to better prepare young people for the world of work and for this to be available to all students rather than limit it to the less academic. The expansion of vocational qualifications from BTEC Nationals to GNVQs and now to vocational A levels (AVCE) has been a long road to follow. For example, when I took over as head of department it offered only the GNVQ Intermediate as a vocational qualification. Now provision is entirely vocational offering the Applied GCSE, BTEC Introductory and First Certificate and the AVCE. In some ways the AVCE is not vocational enough but it has further strengthened the foothold of vocational education in my school by offering a practical orientation in an otherwise traditional A level curriculum.

The AVCE is well placed to develop students' skills so that they can confidently enter the labour market. Through its project-based approach the AVCE, as will the new GCE Applied A level, equips young people as self-learners, with good research skills, who are motivated, have initiative, good communication, numeracy and ICT skills and can work to deadlines. This is what employers say they want and this is what the AVCE provides.

Aims of the AVCE

The AVCE in Business is an attempt to provide a broad vocational background in business allowing students to make good choices for post-18 study or employment, so that they can easily go on to a degree at university, or undertake an NVQ or a Modern Apprenticeship. In essence, the AVCE provides an opportunity for students to

- Demonstrate and apply knowledge and understanding of business using appropriate terms, concepts, theories and methods to address problems and issues;
- Plan and carry out investigations of issues by gathering, selecting, recording and analysing relevant information and evidence; and
- Evaluate evidence, make reasoned judgements and present conclusions:

Having taught both A level and the AVCE, in my opinion it is the AVCE that better develops research skills, self-motivation and the ability to discuss issues and meet deadlines. The AVCE also uses information and communications technologies (ICT) as an intrinsic part of the course, and students must complete presentations, sit examinations and produce several pieces of much-researched portfolio work. The AVCE enables students to develop knowledge and understanding of business through the investigation of a range of business organisations. This prepares them for employment, further education or training.

Objectives

Using the criteria of transparency, consistency, reliability and validity the AVCE can be compared to the traditional A level, often referred to as the 'gold standard'. My point here is that the AVCE not only matches this standard but in some ways offers advantages.

One of the main aims of the AVCE is to be completely 'transparent', and it does this by setting out exactly what students have to achieve to gain a certain grade. The A level does go through similar stages, but the criteria for coursework are not as transparent as those for the AVCE portfolio units. The AVCE and the A level are both 'consistent' and to date the criteria for each of the AVCE units have not changed. Notwithstanding the annual debacle when results are published, the A level is often seen as a very 'reliable' qualification in its outcome because of its mainly external assessment and moderation processes. In my view, the AVCE has to be regarded as having at least the same reliability as the A level as it has the advantage of greater teacher involvement in assessment through internal moderation which is then checked by an external moderator. Undoubtedly, this requires a greater commitment on the part of the teacher but it does produce a better articulation between teaching, learning and assessment (see Chapter 5). As regards 'validity', the AVCE is designed to be a broad vocational qualification. Students have to undertake research, complete presentations, keep to deadlines, be self-motivated, use ICT and sit examinations. Knowledge content has to be gained from studying businesses at first hand.

Course structure

The current AVCE course and coursework assessment is designed to provide a range of teaching, learning and assessment styles to motivate students, to help them achieve the best they can and to empower them to take charge of their own learning and development. Assessment is designed to give credit for what students can do. It is based on Portfolio Evidence from Units 1 and 3 for AS equivalent students; add Units 4 and 6 for A level equivalent students; and for Double A level equivalent students, add four more optional units. The qualification is also based on unseen written examinations relating to a pre-released case study. AS equivalent students complete Unit 2 while A level equivalent students add Unit 5. Double A level equivalent students take two more externally examined units. The Portfolio Evidence assignments are set and assessed by the teacher and moderated by the examination board. External moderation begins when the teacher sends his/her marks to their examination board. A moderator may visit the school/college or they will send a form listing which units from which students they wish to sample. The sample will always include the work of the students who gain the top and the bottom marks with the rest being a spread across the range of marks and units. The examination-based units are set and marked by the examination board.

The units studied

The mandatory units for the three- (AS), six- (A) or twelve-unit (2A) AVCE are shown in Table 8.1. Students taking the 12-unit or Double AVCE must take six further units. The examination boards provide many of their own optional units from which students must choose four portfolio units and two examination units.

Table 8.1 Mandatory units for the AVCE

	Title	*Type of assessment*	*Weighting AS / A / 2A*
Unit 1	Business at Work	Portfolio	33% / 17% / 8%
Unit 2	Competitive business environment	External	33% / 17% / 8%
Unit 3	Marketing	Portfolio	33% / 17% / 8%
Unit 4	Human Resources	Portfolio	17% / 8%
Unit 5	Finance	External	17% / 8%
Unit 6	Business planning	Portfolio	17% / 8%

The portfolio units are teacher-assessed and moderated by the examination board, and this can take place in either January or June. This means that a student can re-submit a unit for an improved mark twice a year rather than just once.

The external units are set and marked by the examination board. The Unit 2 'Competitive business environment' examination lasts two hours while Unit 5 'Finance' lasts one and a half hours. The optional examination tests vary depending upon the examination board. They are available every January and June and students are able to re-sit them as many times as they like to gain the best mark possible.

To make sure the students complete on time it is useful to have a timetable for them across the course. Clearly, meeting the criteria, undertaking the work, carrying out investigations, producing the written evidence and working to deadlines are all the responsibility of the student. However, it is wise to set fixed dates for the students to achieve sections/units, although, at the same time, dates must be flexible enough for students to overcome problems such as contacting firms, administering questionnaire surveys and undertaking visits. Overall, the AVCE is about learning by experience, and this must be student-led. Nevertheless, teachers should set a final deadline around a month before they have to send their final marks and portfolios to the external moderator.

Marking the portfolio

Each Portfolio Unit is marked by an Assessor (who is usually the student's teacher) according to the criteria in the Unit Recording Sheet. This recording sheet is completed when work is assessed and included in the final portfolio. It must be page-numbered and cross-referenced to where evidence can be found in the portfolio. The student should do this. Each column in the grid comprises a strand (E/C/A). If the student achieves the entire E criterion, then they gain a Grade E for this portfolio. If the student adds to this the achievement of the C criterion, then they gain a C grade for this portfolio. If the student adds to this the A criterion, then they gain a Grade A for this portfolio.

A unit is marked out of 24. Each criterion achieved by the student attracts marks. The minimum mark to achieve the E criterion is 7 out of 24, for the C criterion it is 13/24 and for the A criterion it is 19/24. When a portfolio is assessed the assessor will initial the criterion achieved on the 'Unit Recording Sheet', and for those not yet achieved but attempted, the assessor will write notes on what the student has to do.

Before the marks are sent to the examination board, there should be internal moderation by another teacher in the school/college. The board's moderator will then select from each unit a sample of the students' portfolios that cover a range of grades. Either the board's moderator will agree that the marks are within tolerance of the national standards or they will change them to be within them.

The examination board will then convert the mark out of 24 into a 'Unit Uniform Mark' out of 100. The 'Unit Uniform Mark' is then aggregated and compared to the pre-set boundaries. Final results for the qualification will be awarded on a scale of A to U for the three- and six-unit students, with AA to UU being recorded on the certificate for twelve-unit students.

The scheme of assessment consists of one tier covering the whole of the ability range A to E. Candidates achieving less than the minimum mark for Grade E will be unclassified. Students can re-sit each assessment as many times as they like and the best mark counts towards their final grade.

From my experience, teaching the externally examined units is very similar to teaching the traditional A level. For the portfolio units it is very important that students strictly follow the Unit Recording Sheet (URS) criteria, as the external moderator will use these in making his/her judgement. Assignments could helpfully be planned so that they reflect the assessment criteria, and in turn, students could be encouraged to lay out their portfolios to ensure that they demonstrate each criterion. When the portfolio is complete, the students should page-number their assignment and enter on the URS page numbers for each criterion. The external moderator can see the students' evidence for each criterion and whether the student has achieved it. This also makes it much easier for the internal assessor to tell the student what they have to do and see whether the student has achieved all the criteria. In addition it makes it easier and more transparent for the student to see exactly what they have achieved and what they still have to do. Getting it right first time and getting the best grade possible is preferable to waiting for the next re-sit opportunity, which is time-consuming for teachers and students and undermines students' morale.

The future of vocational education

The AVCE is an excellent qualification as it certainly motivates students and allows them the opportunity to gain the highest mark they can for each unit. It built on and improved on the GNVQ Advanced Qualification and criterion-led structure by simplifying the criteria and replacing the 'mastery' concept with the more practical 'compensatory' method.

In September 2005 the AVCE is being replaced by the new Applied GCE A level in Business. Because there is still an existing A level in Business it has the word 'Applied' attached whereas in Health and Social Care the word 'applied' is not used. The new qualification will use the same system of assessment as the current Applied GCSE. It will be available as an AS single award (3 units); an AS double award (6 units); an A level single award (6 units); and an A level double award (12 units). The 3 units of the AS single award will be the first three units of all the above qualifications, with each examination board producing its own units. These units will provide the core knowledge, understanding and skills of the business criteria.

A difference between the existing AVCE and this new qualification is that in the AVCE all of the units are of the same standard whereas in the new qualification some units are designated at AS level and others at A2 standard. The new qualification will also be very different in its aims and nature from the AVCE. The new qualification will concentrate on the categories of the practical, presentation, personal, interpersonal and cognitive. These will be developed through skills, knowledge and understanding in realistic business contexts. This new qualification also explicitly requires students to investigate how businesses respond to environmental, social and ethical issues and to complete topics on areas such as enterprise and innovation. One similarity with the AVCE, though, will be that a third of the units completed by the students will be through external examination.

Summary

In England and Wales there are proposals to move towards a diploma-style award in post-14 education which encompasses what we currently refer to as 'academic' and 'vocational' subjects. Indeed, an outcome of such proposals will be the eradication of this division. In Wales, the introduction of a Welsh baccalaureate seems likely to come about in the next few years, but in England proposals are still at an early stage.

According to Tomlinson's Interim Report, in England there are still too many students finishing education too early and failing to progress. Too many students are unchallenged; both students and teachers are constrained by the current curriculum structure and methods of assessment; there is still not enough post-16 participation and achievement; and there is a fragmented framework of vocational qualifications. The report reminds us that employers think that school leavers do not have the required basic knowledge, skills and attributes, and they find education confusing and are unclear about the relevance and value of students' qualifications. The answer seems to lie in a more co-ordinated system designed to meet the need of the 'knowledge economy', based on greater workforce knowledge, skills and flexibility.

Tomlinson proposes a flexible ladder of progression through a Diploma at four levels: Entry, Foundation, Intermediate and Advanced. This will have a compulsory core of learning – Maths, English and ICT. The Diploma will also include learners' development and achievements to allow differentiation, and Modern Apprenticeships will link into the Diploma. The pre-16 Diploma will follow a statutory curriculum in which students can opt for many broad vocational units. The post-16 Diploma will give a choice of a Specialised or an Open Diploma offering academic/vocational units. Students will be able to choose their units but all will include units in Maths, English, ICT, an extended project, work/community experience and personal planning.

Vocational units will be on a basis equal to the academic units. Students will not have to choose an academic or a vocational path but can have a mix. This mix should not only be encouraged but should be made compulsory so that all our students have a broad education.

Research skills for post-16 students

Ian Abbott and Brian Sanderson

Introduction

The development of research skills in 11–18 education is not a new strategy. It has always been an important part of teaching, as teachers have attempted to provide learners with the tools to undertake independent learning. However, these skills have become increasingly vital in recent years, especially to post-16 students who are being required to undertake significant amounts of research as part of a range of examination courses.

Research skills have become an integral part of many post-16 courses in business and economics as a range of different teaching, learning and assessment styles have been introduced. There has been a movement away from more traditional methods of teaching and assessment and greater emphasis has been placed on learners taking responsibility for their own learning. In particular the growth in the amount of coursework in post-16 courses has led to much more emphasis on the development of research skills.

Why develop research skills?

- Most teachers would accept that there is a need to develop research skills in general for all learners. At post-16 this builds and develops some of the skills that are initially assessed at Key Stage 4 during GCSE programmes. At Key Stage 4 learners will already have demonstrated their research skills in the many pieces of coursework they had to produce for the majority of subjects at GCSE level.

- Many of the research skills learners require to be successful in business and economics are generic. Since many of the skills needed are transferable, a whole-school approach to the development of research skills may be worthwhile. For example, the maths department could provide support with the analysis of questionnaires, or the English department could help with questionnaire design and how to carry out interviews. These skills could then be transferred into all other subject areas that require research skills, including business and economics.

- Teachers should encourage learners to adopt an enquiring approach and give the learners the necessary skills to carry out research in a variety of contexts.

- Research skills are important skills which will be of use when learners enter the labour market and apply to higher education. As learners develop teachers should be making every effort to encourage them to become independent learners and to provide opportunities for further research. In the past there has been a tendency to 'spoon-feed' learners with all the information they need. Teachers have justified this on the grounds that it saves time and is less trouble. Given the requirements of many courses this approach is no longer possible. It has often been the case, for example, with ICT access where it is easier to give the learner the information direct rather than allow them to find out for themselves. Ultimately this approach will lead to learners becoming over-reliant on the teacher. It will encourage a more passive teaching and learning style which is opposed to the current emphasis on active learning. Employers prefer potential employees to possess skills that will prepare them for employment or further education. Learners need to acquire skills that will enable them to 'learn for life'.

- Research skills can also be coupled to key skills, for example carrying out research and then undertaking analysis and presenting data in a variety of formats. This is a valuable method of getting learners to display certain key skills – Communication, ICT, Numeracy. Group work and research can also contribute to the key skill Working with Others. Research activities are often excellent opportunities for teachers to develop group work. The collection of data and the planning and production of presentations provides learners with the opportunities for interaction, organisation and delegation.

Research skills in practice

Research skills are required in a number of areas of business and economics. Some examples might include the following.

Economics

Produce a report on the UK economy looking at the following key indicators:

- Economic growth
- Inflation
- Unemployment
- Balance of Payments.

What are the prospects for the UK economy for the next 12 months? The setting of a project of this nature allows learners the opportunity to work together, to gather information from a wide range of sources (which they can then use again for other tasks) and to make informed predictions.

● Give the learners a list of five countries and using economic data (Human Development Index, National Income statistics, etc.) place them into an order of economic development. Then use economic theory to compare the countries' economic performance and development. For example Rostow's stages of economic development or the Harrod-Domar model could be used. The data gathered can be used for discussion of the key areas of economic growth, such as the common characteristics of less developed countries.

Business studies

In business most areas of the syllabus provide ample opportunities for individual or group research. For example, an introduction to human resources management (HRM) could be developed by giving a group of learners a famous motivation theorist to research, such as Maslow, Herzberg or Mayo. Then the teacher can ask the learners to compare their findings by giving a presentation or taking part in a debate.

A visit to a local shopping centre could be a particularly relevant way to introduce a number of subject areas. Individuals or groups can be given a specific research task, for example looking at customer service, health and safety, the marketing mix. The data collected by the learners could then be related to theory or provide relevant information for coursework.

Research skills for learners taking traditional A levels

For the purposes of this section we will classify the traditional route as being AS and A2. The assessment of research skills in the post-16 traditional A level route only really occurs at A2 level. AS assessment, by the three main examination boards for business and economics, is almost exclusively by case study. Most often the case study material is pre-released by the examination board. It is likely therefore that teaching in Year 12 will be based around preparing students for this style of examination.

However, research skills will still be required for learners who continue to A2 in Year 13. Therefore it is vital to continue to develop research skills. It would be extremely shortsighted of any teacher to leave out research skills development at AS level in Year 12 simply because they are not being assessed and then expect students to switch back on to these skills with A2 coursework. As previously stated, it is a vital and enjoyable form of active learning, and can motivate learners. In addition, developing research skills will also help learners to develop the higher-order skills of analysis and evaluation.

At A2, research skills are needed to produce coursework. Teachers commonly choose the coursework option because they are aware that often the grades gained are higher on coursework units in comparison to examination units. Choosing the coursework option provides variety to the course and the opportunity for the development of research skills. However, the downside associated with this choice is that it will create extra work for all concerned. The coursework is usually internally marked and moderated, and this can significantly increase the workload for both the teacher and the student. Typically business studies coursework will be an investigation into a real business problem. This in itself can sometimes cause problems, for example, if a student identifies the following issue: 'How can company X improve the motivation of its workforce?' The assignment must be a real business problem, but business managers may be extremely reluctant to allow sensitive issues to be investigated, especially if the recommendations are likely to be critical of their role! In a school with a large A level entry finding genuine business issues every year can be very time-consuming and may lead to fairly vague titles being chosen, such as 'How can company Y improve its marketing mix?'

Once a working title has been established the requirement to collect primary and secondary data becomes a necessity. Without quality data the coursework is bound to be of a low standard. It is therefore necessary for learners to develop effective research skills. The main research skills required by learners in business and economics are:

1   *The collection of primary data*; how to design questionnaires; setting up interviews; provision of data in the appropriate format.

2   The development of the internet has transformed *the collection of secondary data* and significantly changed the skills needed by learners. There is an obvious danger of information overload and also serious issues about plagiarism. The ease of acquiring data, and the sheer volume of data, available on the internet has made some learners lazy and non-selective. In some cases there is a tendency just to copy, cut and paste.

3   Once you have the data in an appropriate format you can then *apply the assessment criteria*. For example for the AQA A level Business Studies course this would be:

   ● Knowledge (8 marks) – understanding and using appropriate business terminology.

   ● Applying knowledge (8 marks) to the business enquiry.

   ● Analysis of the effects (8 marks) that the data collected is having on the business.

   ● Synthesis (5 marks) – report format and the presentation of data in a logical and coherent order that 'flows'.

   ● Evaluation (11 marks) – judgements/recommendations based on the data.

Research skills for vocational courses

The assessment load in AVCEs is more heavily weighted towards coursework, with 66 per cent of the marks available devoted to coursework. Developing relevant research skills therefore becomes even more important for AVCE. This also applies to ASVCE in Year 12. Once learners come into the sixth form on these programmes they are expected to be involved in coursework and research almost immediately. An effective way of preparing learners for this is to run an induction day or week to prepare them for the different requirements of this type of course.

It is also worth noting that many students who take vocational courses post-16 have already experienced this style of assessment, usually in the form of GNVQ Intermediate and more recently Applied GCSE. Entry onto an AVCE programme represents a logical progression from these Key Stage 4 courses. The research skills required by learners in this area are very similar to those for the traditional A level, although the assessment criteria are different. Overall, the coursework required is more specific than A level in order to cover the syllabus of the unit, for example a marketing assignment, or an HRM assignment. There is also more flexibility in the assessment process. For example, role-play exercises or presentations may be used, depending upon the particular examination board.

Research skills and the internet

Before the recent rapid changes in modern technology, gathering secondary data was often time-consuming, frustrating and a costly exercise for researchers. The situation has dramatically changed with the widespread introduction of ICT access in educational establishments, and in addition many learners now have internet access at home. With the wider availability and reduction in costs of broadband access, the role of the internet as a resource provider is going to continue to expand rapidly.

For many post-16 researchers this has led to a fundamental change in the problems they've faced. Researchers have moved from a shortage of information for use in assignments and coursework to 'information overload'. In many cases typing a basic instruction into a search engine can provide thousands of 'hits' with websites being accessible from all over the world. This should enable learners to produce high-quality work which is based on a range of research evidence.

Clearly the internet provides many benefits to the researcher and student of business and economics. There are now many subject-specific sites such as Biz/ed for business students and Tutor2u for economists which provide an array of support and guidance. There are also the websites of thousands of businesses, government agencies and international organisations that provide a range of up-to-date facts and figures about their structure and performance. Currently there is a mass of data available to business and economics learners.

This abundance of information has, to some extent, changed the research skills needed by learners. For example, a major skill is now to refine search skills, to filter out irrelevant sites and limit the amount of data collected. It has always been the case that the quality of the material gathered is of paramount importance. To apply, analyse and evaluate 'poor' secondary data, no matter how much the learner has collected, is clearly going to reduce the overall grade for the research assignment. Learners are often required to reduce the amount of data collected. This can be achieved by refining search skills and being more critical and selective about the origins and accuracy of the data collected.

Despite the quantity and quality of information the development of the internet has had a negative impact on some research students. It has led to an increased acceptance of any data downloaded without questioning its relevance, accuracy and validity. As previously stated there is also a tendency for students to simply cut and paste data and pass this off as research. The problem of plagiarism has become even more of a issue, sometimes it is clearly obvious as in the previous situation – blatant lifting of large chunks of text without any attempt to edit. However, more subtle examples are often more difficult to detect and time-consuming to prove. Rapid change in the availability of materials has made the gathering of secondary data extremely quick and simple, but there is also a tendency to rely on the internet for all the secondary data and not use more traditional methods.

Summary

- Research skills are often transferable across the curriculum and have been significantly tested at Key Stage 4. This will continue to be the case under the recommendations of the review of 14–19 education. However, greater emphasis will be placed on teacher-led assessment, which is likely to further increase the need for learners to develop effective research skills.

- Students should be encouraged to develop their research skills as they will become more independent learners, enjoy the challenge of finding out for themselves and become less reliant on teachers.

- Students need to be equipped with the necessary research skills. It is reasonably straightforward to produce a questionnaire, but to create an effective one requires teacher input and practice.

- Coursework does not usually occur in Year 12 of traditional AS/A2 business/economics, but clearly the development of research skills must remain as part of the curriculum because they will be needed to a very high level at A2.

- Vocational A levels have an even greater need for research skills, but many students will be familiar with this style of assessment from GNVQs and Applied GCSEs. However, a higher level of knowledge and skill will be required post-16.

- The widespread use of the internet provides many opportunities, but can also cause particular problems for teachers and learners.

CHAPTER 10

Supporting learning in business

Andrew Hammond

Introduction

Learning takes place in a variety of settings both inside and outside classrooms and is an outcome of the interaction between students and teachers and between the students themselves. This gives rise to both intended and unintended outcomes. The aim of this chapter is to provide an insight into teaching and learning in business classrooms, focusing on three issues:

- What does it mean to learn business?
- How is learning promoted in the classroom (and beyond)?
- What do both teachers and learners do in the business classroom?

Learning in business

Although we live in a society dominated by the actions of businesses we should not take it for granted that students have the information and critical capacities needed to understand and question business behaviour and its impact on our lives. So, as well as imparting information about the nature of businesses, their structure, organisation and management it is also important to develop in our students a critical insight. This has to be based on a good knowledge base but must go further in terms of developing the skills of analysis and evaluation and requires that students do not only consider business from a business perspective, although this is a necessary starting-point.

What's a business for?

Asking learners to consider this question seems to get at the heart of the issue. Whereas making a profit and the profit motive are central, this does require more than superficial understanding of the nature of business activity and the concept of entrepreneurial activity. Business activity involves both risk and reward, and these have to be balanced in terms of the impact on individuals, the economy and society.

Decision-making and the associated judgement

The development of the sort of critical thinking proposed here requires students to understand and take part in decision-making processes. Business provides examples and contexts which allow students to consider real-world issues by posing problem-based activities. Students will find much of their learning related to the processes of identifying alternative courses of action, and then selecting the most appropriate course based on an analysis of the options. This has to be based on a selection and analysis of information together with the presentation of argument and evidence. Considering the alternatives, especially from differing perspectives, forces a consideration of wider issues than profit. Developing these skills needs, however, to be purposeful and structured so that students develop their confidence and competence to ask their question, seek information and propose solutions to problems and issues. Instinctive thinkers may need this process clarified, since many will not be aware of the process, while other students, perhaps those who can naturally see two sides of an argument as a result of studies in other subjects, will need to be pushed into the need for an actual decision – rather than a possible over-tendency towards fence-sitting. The point is that in the real world decisions have to be made and we have to live with the consequences.

Learning skills

The need to learn the main skills required for business studies examinations is a useful element of learning business. The skills listed below are valuable, but often hugely underdeveloped in students when business studies teachers first meet them. An important part of the learning business experience must therefore be the need to develop and train students in the use of these skills.

- Knowledge
- Application
- Research
- Analysis
- Evaluation

Promote learning in the classroom (and beyond)

A new language

Traditional language-learning methods have been proven to work well. Issuing all new business students with a vocabulary book, a list of words each week and then giving tests at the start of lessons works wonders for rapidly taking on board the key aspects of new terminology needed. This can be done on a weekly basis, with each week's word list itemising the work that will be covered in that week, or was done in the preceding week. By the end of the course, students have equipped themselves with a highly useful business glossary.

Key business words need to seep into the consciousness of students, and one way of doing this is to equip the classroom with a set of self-made posters, one per letter of the alphabet, listing key pieces of terminology. This helps with spelling initially, but perhaps more importantly allows students to spot the key terms that they will need to understand as the course goes by. Each time a piece of terminology is covered in class, students will start to make sense of the word they have spent many hours gazing at while daydreaming through lessons!

It is important, given the need to engage students with the subject's vocabulary, that teachers consolidate this in the course of their teaching. Of course, it will usually be appropriate to remind students of what the term means ('profit – remember that's the difference between revenue and costs'), but they will not use the terminology unless the teacher uses it, day in, day out. This is another illustration of the lessons that can be learnt from language teachers, who will refuse to speak any language other than that being studied during their lessons.

If all of this new vocabulary is making its way into students' minds, opportunities to show off their vocabulary should allow opportunities for recognition. Classroom games can be arranged to run for a small section of a lesson. Familiar formats, such as The Weakest Link, or Who Wants to Be a Millionaire? tend to go down particularly well.

The profit motive

The fundamental driving force behind most business activity – the profit motive – is one that not all students will naturally understand. Though we do not wish to advocate a business learning experience that suggests that the entire subject is centred around maximising profits, it must be important that students who are new to the subject understand the fundamental concept of getting more money back than has been spent. Once explained, the simplest way to generate an understanding of the profit motive will be to challenge students with simulations, giving them an opportunity to try to generate a profit in any given scenario. Moving outside the classroom, the Young Enterprise scheme can provide a useful hands-on experience for youngsters, along with an understanding of the difficulty involved in generating a profit.

The need for an entrepreneurial spark behind business can also be illustrated by classroom simulations, in addition to researching famous examples of serial entrepreneurs. Students may be given deeper research tasks to really get to grips with the history and mindset of a specific entrepreneur, and this particular area is often one of the easiest in which to trigger reading around the subject. Dependent upon contact, local business owners may be willing to come into the classroom to talk to students, although this needs careful negotiation and also an opportunity for students, to prepare their questions.

Decision-making

Business textbooks are not short of case study materials, and it should be fairly straightforward to identify decision-making issues within such cases. There are also many published resources in both text and electronic form (see Part 4 of this book). Whether or not you choose to use questions attached to the case studies is largely immaterial – it is the scenario that can allow you to encourage students to start making decisions. A mixture of individual and group work should be encouraged, since group work allows students to hear the views of others and develop their teamworking skills. However, individual practice is crucial since that is what will be examined in the students' examinations. Overall, it is important that students are able to explain and justify their decisions. This is not simply about giving an answer, but about considering a range of possibilities and assessing the advantages and disadvantages of each. The techniques applied to the study of businesses, such as SWOT analysis, can be applied to the students' own work.

The skills

There are four key areas of development that students on a business course will find themselves needing to develop:

- Knowledge
- Application
- Analysis
- Evaluation

Whereas it is important that students develop and express a point of view, it is as important that this is not only based on sound information and analysis but also links and takes hold of the theories and proposition embodied in the study of business. So, whereas we want students to draw on experience, we also want them to reflect on that experience in the light of the knowledge offered to them through the study of the subject.

The ability to apply their knowledge to real-world scenarios should be an important feature of any student's business learning. Taking a business concept and seeing its relevance for a particular company in a given set of circumstances brings meaning to the work students have done in gaining their knowledge of the subject.

Analysis means a range of subtly different things in varying different business courses. At the heart of analysis must be the ability to break down a complex problem, to see its constituent features and then to bring business techniques to bear in identifying possible solutions to problems or alternative courses of action in any given situation. Analysis must also be founded upon logic, showing an understanding of cause and effect and possibly being able to see a chain of logic within a series of events in a business scenario.

Evaluation, or judgement, must be an important skill if we consider that decision-making is a key feature of business learning. The ability to show judgement, based on a case that has been presented within a student's argument, is critical if decision-making skills are to be enhanced. Many students will need to be encouraged to avoid sitting on the fence, while others will need to be taken from presenting unjustified assertions to creating a well-argued case for one particular side of an argument.

But many courses will also require the development of a fifth major business skill:

- Research

Probably in the preparation of coursework, business students may need to be able to demonstrate their research skills. Clearly some business knowledge of market research, or perhaps time-and-motion study, will enable the students to have an understanding of how business research can be conducted. However, more often than not, students will be required to show that they can conduct research using a *range* of sources, some secondary, some primary, while they will also be required to present their findings in an appropriate manner. Often they will be expected to analyse the data that they gather and show evaluation in some way, perhaps in use of the data or even in their assessment of the validity and reliability of their research.

Classrooms

What do teachers do in the classroom?

Teachers are faced with a number of critical challenges that they must address if they are to ensure that their students manage to get as much from business learning as the subject has to offer.

They know nothing – do you?

All teachers have to face the fundamental problems that most of the time they know a lot more about the subject being taught than the students they are teaching. With the exception of the first time you try to learn something, it can be easy to forget what each topic is like when you know nothing about it. For a student to be able to understand many business concepts as deeply as may be required at advanced level, they must be taken all the way from not knowing what the words 'critical', 'path' and 'analysis' mean when put together, to being able to carry out, comment on, use, discuss the results of and evaluate the usefulness of a particular technique. The teacher's job is easier later on in this process, since a teacher who fully understands the topic being taught should find it relatively easy to stretch students' higher-level understanding of a topic. But to get students to that position they must pass through the earlier, rockier stages of understanding, and it is these phases where we are most likely to be greeted with completely blank expressions! Preparation for the delivery of a topic must include a teacher attempting to think themselves back to a position of complete ignorance. Think what it is like to be a student.

Get the language right

The language of business has already been identified within this chapter as being an important issue for business learners. Business language within the classroom should be used by the teacher wherever possible, referring to a product, for example, as being 'income elastic' should be good practice, if students understand what is being said. An awareness of the language being used is vital if the business teacher is going to effectively explain the subject to their students. Clearly a gradual integration of language is important, since students who do not understand 50 per cent of the words coming from the teacher's mouth will rapidly become disengaged from their studies; yet as students' vocabularies grow, so should the teacher's use of the correct vocabulary and the encouragement for students to use that vocabulary in both oral and written work.

Teach skills as well as content

The previous section of this chapter has identified major skills required by business courses, and students should be informed of these skills. Students should have the assessment objectives of their course clearly explained to them (not presented in exam-board speak), and throughout the business learning experience, skills should be referred to by the teacher, with an explanation of what skills are expected in this type of question and how those skills could be demonstrated. This means more than simply teaching content: content may be the driving force behind the course planning but skills will need to be integrated into the learning experience.

Put everything in context

Business is a practical, real-world subject. Businesses do not exist in the abstract, and this is likely to be the most powerful tool in the business teacher's tool box. If students sitting in a classroom are shown that the work they are doing has relevance to their everyday lives, possibly now, and possibly in their futures, then they are far more likely to be turned on to the subject and keen to find out more about what is being done to them by businesses and why.

What students do in the business classroom

The clearest advice to a teacher is to find out. What students do, think, understand and believe should not be assumed. Teaching and learning takes place in a classroom and is best understood as an interaction, so that the outcomes might be very different for some students than others. Quite simply, what teachers teach and what learners learn may not be the same thing. That said, it is the teacher who is responsible for planning learning and constructing activities but these need to be interactive and problem-based.

Over a period of time students will need to make their way through their business courses, meeting the challenges identified within the chapter. They will learn a new language, becoming comfortable using its vocabulary and being able to understand its meaning. They will begin to understand the fundamental concept behind business activity of the profit motive and the risk-taking element of entrepreneurial activity. They will become practised in the art of decision-making, learning sensible ways to approach a range of choices and methods of enhancing their chance of making the right decision. Finally they should have developed skills such as analytical thinking, and the ability to make rational and informed judgements based on an analysis of a situation with which they are presented, having applied their base of knowledge to that particular scenario.

Summary

A teacher's greatest ally is the world. Students have already lived in it, and they do have plenty of experience of business activity, perhaps so much so that a teacher's job is not just to explain what students already know but to get them to reflect on and look at that experience in new ways. It should be remembered, therefore, that although learning can be embedded in familiar examples, teachers should remain alert to the need to develop in their students the critical insights discussed in this chapter.

CHAPTER 11

Planning coursework

Michael Simpson

Introduction

The use of coursework both as a teaching strategy and as a means of assessment is integral to the majority of business education courses. It enables an in-depth and more extensive exploration of a topic, often including an element of first-hand investigation based either on an analysis of secondary information or on fieldwork in the form of visits, interviews, surveys and questionnaires. As suggested in this chapter, a key to successful coursework is in its planning, the linking to assessment objectives and the support offered to students.

The selection of topics and titles

In some courses the selection of what to do is left almost entirely up to the teacher and student, whereas in others the examination board is more prescriptive. A first point to establish is that a piece of coursework is not just an extended essay. Coursework differs in the way that it usually extends over a longer period of time and requires students to engage in some form of first-hand investigation. A number of constraints often exist when topics are being selected: the word limit, the number of sources to be used, the use of data shared by the cohort of students, the method of displaying evidence, the use of ICT, and of course the date for completion and submission of marks and work to the exam board. For some specifications a pre-issued case study may provide the bulk of the data required for the work, for others it might be the format of the final report itself that attracts marks.

Exam boards provide support and exemplar materials indicating their expectations of students, including examiners' reports and annotated scripts, training events and individualised feedback. External inspections will identify the approach taken to coursework by departments. Good practice is identified and is usually associated with the degree of care with which support is given to students and the independent way students set about producing their coursework. The management of the coursework load for students is also usually commented upon.

Assessment criteria

All coursework is marked according to a published set of criteria, and these tend to be constructed in a cognitive hierarchy in which achieving the higher levels becomes progressively more difficult. Typically a display of knowledge of the topic is essential, then application of the knowledge to the topic is required. Analysis and synthesis of the issues raised by the collection of information usually precedes the final level, where the ability to evaluate and make reasoned judgements is assessed. Additional criteria can include the effectiveness with which a problem has been identified, the quality of the research undertaken, the quality of presentation and communication and explanations of concepts.

In a number of specifications the division of marks between these different criteria is split equally or almost so. For example, 25 per cent of the marks awarded for each of: knowledge, application, analysis and evaluation. The more demanding the course the lower is the proportion of marks allocated to demonstration of knowledge and the greater is the proportion awarded for analysis and evaluation.

Keywords from criteria

- Relevant
- Valid
- Wide range
- Logical

It should be noted that within each criterion there is a mark range. For example, at the lowest level of evaluation a student might make a simple non-judgemental recommendation but at the highest level the student might provide a logical and reasoned argument attaching weight to different elements of the argument and formulating a conclusion arising from the course of the argument.

Example 1

If McTuckins wish to motivate their staff in the workplace my research has shown they need to offer additional pay to staff. The results of the questionnaire I distributed to the staff showed that 85 per cent of the respondents stated the reason they came to work was for money. This recommendation is in line with Maslow's view that satisfying the physiological needs of employees is essential to motivation.

Compare this to

> ## Example 2
>
> When McTuckins' employees were sampled, 85 per cent stated the key factor that motivated them in the workplace was pay. Offering additional pay will not necessarily motivate them more as there is no guarantee that it will move them to a higher level of Maslow's hierarchy. This is supported by the figure that 70 per cent of the workforce sampled felt that pay levels were fair. This would suggest that further research into employee motivation could identify the type of 'dis-satisfiers' that Herzberg identified in his work on hygiene and motivational factors.

In Example 1 the student's assertion is not qualified by reference to sample size, the conclusion is based upon an unquestioning acceptance of the figures, and applied to one theorist's view. In Example 2 a more perceptive interpretation of the result is given by a reference to a more sophisticated use of questioning. The student has also demonstrated a wider and relevant use of knowledge by drawing upon a second theorist to evaluate the proposal. Example 2 demonstrates a higher level of understanding and shows evidence of analysis and evaluation. Example 1 contains knowledge and application but only limited judgement.

Some awarding bodies are explicit that a 'top down' application of the criteria is used. Thus a candidate who displays evidence of the highest level of a particular assessment criterion does not need to meet the criteria of the lower levels as it is held that these lower levels are subsumed in higher levels.

As teachers are frequently required to mark coursework (while the examining body moderate the standards) it is important that the relevant assessment criteria are fully understood. The guide below sets out the typical interpretation made of assessment criteria. The rigour of its application will be also determined by the level of the work to which it is applied such as GCSE, A/S, A2.

Knowledge

The student must show what they know about the topic. Teachers need to check the specification and coursework guidelines carefully. It could be that marks will be earned in the natural unfolding of the work and application of concepts without a requirement that they are listed, glossary-like, before being used. For example, in a finance topic it can be a range of performance, profitability and liquidity ratios; in marketing it may be the marketing mix, the Boston matrix and the product life-cycle. In human resources it could be theories of motivation, leadership and management styles. It could be about the use of fiscal and monetary policy to influence aggregate demand and supply in the economy, or an exploration of the price and income elasticity of demand and the elasticity of supply in the UK housing market. Students should avoid simply citing theory without applying it.

Application

Application of knowledge is at its most effective when the student understands its purpose and relevance to the chosen topic. Negotiation between the teacher and a student can ensure that it is not too narrow and closed off to the higher levels of the assessment criteria. For example, compare 'What has been the impact of Vauxhall's decision to close its Luton plant?' with 'What strategies can the local and national government adopt to tackle the unemployment problem as a result of Vauxhall's decision to close its car plant in the town?' The second title presents a much more significant challenge to a student and opens up many more opportunities to demonstrate the achievement of the highest levels of assessment criteria. It will require the student to apply a wide range of concepts if the subject is to be dealt with effectively.

Analysis

Analysis is concerned with identifying trends, patterns, issues and linkages with data that is collected and then making it meaningful. Good analysis will often critically examine the validity of the data collected by consideration of sample size and collection method, or whether people had fully understood the questions or had been honest in their responses. Analysis can be described as 'joined-up thinking'. The student is looking to make connections with different elements of the data collected and turn them into something meaningful. A student will often identify gender, age and the income of people who have been sampled and present this information in self-contained explanations and then not look across the data to see the patterns that are emerging across the questions. For example, Table 11.1 shows results from a questionnaire employed to help with the focus: 'Are brands important to buyers of trainers?'

Students usually present such information in the form of charts and describe what they show. For example, 'More females than males were surveyed, most were between 21 and 40 years of age. The modal income level was £20-30,000, Nike was the most popular brand and £50 was as much as most people paid.' This tells the reader very little. Good analysis would look for relationships between gender, age, income, and purchases in order to discover where there may be identifiable patterns. For example:

Men and women under the age of 40 were more likely to spend more than £25 and often £75 or more. Older people, 31 years and over, despite having higher incomes spent less than the average amount and tended to buy the less popular and cheaper brands. Women were more likely to wear their trainers only for leisure and proportionately more men wore them for both sport and leisure. People on higher incomes were much less likely to wear their trainers for both leisure and sport. The most popular brand, Nike, was chosen by younger (30 and under) men and women, regardless of income, while older women and older men chose Adidas or the category 'Other'. There was no identifiable pattern between the amount spent on trainers and the use for which they were worn. 16–20-year-olds spent least, tended to chose Nike or Adidas and usually wore their trainers for both sport and casual-wear. However, those men who chose to wear them only for sport were also more likely to have paid between £51 and £75 but only if they were over 30 years old and had an income greater than £20,000.

Table 11.1 'Are brands important to buyers of trainers?'

Gender					
Male 33%			Female 67%		
Age of respondents (%)					
16 – 20	21 – 30	31 – 40	41 – 50	51 – 60	60+
12	30	27	17	12	2
Income (£000 / %)					
0 <10	10<20	20<30	30<40	40<50	50+
21	28	34	9	7	1
Buy trainers branded (%)					
Adidas			16		
Puma			24		
Nike			36		
Reebok			6		
Other (please state)			18		
Have paid as much as ? for a pair (%)					
£25			6		
£50			57		
£75			31		
£100			5		
>£100			1		
Do you wear your trainers for (%)					
Leisurewear only			62		
Sportswear only			21		
Both			17		

The quality of the analysis above could be further enhanced if qualitative data had also been collected. For example, respondents could have been asked for explanations in respect of some of their choices. ICT in the form of spreadsheets could be useful here to help with analytical techniques such as calculating mean values, as well as presenting charts that can help to illustrate the points made in the comments on results.

Evaluation

Many teachers and examiners recognise that the line between good analysis and good evaluation is difficult to draw. The one usually follows from the other, and in the marking of work, centres have often been advised to consider the work as a whole and not always rely on finding specific areas to which only analysis marks or evaluation marks can be awarded. Some students will have a section of work with the title Analysis and one titled Evaluation, but it does not necessarily mean that it is being displayed in the section or that it is only displayed in the so-labelled section. Certain words, such as 'however', 'nevertheless', 'overall', 'in conclusion', and 'on balance', are often associated with good evaluation, although their presence is not sufficient. However, those students that employ them appropriately can find they trigger a fuller response. Poor evaluation will often be identified by a simple judgement based upon the number of arguments for and against rather than attaching any weight to the individual strands of the argument.

Getting coursework under way

The following list offers some practical suggestions:

- Ensure students have appropriate understanding of the subject area that is to be explored.
- Be prepared to show them past students' work or exemplar work.
- Consider using a planning and monitoring template.
- Ensure topics chosen give 'access' to all assessment criteria.
- Be aware of the weightings attached to the different criteria and ensure that students give each criterion due attention.
- Ensure that information can be obtained and is not regarded by a business as too sensitive for release into the public domain – figures for staff turnover, absenteeism and poor timekeeping can be important to measure motivation, but are hard to obtain!
- Make sure that students are aware of the criteria, and know what they mean and how to 'address' them.
- Do not over-rely on readily available publicity material either in printed form or from the internet.

- Regularly monitor the work, possibly identifying specific lessons or weeks as coursework weeks for students to discuss and display their progress.
- Ensure students keep backup copies of their work as they progress.

Planning templates can be drawn up which simply identify the major stages in the production of the work. Giving suggested timings can help, or the use of a diary or logbook in which students record briefly what they have done may assist with time planning and progress checks. To such templates can be added the mark allocations plus other criteria which are identified in the course specification.

Title of coursework. This can be amended if necessary at a later date – the point is to give some form of focus to the work.

Subject theory and concepts. Identify which parts of the course being studied the work relates to, for example concepts and theory in respect of motivation or the effectiveness of trade in encouraging economic development, or marketing and sales.

Sources of information. It is important to identify where the necessary data to support the coursework is to come from. A range of information is needed, and this means a variety that is relevant, valid and up to date and that covers different perspectives. This could be interviews, questionnaires, data from the Office for National Statistics, Social Trends, etc.

Research methods. Students need to have a clear idea about the way in which information will be gathered. This particularly applies to methods of primary research where an effective sampling strategy is usually needed if useful information is to be collected. Secondary data also needs to be obtained in a way that shows careful selection and balance. It is unlikely that just one or two sources will be able to provide the necessary input. Methods for the investigation need to be chosen carefully and a rationale provided. For example, if a student uses a questionnaire then why is it in preference to observation or an interview? What sampling strategy will be used for questionnaire distribution? A pilot study can be useful and may smooth the process of collecting appropriate and accurate data as well as demonstrate the ability to evaluate at an early stage of the coursework.

Analysis. Once the collection of information is under way analysis can begin and should look for links and trends and explain the importance of these patterns.

Conclusions. Most coursework requirements are for students to finish their work by providing an overall conclusion, or set of proposals, or to make a final judgement. It is important these arise from the preceding work and that they do not suddenly materialise without explanation. Where the student wishes to provide original thought it must follow from the logical explanations of what has been discovered, so that such ideas can be substantiated.

In some cases there is a requirement for the student to consider how the work could be improved or how he or she found the whole process. This should not be used as a

Table 11.2 Example template

Important dates

Start date: 1 October 2004
Discuss title with tutor: 7 October 2004
Collect research data by: 1 November 2004
Discuss progress with tutor by: 15 November 2004
First draft for presentation by: 30 November 2004
Final submission by: 18 December 2004

Select a title or area of study

Check there is clear understanding of the chosen subject area of human resources.

Main title

How can rapid staff turnover be reduced at McTuckins Takeaway?

Consideration of assessment criteria

Check that chosen title fits in with coursework requirements and assessment criteria; identify the relative importance of the assessment criteria.

Subject theory and concepts that must appear as a minimum

Motivation techniques, Maslow, Herzberg, labour turnover rates, methods of remuneration, management styles, recruitment methods, training.

Sources of information to use – must be valid and reliable

Manager at McTuckins; questionnaire to staff; food industry data on staff turnover; internet websites relating to working conditions at McTuckins; data from similar takeaway restaurants in the local area; interviews with ex-employees of McTuckins. ACAS (website); CIPD Annual Labour Survey (website); local job agencies; information collected from newspaper adverts on local pay levels and hours of work in similar jobs.

Primary/secondary research methods – ensure a range of sources

Stratified sample of 20 employees to include: ordinary production workers and servers; supervisors; full- and part-time; age range; and both genders. Contact local McTuckins manager plus letter to McTuckins to arrange interview with area manager; contact known ex-employees.

Analysis – what does the data collected show

Present results of secondary research, use to help inform primary research. Collate primary research results and identify relevant factors.

Conclusions – proposals arising from findings

Generate conclusions as to steps, if any, McTuckins could take to help reduce staff turnover.

Review of work

What changes to the work would improve it? What problems were encountered?

Finishing touches

Check title page appears, candidate name and number, relevant headings to sections, page numbers, index, glossary may be useful, acknowledgement of sources used, diagram and tables labelled, spelling and grammar checks.

---

basis for apologising for failing to obtain information but rather as an opportunity to explain how such additional data would have impacted upon the work.

Authenticity

Authentication of coursework is important. Awarding bodies require centres to submit some form of written statement declaring that the work is that of the candidate. Candidates are also required to sign an authentication statement. Plagiarism is a growing problem, but perhaps the best way to overcome this is to require students to show and explain their work as it progresses, allowing some monitoring to take place, rather than waiting until the final deadline.

The amount of support received by candidates from teaching staff will vary. Most guidelines developed by exam boards make statements to the effect that the level of support should be such that the work can still be called that of the candidate. Therefore guidance as to choice of titles, methods of research, concepts to be used and checking the validity of judgements would appear to be generally acceptable. What is not acceptable is a virtual rewriting of a student's work with each paragraph being edited and amended. The level of support should be certainly be sufficient to allow candidates to successfully access the topic and the assessment criteria.

Marking

Marking the work requires a consistent application of the criteria. Internal standardisation is necessary where more than one teacher is assessing the work of a cohort of students and there is the possibility of different interpretations in respect of what mark the candidate should be awarded. To help with achieving this all those that mark the work need to meet and agree upon the marks awarded to the different pieces of work. Such meetings can take several hours and usually require each teacher to bring work with them and allow colleagues to check the marks awarded. If opinions differ then a decision as to how to apply a common standard has to be made. Assuming all those teaching have been consistent, an adjustment to all marks may be necessary; in some cases it may be a tapered adjustment based upon marks awarded rather than an adjustment which is made regardless of the initial mark awarded.

Summary

Although some politicians seem determined to undermine the value of coursework, it remains an important mode of assessment better suited to both promoting and testing a wide range of basic, core and transferable skills. Especially in business education, students need this opportunity to develop their learning and apply what they have learned to 'real world' contexts. At the same time, teachers have an important role in educating them to the rigours demanded by these approaches, including careful planning and attention to detail and in the realisation that coursework is not an easy option.

CHAPTER 12

Enterprise education

Charlotte Davies

Introduction

This chapter aims to define the term 'enterprise', and identify the range of activities that constitute enterprise education. It seeks to develop an understanding of the themes, practices and theories that underpin enterprise education and to link these through to a strategy for good practice for business education teachers.

Defining enterprise education

Enterprise education is a poorly defined term (CEI Warwick University 2001); it can be seen to cover a wide range of educational activities. A useful working definition is provided in the DfES *Enterprise Pathfinders Prospectus* (April 2003), which suggests that the outcomes of enterprise education can be divided into three strands. The first strand is to do with the development of an enterprise capability, that is, to handle uncertainty and change, create and implement new ideas, and assess and act on risks in personal and working lives. In turn this requires the development of the necessary knowledge and understanding of concepts, such as risk, organisation and innovation, decision-making, leadership and risk-management skills and attitudes such as self-reliance, respect for evidence and pragmatism. The second strand is to do with the financial capability needed to be an informed consumer of financial services and the ability to manage personal finances. The third strand is about business and economic understanding giving emphasis to the allocation and use of scarce resources.

In this chapter we are mainly concerned with the concept of 'enterprise capability' delivered through experiential learning, which enables students to find strategies to improve all aspects of their lives, for example:

● time management
● research

- problem-solving and decision-making
- communication
- organisation
- teamworking and interpersonal skills
- and presentation skills
  (Bell 1998)

Experiential learning in this context can be subdivided into:

(a) Short-term activities, typically lasting from 45 minutes to 3 hours. Several of these can be linked together to make one or more days of activity to form industry days/experiences which are usually delivered to students by industry experts.

(b) Long-term exercises, typically lasting for a term or an academic year, such as the Young Enterprise Programmes, the ASDAN Award, the Chartered Management Institute Springboard Programme, the HSBC school bank scheme, Achievers International, and the National Foundation for Teaching Entrepreneurship programme.

(c) Integration of the key skills into the curriculum, making all aspects of the curriculum an opportunity for enterprise education.

Experiential learning aims to change students' methods of working so that they are more effective in their use of key skills in all aspects of their lives; and it needs, therefore, to be developed over a long period.

The importance of enterprise education

The rapid changes in technology taking place in our daily lives are driving schools to re-evaluate their approach to teaching and learning. They are also leading schools to reflect on their preparation of students for a world of rapid change. Students now need to be equipped with a range of lifetime skills that enable them to respond to change and uncertainty.

Consequently, there is a need for an international aspect to enterprise education which is reflected in programmes such as Achievers International and Junior Achievers, the international part of Young Enterprise and World Challenge.

The early years of the twenty-first century are seeing a consolidation of a range of themes that are bringing greater coherence and urgency so that enterprise is now emerging as a more fully supported concept, as can be seen through the Enterprise Pathfinders Scheme, the Work Related Learning initiative and the establishment of specialist Business and Enterprise Colleges.

Experiential learning or 'learning by doing'

Enterprise education takes a pupil-centred approach to learning and requires pupils to be actively involved. So as the following quote suggests:

> Tell me, and I will forget.
> Show me, and I may remember.
> Involve me, and I will understand.
> (Confucius, around 450 BC)

According to Alon and Cannon (www.globalview.org), the important features of classroom-based experiential learning are:

- Active, rather than passive, learning
- Student-based, rather than teacher-based, learning
- Subjective experiences and personal growth
- Learning through evaluation and reflection
- Perception-based, rather than theory-based, learning
- Participative rather than memorisation (rote) learning
- Inductive, rather than deductive, learning
- Exploration, invention and application

Towards a programme of enterprise education

The CEI report (2001) recognises that any subject has the possibility of offering opportunities for an enterprising approach because it is essentially a question of pedagogy rather than subject content. This suggests the need for enterprise education to be developed and managed at an institutional level with input from subject specialists. There is some debate as to whether economics and business studies teachers are the only staff with the expertise to advise on this area of the curriculum. It could be argued that there is a need for subject specialists with respect to the financial capability and the business and economic strands of enterprise education. However, enterprise capability embraces a far wider range of experience and knowledge and requires a contribution from a wide range of teaching staff and external agencies.

There is considerable discussion among inspectors, examiners, designers of enterprise education materials and teachers as to what exactly constitutes 'good' enterprise education. There is broad agreement that there is a lot of poor to mediocre practice that is too didactic and does not allow students to learn by doing.

The Department of Trade and Industry promote a guide to enterprise education on their website giving examples of good practice in all curriculum areas, mapping qualifications to aspects of enterprise education. This website also gives a very useful listing of all Enterprise education programmes including an outline of their schemes and contact details.

The Lifetime Survival Kit framework provides an overview of how the various government initiatives fit together to provide individuals with a coherent means to survive the changes that they will encounter in the external environment in their lifetimes. The core of the Survival Kit are the key skills that empower the individual with the underlying tools to make the most of all opportunities offered to them through curricular, extra-curricular and outside school experiences. The Academic Personal Profiling provides the methodology for the student to continuously improve their performance by reflecting on successes and barriers to development to date and thus identifying strategies for overcoming problems. It is a circular process that should inform a person's development for life.

Figure 12.1 Lifetime survival kit

At the institutional level, for example, whole-school planning must make clear the following:

- the expected learning outcomes, by year group;
- knowledge, skill and attitude progression from Y7 to Y11 (Y13);
- a programme of enterprise activities to which all students will be entitled: this should consider a long-term programme of embedding enterprise into the curriculum;
- long-term and short-term experiential learning exercises;
- evaluation and monitoring of enterprise learning through a student's school life;
- staff training;
- allocation of resources.

Long-term activities

There are a wide variety of exercises that are available for students to participate in over an academic year. As can be seen in the case study below the benefits of students taking part in a long-term experiential learning exercise are that they:

- have time to develop, and take on new roles, such as Marketing Director, Managing Director and so on;
- have time to make mistakes, be lazy, let each other down, reflect on their problems, identify strategies to overcome problems, and finally look back and realise how much they have learnt;
- have time to internalise their new knowledge, attitudes and understanding.

Merton College's Young Enterprise programme began approximately 4 years ago as an add-on to its main AVCE programme in Business and is completed by those students in the second year of their programme.

At the main Trade Fair in Sutton the team won the Best Display Award and got nominated for their Best Traders Award, because they took their goods to the public to raise awareness of their stand and to maximise their sales. The group then became excited and wanted to do more and win more. From never speaking to each other, the team now conversed regularly, just because of the YE programme. *'It showed me how a business should be run and I enjoyed it very much,'* said Kim one of the YE learners. *'I wished we had focused on our product earlier and had gone to more trade fairs',* commented Ophelia, the Production Director.

If one was to take the initial motivation of the group nothing would have happened, but as the link teacher, I stuck with it and worked with the team, feeding them the information they needed. Eventually it paid off and their own motivation took over, they became successful in their endeavours to build a company from scratch and to make it work.

Sandra Bryant
Co-ordinator
GNVQ Intermediate Business

It is advisable for a school or college to allocate curriculum time to these activities. Without staff being given time for long-term enterprise activities, it is highly unlikely that a school could offer all students an entitlement to such an experience or that it will be of a high quality.

Teaching staff who are linked to long-term enterprise experiences need time to recruit and set up students at the start of the activity, observe students' meetings and coach students throughout the year. Ideally, the member of staff will also organise and maintain any relevant industry links and prepare students for any assessments that are part of the programme.

In order for all students to experience a long-term enterprise activity the school or college needs a wide range of activities available that will appeal to all students. These activities might include some of the following programmes:

1 The Young Enterprise Team and Company programmes (www.young-enterprise.org.uk)

2 The National Foundation for Teaching Entrepreneurship programme (www.nfte.org.uk)

3 The HSBC School Bank (www.hsbc.co.uk/hsbc/education/schoolbranch)

4 Running a shop within a school, e.g. the school tuck shop; a PE equipment shop; an outdoor equipment store, which supports the Duke of Edinburgh Award Scheme; or a travel agents (www.ebea.org.uk)

5 The Springboard Management Programme (www.ebea.org.uk)

6 The CHAMPS scheme run by the Chartered Management Institute (www.managers.org.uk, click Scotland on the regions, click on regional news)

7 The ASDAN Award (www.asdan.co.uk)

8 The Duke of Edinburgh Award Scheme (www.theaward.org)

9 The Millennium Volunteers Award (www.go-wm.gov.uk/Connexions/volunteers)

10 The Sports Leaders Award (www.sportsleaders.org)

11 Achievers International (www.achieversinternational.co.uk)

12 Community links working with youth groups such as Scouts (www.scouts.org.uk), Guides (www.guides.org.uk), the Army Cadet Force (www.armycadets.com) and so on

13 Part-time paid employment, although this carries a heavy health warning (www.gmb.org.uk)

Short-term activities

These activities are ideal for cross-curricular work and can incorporate investigations in subjects such as mathematics, science and engineering. They can draw in activities for links with other schools, such as getting pupils at each school to carry out a SWOT analysis of each other's school, or set up a concert together.

Wallington High School for Girls host a three-week visit each year from thirty students from Edogawa High School, Tokyo. The main objectives of this visit are to enhance cultural understanding between the two groups of students, to improve the Japanese students' English-language skills and to enhance the Year 9 Geography curriculum.

As part of the visit the Edogawa students work with the Year 10 business studies students to carry out a SWOT analysis of Wallington High School. This is initially very difficult as the Japanese students have no grounding in business studies and they find it culturally difficult to criticise their hosts. The Wallington students find that they really have to concentrate and think hard about their communication.

'We not only had to tell them about our school, but we also had to teach them how to use camcorders and Powerpoint ... it was fun, but it was more tiring than I had expected,' said one Wallington student.

John Newell
Head of Economics, Business and Politics
Wallington High School for Girls

There are a wide range of organisations providing short-term enterprise activities. Some of these organisations just provide exercises for teachers to organise, others will come into school and deliver the exercise themselves, and other providers will invite school parties onto their premises to take part in games or simulations. Below are a list of short-term enterprise activity providers which have been roughly subdivided by their support level for the activities.

Activities only

- The EBEA website (www.ebea.org.uk)
- The Centre for Education and Industry, University of Warwick (www.warwick.ac.uk/wie/cei)
- On their fundraising web pages, most major charities will have a wide range of experiential activities for students to get involved in to raise funds for the charity.
- Oxfam will support you with a fundraising toolkit (www.oxfam.org.uk)
- Save the Children Fund have a special section on their website for youth fundraising activities (www.savethechildren.org.uk/youngfundraisers)
- Christian Aid (www.christianaid.org.uk/learn/schools) market a series of economic development games.
- World Aware has Economic Geography resources (www.worldaware.org)

- BT offer a website building resource (www.schools.ik.com)
- The Royal Geographic Society (www.rgs.org)

Activities supported by the organisations coming into school

- The Construction Industry Trade Board (www.citb.co.uk)
- CRAC (www.crac.org.uk)
- The Centre for Education and Industry, University of Warwick (www.warwick.ac.uk/wie/cei)
- The Army Careers Advisers through their Active programme; contact your local Army Careers Office.
- Science, engineering, technology and mathematics are supported by SETPOINT (www.setnet.org.uk)
- The Royal Society of Chemists (www.rsc.org)
- Young Enterprise, Master Class Programme, the Learn to Earn Programme, Project Business and so on (www.young-enterprise.org.uk)
- BT have a variety of resources (www.btplc.com)
- Natwest Face 2 Face with Finance (www.natwestf2f.com)
- The Chartered Management Institute (www.managers.org.uk)
- Local Education Business Partnerships; contact your local office or use the website of the national education business partnership association (www.parawebsol.co.uk)

Activities organised on the companies' premises or away from the school site

- The Army: contact your local Army Careers Office.
- Most major companies will have some programme for students to visit their premises.
- BP has a schools link schemes for schools near its office and refinery sites (www.bp.com/schoolslink).
- BAA will work with schools which are looking at issues surrounding airports. Contact can be made with the public relations department at each airport.
- Most town centre managers will work with schools to look at the issues surrounding their town centre development.
- Supermarkets and banks tend to be the easiest local links to access.
- Local corner shops, cafés, railway stations and council facilities such as parks are very accessible for students to develop an enterprise investigation around. This can have the benefit of helping a local business develop by identifying new products or services they could offer or how they could save costs on, say, ineffective advertising.

- Smaller groups of students can far more easily access external partners, so it might be more profitable to send different groups of students off to interview or work with different stakeholders on a particular issue. This way the report back in the classroom is of genuine interest to everyone as each group of students has something different to say.

Many organisations simply do not know what schools want from them, and schools need to think carefully about what they are going to achieve from their link with an organisation. Going to see a company and staring at their operation is probably of very little use and it is terribly difficult for students to think of sensible questions to ask. To bridge this gap teachers need to identify curriculum areas which could be enhanced by input from external expertise and then work with the company on setting up a problem for students to solve which requires them to interact with the company's personnel. The company will then have an educational product that they can offer to other schools and the school will have a strong professional relationship with an external partner.

Summary

It is clear that enterprise education is to do with much more than just running business activities in schools and colleges. It is about making links with and drawing on businesses and the world of work to enhance learning in simulated and real situations. This gives students an opportunity to develop and use a range of skills in practical, applied and relevant settings in which they are active learners. This needs careful planning on the part of teachers, who can exploit the opportunities for both short- and long-term activities. The challenge is to make these learning opportunities available to many, if not all, students at a school or college. Clearly, enterprise has much to offer in meeting the requirements set out in the proposals for the reform of the 14–19 phase of education.

References

Bell, G. (1998) 'The Personal Effectiveness Programme Initiative', *Pastoral Care in Education* 16(2), 20.

Centre for Education and Industry (CEI) Warwick University (2001) *Independent Research into Learning for Enterprise and Entrepreneurship*. DTI website.

Goldsmith, W., and Clutterbuck, D. (1984) *The Winning Streak*. London: Weidenfeld & Nicolson.

Maslow, A. (1954) *Motivation and Personality*. New York: Harper.

Kolb, D. A., with J. Osland and I. Rubin (1995) *Organizational Behavior: An Experiential Approach to Human Behavior in Organizations*, 6th edn. Englewood Cliffs, NJ: Prentice Hall.

Rogers, C. (1961) *On Becoming a Person*. Boston: Houghton Mifflin.

External assessment: an examiner's perspective

Ian Marcouse

Introduction

This chapter gives the benefit of the experiences of one chief examiner from a leading examining board in the hope that both students and teachers have much to gain from an understanding of the external assessment process.

Preparing an exam paper

Before starting

An exam paper starts with the specification. Within AS/A Level, each of the six units of examination has its own role. This role is governed by the subject content it must test, and the assessment objectives it must meet. For example, the AQA A level Unit 1 examines AS Marketing and Finance through the assessment profile in Table 13.1. By contrast, the synoptic Unit 6 exam tests A2 External Influences and Objectives & Strategy with the profile in Table 13.2.

Table 13.1 Assessment profile for AQA A level Unit 1

Knowledge and Understanding	Application	Analysis	Evaluation
33%	33%	24%	10%

Table 13.2 Assessment profile for AQA A level Unit 6

Knowledge and Understanding	Application	Analysis	Evaluation
20%	15%	25%	40%

As can be seen, knowledge and application are of overwhelming importance in Unit 1 (33% + 33% = 66% would mean an A grade) but of much less direct significance in Unit 6 (20% + 15% = 35%, which might be a fail). By contrast, evaluation rises from inessential luxury in Unit 1 to necessity in Unit 6.

The above variations lead to differing approaches to assessment. The AQA Unit 1 is examined through a data response paper with several small-mark-allocation questions, including 2-mark definitions of terms suggesting that it is very knowledge-driven. Unit 6 is a sweeping case study covering a major strategic issue for a major, real company. For instance, in June 2004 it looked at the battle between Boeing and Airbus, with the questions targeted at huge debates such as government intervention, ethics, takeovers and competitive forces.

These different styles of exam make it possible to give students the opportunity to show different skills, as appropriate to the assessment profile. For example, the Unit 6 paper raises open, discursive issues that enable students to debate and to make judgements and, therefore, gain marks for evaluation. A June 2004 question, for example, asked students to 'Consider whether Boeing should make a takeover bid for easyJet.'

So what exactly is meant by these assessment objectives and what, therefore, do students have to be able to do to gain the marks? AQA Business Studies mark schemes start with these explanations to examiners:

1 Knowledge and understanding: accurate definitions or explanations of relevant terms should always be credited within this category; candidates can also gain credit for knowing and explaining a point relevant to the question, e.g. an advantage of factoring.

2 Application is the skill of bringing knowledge to bear to the business context faced by the candidate. No reward should go to a candidate who simply drops the company name or product category into an answer; the response must show recognition of some specific business aspect of the firm, its management or its situation.

3 Analysis: building up an argument using relevant business theory in a way that answers the question specifically, and shows understanding of cause and effect.

4 Evaluation is judgement. This can be shown within an answer, through the weighting of an argument or in the perceptiveness shown by the candidate (perhaps about the degree of crisis/strength of the XYZ company). It can also be shown within a conclusion, perhaps by weighing up the strength of the student's own arguments for and against a proposition. Evaluation is *not* shown by the use of drilled phrases such as 'On the other hand' or 'Business operates in an ever-changing environment.' It is shown through the weighting of the candidate's response plus the logic and justification of his/her conclusions.

Writing a paper

Exam papers are supposed to be finalised about 18 months before they are sat, ensuring that there is always a spare paper ready in case a security leak invalidates the planned one. It follows that writing an exam paper might begin nearly two years before the exam session and creates huge difficulties for paper-setters who want to include some realistic macro-economic data within the exam.

An exam may originate from a number of different stimuli. Often the prevailing business mood is important, such as if manufacturers are complaining about an over-valued pound. There may also be a nagging feeling in the paper-setter's mind that recent underperformance on an element of a recent exam means that a subject requires exposure. For trails to this kind of thing, do not look at the most recent chief examiner's report, but the one before, that is, hints on the June 2005 exams are most likely to appear in the summer 2003 report.

A further influence upon content comes, of course, from previous exam papers. Most obviously, an examiner who has not tested a substantive topic for some time will feel compelled to do so. Despite this truism, it rarely bears fruit to guess the up-and-coming question topics. In business studies, there tend to be too many options to make predictions a worthwhile game.

Evaluating the paper

After the exam paper, questions and mark scheme are completed, all are sent to a Reviser. This person checks the content for clarity, accuracy and overlap between papers. Then a full day is spent by a question-paper evaluation committee dissecting each paper – the prose, the data, the questions and the mark scheme. The committee members focus mainly upon the questions to check that they say exactly what they mean to say.

What makes a good paper?

After a paper has been sat, the immediate feedback from teachers focuses upon accessibility and predictability. No-one ever writes in to complain about a paper because the questions were bland or too straightforward. In fact, the job of an examiner is to give students an opportunity to use their ability, and this requires an exam with enough of an edge to give the stars a chance to shine. Well-pitched exams are tough enough to force candidates to think, to reflect and to push themselves. Many students find this uncomfortable and may come out saying it was awful. Experience shows that this is a better predictor of success than a gleeful statement: 'That was easy.'

How to maximise the chances of student success

To succeed at high-mark-allocation, discursive questions, students need the confidence to address the question directly. In other words, they must not write what they think 'Miss' might say, or rehash the textbook, or write what they believe the examiner wants to hear. The correct approach is to formulate arguments based upon the contextual evidence, using relevant theory. The Radio 4 programme *Just A Minute* gives an appropriate, if extreme, illustration of the need to answer 'without deviation, hesitation or repetition'. Questions must be tackled directly by students who are used to thinking for a moment before they put pen to paper. In fact, many answers begin with wordy rehashes of the question, then drift towards pre-learned, all-purpose prose. Stock answers about ethics or motivation or economies of scale leave examiners cold. They want evidence of thought, not memory. Good teaching empowers, even liberates. Poor teaching hammers home what are believed to be eternal truths. In some subjects there might be an excuse for inculcating 'facts'; in business studies and economics the key is to open up debates.

To encourage a confident approach to answering questions, the key is to make debates a key part of the classroom, and to create many situations in which students are forced to make decisions. This can be done via role-plays or simulation exercises, or in more standard ways by providing data that must be assimilated before discussion and then a decision by an individual or a group. In AQA Business Studies the A2 Unit 4 exam is a decision-making case study and the Unit 5W report requires a decision to be made and justified. Past papers provide many examples of decisions, such as whether or not to sell a business; to move location; to launch a new product; to close a bakery.

What happens after the exam?

The marking process

Four or five days after an exam is sat the Principal Examiner runs a series of meetings to co-ordinate the exam-marking. Five or six exam scripts are selected and photocopied for all markers to have a go at the same answers. After the co-ordination meeting, the first ten scripts marked by every examiner are sent to his/her supervisor. This goes up the hierarchy so the supervisors' marking is checked by Assistant Principal Examiners, whose marking is, in turn, checked by the Principal. Feedback is given at that stage, such as, 'You're a bit harsh on Application, but a touch generous on Quality of Language.' If the ten are competently marked, the examiner will continue through his/her allocation of perhaps 250 scripts. Along the way, 50 are sent to the supervisor, who will randomly select 15 for a further check. If these are fine, no further checks are made. If an adjustment is thought necessary, such as adding 2 marks to every script marked by a marginally mean examiner, a further 10 scripts are checked at that stage.

Later still comes the Grade Awarding meeting. In the summer, this is at the end of July or beginning of August. A group of perhaps eight people look at a range of scripts at around the A/B and E/U borderline for each exam unit. From reading scripts, the Awarding Committee will decide whether the minimum mark for an A grade on a paper marked out of 84 should be struck at 55 or at 54. The more generous the committee decides to be, the more students will get an A grade. It should be pointed out, though, that the statisticians at the exam board will have analysed the data to predict how many students are likely to get an A Grade, based upon their aggregate GCSE scores. If the Awarding Committee appears too generous with As or passes, the Board will be reluctant to allow 'grade inflation'.

Does all this care and attention mean that all students always get the right mark and grade? Sadly, not. Mistakes will happen, which is why it is sensible to ask to see a photocopy of your candidates' scripts, if you believe the marking to be unjust. Sometimes you will then realise that the fault was that of your candidates, but on other occasions you will want to get the work re-marked.

The results (the extraordinary UMS system)

Although this topic seems arcane, it can have a direct bearing upon candidate results. This is because the Government's measure for declaring AS and A level module results (the UMS or Uniform Mark Scale) exaggerates the real level of student performance. Candidates can end up thinking that it is pointless to re-sit an exam unit because their performance seems better than it really was. This method is used across all subjects and all exam boards.

The UMS is a synthesised version of percentage exam result. It presents results in a format that consistently shows 80%+ to be an A and 40%+ to be an E. In fact, though, the grade-awarding committee may have decided that the A grade boundary on a difficult exam should be set at 60%, for example, 30 out of 50 and that the E grade boundary should be at 36%, for example, 18 out of 50. In this case, the following will occur. In Table 13.3 the column headed 'Max 50' shows the actual grade-awarding decision. The 'Max UMS 100' shows the UMS points the student will receive on their exam results slip. The 'approximate egs' show how confusing the results can be for candidates. Take for example the student whose UMS result is 73/100. S/he may well say 'I've never beaten 73 per cent before so there is no point in me retaking the exam next time.' Yet, the actual mark in the case below was just 56 per cent – which sounds a great deal more beatable.

A further confusion comes from the fact that a maximum UMS result of 100 points does not mean what you might expect. It is not a perfect script. As teacher/examiners tend to be mean at the top end of the mark range, the computer that generates the UMS scores in effect ignores the top band of marks. In this case, with the A grade set at 60%, there may be very few candidate responses that scored more than 40 out of 50 (80%).

Table 13.3 Grade-awarding decisions using the UMS

	MAX 50	Max 100 UMS	Approximate egs
A	30	80	30 (60%) appears as 80/100 = 80%
B	27	70	28 (56%) appears as 73/100 = 73%
C	24	60	25 (50%) appears as 63/100 = 63%
D	21	50	
E	18	40	

Therefore, the computer says 'let all results of 40+ be given a UMS score of 100', leaving the majority of the A grades to be given UMS scores between 80 and 100. If 40 is to receive a UMS of 100, 35 will get 90. Once more, this is very confusing for anyone to deal with – and can be seen by a candidate as a reason to avoid further work.

Broadly, it is fair to assume that if an AS student gets a UMS of 73/100 on a paper taken at the end of the first year, there is a significant chance of beating that score at the end of the second year. The 27 UMS marks left for this student to get are likely to be far easier to obtain than an extra 27 UMS marks on a tough A2 paper. So re-sits should be regarded as a natural part of the process.

Exam marking and mark schemes

There are three main strategies used by examination boards in the marking of candidates' work.

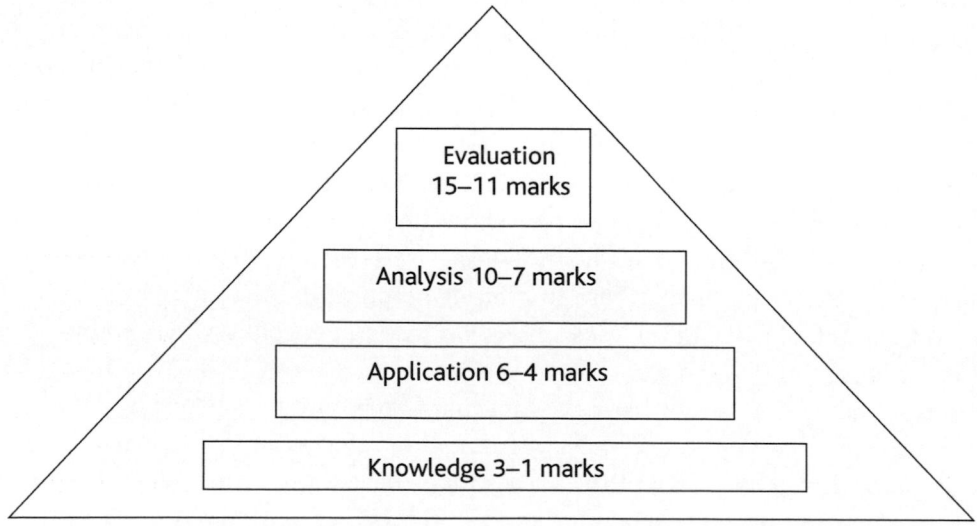

Figure 13.1 Single-pyramid marking

1 Single-pyramid levels of response

This approach is based upon Bloom's taxonomy, in which the mark is based upon how high up the pyramid the student response reaches (see Figure 13.1). The advantage of the single-pyramid approach is that it is quick to use. The examiner need only make two judgements: (i) What skill level does the candidate reach? (ii) How good an example of that skill is contained within the answer? So for example if the skill level reached is analytic, the student scores 7–10 marks out of 15; and if the analysis is good, the student gets 10.

The downside is that a poorly analysed script with some plausible evaluation may be scored at 13/15 by marker A, but 7/15 by marker B. This, in turn, may encourage candidates to focus purely on a rather general, evaluative style of writing that may contain too little evidence of specific knowledge or mastery of the business context.

2 Assessment objective grids

In this approach, the four components of Bloom's taxonomy are marked separately. This allows a marker to give a script full credit for Knowledge and Analysis, but perhaps zero for Application and little for Evaluation. It takes longer for the marker, who has far more decisions to make. The hope is that it is more reliable for candidates, and it is unarguable that it gives a greater incentive to teachers and students to master all four assessment objectives. Table 13.4 is drawn from the June 2004 AQA Unit 3 Business Studies exam.

Table 13.4 Marking grid for Unit 3 Business Studies exam June 2004

Marking grid (out of 15)			
3	3	4	5
Knowledge	Application	Analysis	Evaluation
			5
			Judgement shown in weighing up whether Andrew was *always* acting for *all* stakeholders, with clear conclusions
3	3	4–3	4–3
Good understanding shown of shareholders and stakeholders	Relevant issues applied in detail to the case	Analysis of question set, using relevant theory	Judgement shown in weighing up Andrew's approach to the interests of stakeholders in this case
2–1	2–1	2–1	2–1
Shows some understanding of the relevant terms	Relevant issues applied to the case	One or two points applied in a limited way to analyse the question.	Some judgement shown in text or conclusions

3 Integrated mark bands

Some awarding bodies merge the assessment objectives within mark ranges that describe particular types of answer. These statements are often quite long and could be taken as a description of a stereotypical A grade, B grade, etc. answer. For example:

15–12 marks. A very well-written answer focused on the question, revealing a good understanding of the context and weighing up both sides of the argument. From this a mature conclusion is reached that is well justified.

11–8 marks. A well-structured answer to the question, showing understanding of the context. Both sides of the argument may be looked at, but without insight, or the answer may be one-sided. Some conclusions are reached but lack justification.

And so on.

The concern about this style of marking is that it seems to place written fluency above all other considerations.

Summary

On exam marking

The teacher's task is to find out the approach used by the relevant exam board, then make sure to reflect that approach in their marking. The grid system is especially helpful in identifying for a student his or her strengths and weaknesses. Some will master application quite quickly, while others will struggle. It is also helpful that it may highlight that the candidate has some undoubted strengths as well as some aspects upon which s/he 'could do better'. Whatever the system, though, students need a great deal of preparation to be able to mould their style of answers around the examination board's methodology. To ignore this issue is to risk condemning students to underperformance.

Years ago, exam marking was a mysterious process conducted in secrecy. Today it is highly transparent. The awarding bodies are happy to make their mark schemes available to all on the internet, together with their essential companion, the Chief Examiner's report. For full details see:

www.aqa.org.uk

www.ccea.org.uk

www.edexcel.org.uk

www.ocr.org.uk

www.wjec.co.uk

Perhaps there is no better way of understanding the examination system and passing the benefits on to students than becoming an examiner!

Initial and Continuing Teacher Development

Initial and continuing teacher development

Ian Abbott

Introduction

The purpose of this part of the book is to develop some of the issues relating to initial teacher education and the continuing professional development of teachers (CPD). In particular, it will look at some of the recent policy initiatives that have had a major impact on business and economics education. This chapter and the rest of Part 3 will focus on the way these initiatives impact on individual teachers and the effect they have on school and classroom practice.

Initial teacher education

The demand for teachers of business and economics teachers from schools and colleges remains at a high level. Recent developments within the subject area have contributed to this high level of demand, especially the continuing growth and popularity of vocational programmes. Schools have recognised the contribution business and economics can make to the curriculum and the key role they play in retaining learners post-16. Over recent years the proliferation of new programmes has resulted in improved employment opportunities for business and economics teachers.

Most new teachers of business and economics are trained through the one-year Postgraduate Certificate in Education (PGCE) route. Given the nature of the subject area, trainee teachers are recruited from a variety of subject backgrounds, including business studies, economics, accounting and finance, management and human resources (HR). Increasingly entrants to PGCE programmes have significant business experience, which they are able to utilise to good effect in the classroom. These skills are also often employed across the school, although it is still relatively unusual to find business and economics specialists in senior management positions. Hopefully this situation will change over the next few years as the skills developed by business and economics teachers are fully utilised and more teachers from the subject area obtain positions of responsibility.

In most cases the PGCE is organised as a partnership between a higher education institution (HEI) and local schools and colleges. However, in recent years a number of alternative programmes have been developed, including the Graduate Teacher Training Programme (GTP) and School Centered Initial Teacher Training (SCITT). Neither of these two programmes have had a significant impact on the training of business and economics teachers, but they have contributed to the development of different approaches to initial teacher training. In a PGCE programme a trainee teacher will spend approximately 66 per cent of their training year based in school or college, with the remainder of their time at the HEI. During this year trainee teachers are expected to develop their subject knowledge in addition to developing a range of teaching competencies. In England the system is heavily regulated by the Teacher Training Agency (TTA) who lay down professional standards for Qualified Teacher Status (QTS). In addition the TTA set, control and allocate, on an annual basis, the number of trainee teachers each institution can recruit. The initial training of teachers is further controlled by an inspection regime carried out by Ofsted. The inspection system is designed to monitor how effectively the trainee teachers are being prepared for the classroom and to ensure compliance with the standards. Any institution offering PGCE courses that are non-compliant is at risk of losing its 'licence' to train teachers. So the Ofsted inspection process is of great significance to providers, who are under pressure to meet the targets that have been set.

The TTA has been determined to increase the quantity and quality of entrants to the teaching profession. Consequently they set high standards for new entrants to the teaching profession:

> Just as teachers must have high expectations of their pupils, so pupils, parents and carers are entitled to have high expectations of teachers. Teaching is a creative, intellectually demanding and rewarding job, so the standards for joining the profession must be high too. Skilled practitioners can make teaching look easy but they have learned their skills and improved them through training, practice, evaluation and by learning from other colleagues.
>
> (TTA 2003: 3)

Trainee teachers have to meet the specific standards laid down by the TTA, to achieve qualified teacher status (QTS). The standards are organised into three sections:

S1 Professional values and practice

These standards outline the attitudes and commitment to be expected of anyone qualifying to become a teacher, and are derived from the professional code of the General Teaching Council for England.

S2 Knowledge and understanding

These standards require newly qualified teachers to be confident and authoritative in the subjects they teach and to have a clear understanding of how all pupils should progress and what teachers should expect them to achieve.

S3 Teaching

These standards relate to skills of planning, monitoring and assessment, and teaching and class management. They are underpinned by the values and knowledge covered in the first two sections. (TTA 2003: 3)

These general standard areas are further broken down into a series of smaller statements. For example, the standard relating to knowledge and understanding is broken down into eight criteria:

> *S2.1* They have a secure knowledge and understanding of the subject(s) they are trained to teach. For those qualifying to teach secondary pupils this knowledge and understanding should be at a standard equivalent to degree level. In relation to the specific phases this includes:
>
> *d.* For Key Stage 4 and post-16, they are aware of the pathways for progression through the 14–19 phase in school, college and work-based setting. They are familiar with Key Skills as specified by QCA and the National Qualifications Framework, and they know the progression within and from their own subject and the range of qualifications to which their subject contributes. They understand how courses are combined in students' curricula.
>
> (TTA 2003: 9)

From the example above it is clear that in England the system of teacher training is heavily regulated, and organisations and individuals involved in the process have relatively little room to manoeuvre. A centralised system has clear advantages because it has enabled common standards to be developed across the country. There are also clear guidelines about the characteristics of a competent teacher and what constitutes effective teaching. The standards laid down by the TTA have also led to an increase in the amount of time trainee teachers spend in school. However, over-regulation can lead to a decline in innovation and encourage trainee teachers to just adopt an approach that will be sufficient to meet the standards. While there is general agreement about the characteristics of good teaching, there has to be room for innovation and a range of alternative approaches.

Continuing professional development

For the purposes of this section I will use Day's (1994) broad definition of continuing professional development (CPD). This includes an acknowledgement of formal and informal training and learning:

> Professional development consists of all natural learning experiences and those conscious and planned activities which are intended to be of direct or indirect benefit to the individual, group or school, which contribute through these, to the quality of education in the classroom.
>
> (Day 1994: 4)

CPD is not then just related to in-service training or on-the-job learning. It should encompass all aspects of a teacher's work and training, including the specific opportunities provided for formal training. There is strong evidence to suggest that a robust system of professional development contributes directly to school improvement. Research into improving schools, for example, shows that improvement is facilitated by a series of training opportunities, discussion and dialogue at a variety of levels (Harris 2002). Recognition of the importance of continuing professional development is clearly acknowledged by the TTA at the start of a teacher's career:

> Of course, initial training in not an end in itself, but the start of a long-term process of professional development, and effective teaching depends on working well with everyone else who has a stake in the education of our children.
>
> (TTA 2003: 1)

At the end of the PGCE newly qualified teachers have to complete a Career Entry and Development Profile (CEDP). The CEDP is a bridging document, which should contain details of the areas requiring further professional development during the induction period, which is normally one year.

So there is a clear recognition that every teacher should undertake professional development at the beginning of their career and this should continue in subsequent years. Given the changes that have taken place over recent years in education and especially within business and economics it is difficult to imagine any teacher who has not had to undertake some form of professional development. So what form does this training take?

In the past a great deal of training and support was provided by the local education authority (LEA), who may have had specialist advisers in a range of subject areas. However, business and economics was not well served by this system with many LEAs not employing specialist advisers in the subject area. In recent years the role of the LEA has been weakened by the policies of successive governments who have directed resources away from the LEA and directly to individual schools. Part of this process has been the delegation of money for staff development directly to the individual school. This has changed the pattern of provision of CPD as schools are able to buy training and staff development from different sources. As a consequence of this policy a range of providers have entered the market to provide professional development training for teachers. Due to the frequent changes that have been made, many teachers of business and economics have had to attend training on new examination programmes and related assessment issues. In many cases training is provided by the examination boards, who are keen to encourage teachers to enter candidates for their examinations.

Other groups such as the EBEA have also entered the market and now offer a range of training programmes. However, it is difficult to escape the importance to teachers of the training associated with examination programmes. Teaching and assessing GCSE and A level are clearly of great significance to teachers in the subject area.

The introduction of Advanced Skills Teachers (ASTs) might also have an impact on the ability of business and economics teachers to work together and undertake professional development. The AST has a clear role within their school, but they also have wider responsibilities for developing good practice within the subject area. However, only small numbers of business and economics teachers have become ASTs, and the funding for this area of work looks problematic.

Higher education institutions have traditionally provided a range of long and short courses for teachers. While these are still available, the cost, especially of longer courses, has prevented many teachers from undertaking this type of activity. The opportunities for secondment have also become more difficult, and many teachers are reluctant to study for a higher degree on a part-time basis, although a number still do. However, the opportunities for undertaking classroom-based enquiry using action research are likely to increase in the future. This may encourage more teachers to become involved in programmes provided by higher education institutions.

Of greater significance have been the networks established by higher education institutions as part of their teacher training remit. The opportunities for business and economics teachers to meet as a group have become more limited, and the regular mentor meetings organised by higher education tutors often provide opportunities to share ideas and good practice. Certainly recent government policies have been keen to promote greater co-operation between individual schools in place of the outright competition that was a feature of the previous decade. This is especially true in urban areas and there is likely to be greater emphasis on the sharing of good practice over the next few years. The establishment of a number of specialist business and enterprise schools is likely to continue this process with increased opportunities for the sharing of good practice.

Working with business has also provided significant opportunities for staff development for teachers of business and economics. Training programmes offered by organisations such as the Centre for Education and Industry and placements facilitated by Education Business Partnerships have been extremely popular. Many subject teachers have been able to update their understanding of business through placements. This has had an impact on teaching and learning and has led to a range of teaching materials being developed. Undertaking a placement in a local business has been a successful option for business and economics teachers, especially with the proliferation of vocational programmes and the requirement to provide 'real life' examples and materials for learners.

Summary

There is a continuing demand from schools and colleges for teachers of business and economics. The initial training of teachers has been fundamentally reformed with the introduction of the standards and the continuing role of the TTA. Teachers are fully involved in the training process, working closely with HEIs, and they have played a major part in the reform of the system.

Teachers want to be able to do the best job they can for their pupils, and generally they are keen to receive appropriate training and support. CPD will provide them with opportunities to develop new strategies and approaches. At one extreme will be the courses designed to instruct teachers about new examination requirements and systems. Clearly this is important and necessary, but it is also important not to lose sight of the importance of the sharing of ideas and approaches and the need to communicate with colleagues. Professional development should be about more than just being prepared to teach the newest syllabus or understand the latest assessment techniques. While this is clearly important, there should also be the opportunity to develop new ideas and new approaches.

On a wider level there is growing recognition that raising educational standards is ultimately dependent on what teachers do in the classroom. David Hopkins Director of the Standards and Effectiveness Unit at the DfES, recently identified the importance of the teacher in this process:

> The emphasis on transformation is key – reform strategies can no longer take only an incremental approach to change. The raising of standards of learning and attainment for all our students now needs to be seen within a whole school or systems context and to impact both on classroom practice and the work culture of the school.

> (Hopkins 2003: 3)

Continuing professional development is going to continue to be important for teachers. The drive to improve standards of educational achievement is at the core of this process. However, for individual teachers the significance of any training is the impact it has on teaching and learning. Therefore any judgements about the effectiveness of any professional development programme undertaken by teachers has to be the impact it has on classroom practice.

References

Day, C. (1994) 'Quality assurance and staff development', *British Journal of In-Service Education*, **17**(3), 189–95.

Harris, A. (2002) *School Improvement: What's In It for Schools?* London: Routledge Falmer.

Hopkins, D. (2003) 'Transforming schools', keynote address to DfES *Transforming Schools* conference, London, September 2003.

Teacher Training Agency (TTA) (2003) *Qualifying to Teach: Professional Standards for Qualified Teacher Status and Requirements for Initial Teacher Training.* London: TTA.

The changing face of initial teacher education

Paul Clarke

Introduction

Initial teacher education (ITE) has undergone a number of significant changes over recent years. A national curriculum with published criteria (DfEE 1998), an inspection regime with a three-year cycle (Ofsted/TTA 2002) and a funding provision linked to inspection grades have shifted the balance for training institutions used to managing their own courses with partner schools. In some ways, the idea of a consistent training programme producing nearly 20,000 new secondary teachers who meet a guaranteed standard is attractive, and given the number of different providers now, some degree of regulation would be seen by many people as a sensible measure. In 2003–4, there were some 130 providers of ITE in England and Wales, with 90 organisations offering employment-based training routes and 59 school-based consortia, 35 of which operated at secondary level. Business and economics training has a relatively modest role within this overall picture with 25 providers in England and Wales and four in Scotland preparing roughly 760 new teachers. Four of the providers are relatively new school-based consortia. The majority of the courses focus on business studies with some ICT while a minority provide some training in economics.

Providers clearly have an eye on the needs of schools who employ new teachers, and the trends will be familiar to those preparing students for examination courses in schools. A growth in business and applied vocational numbers at pre- and post-16 stages, a reduction in the numbers sitting economics and a rapid increase in the uptake of ICT at all levels is reflected in the content of training courses. In the West Midlands, for example, one course integrates ICT and business and the majority of trainees' placements are in 11–16 schools where a teaching timetable is likely to involve an equal weighting of KS3 and KS4 lessons. Another institution links to schools where pupils transfer to high school at 12 and 13. Here the partner schools have a tradition of teaching sixth-form economics as well as business, and trainees join a course which places an emphasis on both subjects.

Subject knowledge

Business education is a complex mix of subjects, and this raises interesting questions about trainees' subject knowledge and the expectations on both them and providers to ensure a good quality experience. Inspectors have grown used to referring to the term business education to cover all that is taught by specialist departments in school. Should, therefore, a trainee be expected to be competent to teach at an advanced level in business, economics and information technology? There are few graduates emerging from university courses with a firm grounding in all areas and 120 days teaching and observing in two schools supported by 60 days study with a training provider are not sufficient to develop a graduate understanding of all three subjects. The need to update and develop trainees' subject knowledge raises issues that equate with those of school departments trying to cover National Curriculum content. The breadth of a trainee's knowledge may be developed at the expense of the depth of their understanding.

Governments of all political persuasion assume that trainees come into teacher training with a complete subject expertise and the main job of trainers is to focus on teaching strategies. The reality for many trainees is that they have to reinterpret their subject knowledge in order to communicate with learners of different ages and abilities. Challenging situations arise in school when a pupil asks an unexpected question or offers an unusual answer to a question, or when a trainee is asked to prepare material for a course or a context beyond their experience. Thomas (1996) has written about 'knowledge and theory in action', where she argues for the need to be able to reinterpret knowledge and principles each time they are encountered in new contexts. This is a major issue for new teachers, and it could be argued that it takes several years of experience of the cycle of examination courses before anyone is really comfortable with their subject knowledge.

The Teacher Training Agency (TTA) has recognised the problem and supported trainees with pre-course subject top-up training, but, as with many initiatives, the provision only covers main National Curriculum subjects. Business trainers have used a number of strategies including distance-learning study packages and detailed subject audits accompanied by targeted action plans for trainees. Some school partners provide time in their programme for trainees to observe and to discuss teaching sessions on less familiar topics. The focus of first school placements tends to be on topics most familiar to trainees while they learn the fundamentals of class management. Later placements offer the opportunity to explore some topics in more depth. However, there are always going to be differences in schools' abilities to offer trainees experience across a subject range and in different course contexts. Some schools and colleges prefer to have trainees with a strong subject background, especially if they are to teach on post-16 courses.

Some schools work with trainees in a very supportive and collaborative way while others expect trainees to sort out their own subject knowledge issues.

In this new era of accountability, Ofsted holds training providers to be responsible for ensuring the development of trainees' subject knowledge. Reports do indicate progress in general:

> Nine out of ten trainees who were observed teaching, demonstrated secure understanding of their subjects. The general improvement in standards of subject knowledge reflected the greater importance placed on subject understanding at recruitment, and better strategies adopted by providers...On a few school-centred courses several locally-recruited trainees were less qualified in their teaching subjects and this affected their achievement.
>
> (Ofsted 2003: 8)

Providers are expected to promote pre-course study for their recruits at interview and are then asked to assure the quality of the two-thirds of training time spent in partner schools. School mentors and university tutors provide supporting programmes, but still expect trainees to take responsibility for much of their subject knowledge development. In many ways, the expectations of trainees' knowledge and understanding has also increased because there are some cross-curricular themes to embrace as well as specialist business examination courses. Trainees need to know about the proposals for enterprise education (Davies 2002), and how best to contribute to a citizenship agenda for Key Stage 4 QCA (2002) which includes knowledge about 'how the economy functions'. The standards laid down by the TTA also include knowledge of NC courses, of pupil differences and needs, and of learning strategies and related educational research under the broad remit of 'Knowledge and Understanding'.

It is an impossible agenda if viewed as something to accomplish in one year. The reality is that for most trainees at interview for a new teaching post, subject knowledge expectations have not changed so dramatically. Questions refer to trainees' academic background and explore their understanding of specialist topics with reference to their modest teaching experience. They would not be expected to know how to teach everything from an exam course, but would need to identify the degree of support they expect in the process of planning, teaching and assessing topics new to them. Some training providers also work with schools and LEAs on supporting trainees through their first years of teaching, and there is a greater emphasis in evaluating the impact of the ITE year on the retention of new teachers. This provides a more measured view of the process of training and suggests that our expectations of new trainees and of providers should be viewed across a five-year period rather than squeezed into a precious 180 days.

New routes

The introduction of new training routes has also 'shaken and stirred' the ITE cocktail. A prospective new teacher can train on a traditional full-time course led by a university department of education but can also choose a part-time version – an alternative led by a cluster of schools, a fast-track route at a limited number of venues, and an employment-based training programme which leads to a teaching qualification without postgraduate university accreditation. This diversity has certainly encouraged providers to take the individual interests of trainees into account at a recruitment stage and, within each region, led to a degree of competition for trainees and for training placements in schools. The TTA expects providers to bid for an allocation of trainees and has encouraged new ventures such as the 'Training School' through specific financial incentives.

It is a positive development that there are now some trainees who have the opportunity to become teachers who before would have been unable to manage training alongside other commitments, or cope with a dramatic fall in income while they trained. There are more mature entrants to teaching partly as a result of targeted TTA recruitment campaigns and many are ideally suited to part-time study where they have to be confident and assertive and adept at managing their own time and resources. Trainees with their own businesses or current employment also have a real advantage when they work with pupils because of the status given to first-hand experience.

Providers have had to explore new patterns of provision, for example with flexible start and finish times, with distance-learning materials and with modular in place of linear course structures. However, it has also revealed some of the strengths of existing courses. There are economies of scale in the way many school and university providers operate with clusters of business trainees and with mixed subject groups. Schools find the logistics of managing trainees' time in school easier when there are accepted patterns for placements, for report-writing, for research tasks. The support of a critical mass of other trainees is important, not only for the sharing of experiences and for the boost to morale, but also for challenging other views of good teaching and learning. Finally, the momentum of a training year sees some trainees through to successful completion, and it has been hard for some part-time trainees to return to their studies and their practice after a period away from school and university.

Employment-based training has been especially valuable to business teachers transferring from further education to school contexts. The school benefits because it is assured of a recruit with suitable subject knowledge and teaching experience. The trainee can accredit prior experience and, in some cases, move quickly though a placement to the point where a final assessment is possible and employment proper begins in a familiar setting with familiar classes. On the other hand, it can be difficult to ensure a quality training experience when the school is under pressure to put a teacher in front of a class. The most recent modification portrays the trainee as supernumerary to the school staff and not as an immediate replacement for a teacher with a little 'on-the-job' training. The employment-based route has now to be supervised by a training body registered with TTA (and inspected by Ofsted) and the school completes a training plan as part of the process of bidding for the trainees' 'salary'. Enterprising training managers have appeared in some schools where the combination of a potential recruitment path and an above average source of finance has been seen as an attractive option. There is a risk that established placements of local HE/school partnerships are displaced for reasons that may benefit a school more than a trainee.

The proportion of business trainees on programmes led by school clusters is relatively small, but these schemes have proved popular with trainees who value the immediacy of a school environment. In some schemes, central training is organised in partnership with LEA staff, while in others, a lead school provides the core training for a group of schools who between them provide two placements for each trainee. The TTA reports a good retention rate of new teachers who have trained by this route. However, Ofsted have been critical of some of the quality assurance measures established in the early stages of these schemes. Trainees enjoy the strong contacts with business departments, but training managers have to work hard to ensure that trainees have a breadth of vision and understanding of educational issues.

Working in school

One of the biggest tensions in the training year, no matter what route is taken by trainees, is the degree to which they are expected to work in collaboration with others, or to show success in managing the teaching job single-handed. The vision of what 'learning to teach' is all about colours almost everything a mentor in school says or does with a trainee and is the basis of how HE institutions and others structure their courses.

Ralph Tabberer has described initial teacher education as an essential partnership between schools and HE institutions and has underlined the role of the TTA in promoting teaching as a collaborative venture (TTA 2004). The Qualifying to Teach (QTT) standards refer to a trainee's ability to contribute to the corporate life in school, to work with others (such as teacher assistants) to orchestrate pupils' learning, and to be able to work with others in giving and taking advice as a critical friend.

Some of the experiences provided by an HE/school partnership include paired placements in school where trainees plan, teach and review lessons together. They both have a shared interest in a lesson and how it is managed, provide detailed information for each other on the way in which tasks work, and review the kinds of discussion which take place between pupils. The pairing provides a supportive climate in which to share any fears about class management or weaknesses in subject knowledge, and when it works well, provides a trust which allows two trainees to challenge each other's perspectives.

In another example, time in university is spent in preparing a whole day's event in one partner school where a group takes responsibility for teaching a year group. The research and lesson design, the interaction between teachers and between pupils, and the recording and reviewing of evidence, provides a very rich experience for trainees to think through their ideas of good business education, of effective use of ICT and of high-quality assessment. In a recent case, some trainees set up a simulation where pupils were emailing their responses to a business development to the 'press office' managed by teachers. Some of the trainees were using digital cameras to record pupils' group work and to 'interview' them for a mock TV broadcast. The 'public inquiry' which completed the event had pupils, trainees and teachers intermixed in a way new to the school. All involved felt they had learned new strategies and were planning to try out different ideas in their various school settings. In this setting, trainees may become the leaders and mentors the learners in a new kind of collaboration.

A final example is taken from near the end of a PGCE course where trainees are asked to work together with the department in which they are placed to undertake curriculum innovation. Several trainees have worked on intranet sites for their mentors and have developed different interactive tasks for pupils to use. Another trainee researched local businesses and developed a module for vocational business with a company providing a study base for pupils. The activities usually have a sound theoretical base in accelerated learning with good differentiated materials and tasks. The mentors have helped to root the tasks firmly in their school contexts, and the trainees have an understanding of curriculum development tasks and collaborative work.

The benefits of these collaborative experiences are obvious to those who participate, and a current debate at higher education level is at what level such work should be accredited. Some of the more reflective pieces are worthy of a higher degree award. The experience of collaborative work and the skills acquired are those expected of teacher development networks and could easily help to ease the path from trainee to NQT, to action teacher researcher on a postgraduate course.

On the other hand, there are mentors who argue that weaker students are over-supported through these collaborative approaches and that the reality of the classroom is that trainees must be able to stand on their own two feet. The time-management pressures on a modern teacher are such that a trainee should have the fullest teaching load as soon as possible in a training year. The balance here is one of quantity against quality, and rests on a particular perception of teaching. Many trainees experience a school timetable which includes an A level lesson where teacher presentations are expected, a vocational lesson where a teacher facilitates portfolio work and an ICT-focused lesson where pupils have a mix of tasks. What should be the assumptions about an 'adequate time' in any of these teaching contexts? Given the ever-present need to prepare for external examinations, how much time should a trainee spend with sole responsibility for a group?

Summary

There appear to be a number of issues facing ITE providers. An ideal training course meets the individual needs of trainees, and these needs are becoming more diverse in their nature. Diversity should be encouraged and providers ought to be able to develop their own particular niches within business education training. At the same time, schools are becoming reluctant to take on too many trainees when their core business is educating pupils. They prefer streamlined systems and, if anything, would prefer partner higher education institutions to be operating more consistently and to be using common placement frameworks.

The TTA argues for good partnerships yet appears to be funding training schools and employment-based training routes at a higher rate than conventional higher education/school partnerships. Some education departments in universities are surviving by the narrowest of margins and believe that if they are not better financed, the tradition of training in a culture where research informs teaching could be lost. Should the message of a training year be one that says experience of school is everything or one that trains teachers from the outset to combine practice with measured reflection and a culture of curiosity?

Schools wish to employ new teachers who bring flexibility as well as specialist expertise to their first post. It seems a good idea to encourage business trainees to learn their craft in specialist 14–18 course contexts yet also to develop other strings to their bow wherever possible. Key Stage 3 experiences can include ICT, a second subject taster, cross-curricular work and citizenship activities. The Ofsted version of accountability coupled with the QTT standards has led to a provider being considered as 'non-compliant' if trainees are teaching in a non-business-related KS3 context. As a result, a large number of business providers have re-designated their courses as 14–18. It seems to be a difficult decision to balance the reality of school expectations with those of government agencies.

Finally, whatever the expectations of partner institutions and wherever the training takes place, the relationship between tutor/mentor and trainee seems to be changing as a result of ICT developments. The ability to share ever more complex documents using an increasing range of software and hardware at distance as well as within an institution has changed the use of contact and non-contact time. A visit by a tutor to a school partner can now be prefaced by a regular exchange of lesson plans, lesson reviews, targets and action plans, lesson evaluations and meeting summaries. Video-conferencing allows even that visit to take place from a distance and lesson observations and reviews are possible with some of the better systems. Trainees are becoming used to submitting drafts of almost anything and expecting almost instant feedback. The technology makes it possible, but the time management becomes difficult. How important is face-to-face contact? How much support should a trainee receive in framing a lesson, a report, an assignment? How much contact should trainees and mentors have across schools, as well as between school and tutor? How important is the need for measured responses and time to mediate on exchanges between partners? What of the risk of cultivating a 'just-in-time' mentality because the technology allows it to happen? How best to develop criteria to assess trainees' work when the final product can include hours of DVD-based evidence but a limited amount of writing? These are ever-changing, sometimes frustrating but certainly exciting times to be a trainer and a trainee.

References

Davies, H. (2002) *Review of Enterprise and the Economy in Education.* London: HMSO.

DfEE (1998) *Teaching: High Status, High Standards.* London: DfEE.

Ofsted/TTA (2002) *Framework for the Inspection of Initial Teacher Education.* London: TTA.

Ofsted (2003) *Quality and Standards in Secondary Initial Teacher Training.* London: Ofsted.

QCA (2002) *Citizenship Orders.* London: QCA.

Thomas, L. (1996) 'Promoting economic thoughtfulness', in S. Hodkinson and M. Jephcote (eds) *Teaching Economics and Business.* London: Heinemann.

TTA (2002) *Qualifying to Teach: Professional Standards for Qualified Teacher Status and Requirements for Initial Teacher Training.* London: TTA.

TTA (2004) *Collaboration as the Key to Training and Developing the Wider School Workforce: Report on TTA Stakeholder Day.* www.tta.gov.uk/stakeholderday

CHAPTER 16

The newly qualified teacher

Vivianne Lawson and John McAfee

Introduction

> 9.00am the bell rings, I grab all my resources and head into the classroom – 25 young people whom I've never seen before. Will I be prepared enough? Why the hell am I doing this? They're bound to see straight away that this is my first day.

Perhaps every newly qualified teacher (NQT) has experienced this feeling. Despite the hours of classroom experience gained on an initial teacher training course, that first class of a new term fills the most determined of us with nerves and trepidation. However, we have now survived our first year of teaching, and we aim to relay some truths about what can be expected in teaching economics and business studies.

The formal induction programme

For teachers in secondary schools the statutory induction programme aims to ensure that professional development and support for an NQT are secure. During this period new teachers have to demonstrate that they have continued to meet the standards of qualified teacher status (QTS) and meet all the induction standards. They will have an individualised programme of support and a designated induction tutor. The programme will involve classroom observation of the new teacher and a professional review of progress at least every half term.

The truth about economics and business studies

As classroom practitioners, we are committed and passionate about our subject. We know that it is relevant, useful, interesting and a vital component in the development of students' life skills. We acknowledge that teachers of other subjects feel exactly the same way about their areas of expertise. It is therefore inevitable that micro-political conflicts can arise within any school. These can manifest themselves in several ways:

- Competition for student numbers
- Squabbles over financial resources
- Possessiveness over teaching facilities such as ICT
- Limited cross-curricular interaction
- The formation of departmental 'cliques'

Inevitably, there are winners and losers, and it should be accepted that the core subjects, the bigger departments, will have greater negotiating power. As we teach our students, bigger is not necessarily better, but getting the true recognition for economics and business can seem like an uphill battle at times. As an economics and business studies NQT just arrived from a specialist PGCE there is obviously a great degree of loyalty to the subjects and an interest in taking an active and decisive role in defending and promoting them. The most effective strategy in raising the profile is to be the best classroom practitioner that you can be. Enthusing students and gaining their commitment and support will filter throughout the school and to parents. Building the reputation of the subjects will pay off in the ways in which they are regarded by other teachers and show itself in the ways in which students make their subject choices.

The truth about getting to know colleagues

The importance of the relationship that is developed with colleagues should never be underestimated. Even in the most difficult schools where there are issues of social deprivation, difficult classroom management and poor resources, it is the shared experiences and support offered to NQTs by more experienced teachers that can make the most difficult times bearable.

Formal relationships will include those with heads of department, subject mentors and the school's NQT co-ordinator, who is usually a member of the school's senior management team (SMT). Each of these will provide useful support at varying times throughout the year. Sometimes it can be difficult to request help, particularly if you feel that you really should be able to deal with a given situation yourself. A departmental colleague may well be responsible for your career progression and future promotions and you may not want to admit to him or her that you are struggling. If this is the case, it is a good idea to have considered one or two potential solutions yourself before speaking to them about a problem. In most cases colleagues will be sympathetic, happy to offer advice and assistance, and in all probability an NQT will be able to cope from then on. The point is that new teachers can tap into a wealth of accumulated experiences and, in the main, those with this experience are only too happy to share it.

The essence of mentor relationships is professional, and as an NQT it is important to remember that demands on colleagues' time are varied and frequently onerous. However, it may be necessary to manage this relationship and at times to be assertive in requesting their time/support while at the same time respecting their other commitments.

Institute of Education research carried out in 2002 showed that many induction tutors regarded being a tutor as one of the most rewarding parts of their job – but also felt guilty about not always fulfilling the role properly. Tutors are generally asked to undertake this role because they have the necessary skills and experience – the snag is that they do not always have the time it requires (one to two hours per week). The tutor can call on others to help – but still has the task of supporting, monitoring and assessing the NQT, enabling him/her to develop into an effective teacher.

Sara Bubb – *TES* Friday Magazine – 6 September 2002

Less formal relationships help NQTs assimilate into their new environment. Remember that a friendly smile to a new colleague in a corridor can brighten a dull day!

Opportunities to mix may include:

- Parties/nights out
- Staff sports teams
- Weekends away
- The pub after work!

Building a wide range of informal relationships allows an NQT to share experiences, and to appreciate that other more experienced teachers have similar problems and will also help in the development of coping strategies. It is, therefore, important not to neglect this social aspect of working in a school and to both contribute to and benefit from the camaraderie that exists. Other people will provide a sense of perspective and just having someone to laugh with at lunchtime can be a major source of stress relief!

'Gooooal' – and now we were 3-nil down. As I stood in the drizzle, wearing the ill-fitting school strip, I started to wonder how I had been convinced to play for the teacher football team. Later, in the pub, as we lamented our lack of ability I quickly realised that these new friends would not only help improve my jaded football skills, but their varied teaching experiences were going to be invaluable in honing my teaching skills. Any doubts about whether to turn out for the next game vanished with that realisation.

The truth about students

With a well behaved class, teaching is one of the most wonderful jobs in the world.

(Cowley 2001)

We fully endorse this view. However, even the most consistently trouble-free class is made up of individuals whose motivation to learn will vary according to events in their lives and the teacher's ability to connect with the group. Getting to know your students is a vital component in achieving good classroom management, and learning their names is essential.

Information about students is available from a variety of sources within school. Class lists may be enhanced with information such as SATs scores, YELLIS or ALIS results. These can be very useful in identifying students for whom differentiated work may be necessary. The special educational needs co-ordinator (SENCO) will provide individual plans for students who have been identified as having special needs. If you are taking over a group from another teacher ask for a copy of his/her mark book for the class. Having such information at your fingertips from the very beginning not only makes you a more effective teacher but also boosts confidence and levels of professionalism.

Part of general school induction will involve the issuing of a Staff Handbook. It is vital that some time is spent reading sections on the discipline policy. There is nothing worse than having a student who has not responded to your best efforts to gain good behaviour, and not knowing what to do with him/her. Your responsibility is to educate the majority, and if the behaviour of the minority adversely affects your ability to do so, then the problem must be removed so make sure you know how to do this!

It is important to appreciate that students are also getting to know their teacher. Consistent behaviour – firm but fair – will pay dividends in the long run. As an NQT you must remember that respect from classes needs to be earned; so never assume that just because you are a teacher, students in your classes will automatically bestow it.

> I used to think that everyone automatically respected teachers – I did, I thought that was the norm. However, when I became a teacher I quickly realised that many pupils do not share this sentiment. I realised how hard my own teachers had worked to gain my respect and trust. I also remember that my best teachers were the ones I respected most. So I vowed to work hard to ensure my students respected and trusted me. I want, when they eventually look back on their school days, to be regarded as one of their best teachers.

Most NQTs undertake the duties of a form tutor. Here the relationship with students is different. The roles NQTs will be expected to play include confidante, conveyer of messages, careers advisor, 'policeman' – in short acting *in loco parentis*. Despite all the

PGCE training and classroom experience, this is a role that will evolve in its own way. Even the most experienced of teachers will come across unique difficulties with their tutees, for which they are not prepared. Marland and Rogers (1997: 9) point out that 'the central reason why tutoring is so difficult is that the tutor's main contribution is culled from those less-defined aspects of a teacher's professional concerns'. An NQT should not feel intimidated or worried about not having all the answers. Senior tutors and heads of year should be relied upon for guidance and support.

The truth about marking

> Many new teachers fail to appreciate the additional workload that marking presents. For those who lack practice this task can take significantly longer than their more experienced colleagues... Correct time management is imperative to maintain a healthy work/life balance...

Marking is informative and is after all the best measure of a student's progress and performance. There is no escape from marking. However, the task can be extremely boring, onerous and one which it is tempting to push to the bottom of a 'to do' list. Coping mechanisms need to be developed for managing this aspect of the job. Key essential techniques are:

- Having a clear mark scheme for all pieces of work set
- Marking the whole class's Question 1s before moving on to 2, etc.
- Moving to quiet offices/classrooms to mark to avoid distraction
- Using free periods during the working day rather than taking work home.

While these appear to be common sense, many NQTs do not always implement them and find themselves overwhelmed with marking in addition to lesson preparation. If this is the case, the quality of the feedback given to students through marked work will be incomplete and a golden opportunity to improve future performance will have been missed.

The truth about vocational courses

Education in the 14–19 sector has moved firmly towards vocational courses and enterprise education. Economics and business studies are at the forefront of this initiative. This is an exciting time to join the profession!

The DfES describes vocational courses as:

Courses of study that introduce students to a broad sector of industry or business. They encourage understanding and knowledge of the sector and develop some capability in the skills used within it...GCSEs in vocational subjects are designed to provide a more hands-on approach to learning. They will emphasise practical skills and the application of knowledge and understanding. (www.dfes.gov.uk)

The delivery of vocational courses presents teachers with unique opportunities and challenges. The requirement to incorporate strong practical vocational elements makes demands of the NQT to be a conduit between businesses and schools. Without a significant network of connections this can be incredibly difficult. Advice on how to overcome this is usually available from careers advisers, HODs and education business link organisations run by local councils. From the perspective of a new teacher, significant amounts of time can be spent arranging visits, negotiating with third parties and developing connections. The danger is that the activity/speaker/visit does not actually complement the students' learning. Teachers must be clear about the desired outcomes and must communicate this effectively to the outside organisation. For example, consider the following two scenarios:

A guest speaker was invited in to address AVCE students on quality management. The speaker was asked to cover various issues, which were on the specification. He delivered a very slick Powerpoint presentation, showed videos, and covered all of the relevant points. However, it was clear that students were not engaged, and that the experience was not supporting their learning.

The problem was that the expert was used to delivering to professional audiences – the language and terminology used were too sophisticated and technical for students to access. The NQT teacher had not briefed him fully as to what prior knowledge students had, and how they would be using the information given. The overall effect was a mismatch, and an unsatisfactory session.

A trip – with a talk - organised by the same teacher some time later involved sending the speaker a full copy of the assignment students were working on, a list of questions which they needed answers to and a copy of the course specification. There were also several telephone conversations in the time leading up to the trip. The result was much more satisfactory. Students gained valuable information and understanding, they were engaged because they could see the relevance of what was being said, and they used the material extensively in their work.

Most vocational courses have a strong coursework element. Some students will happily complete entire projects with minimal input from the teacher whereas others will require significant support, encouragement and cajoling throughout. Preparation of timescales associated with deadlines for submission of work, marking and moderation is absolutely essential to the successful delivery of these courses. Failure to do so will result in stress for both students and teachers (as experienced first hand by both of us!).

The truth about meeting parents

Parents' evenings and meetings can be daunting for all involved. Teachers have a multitude of questions and doubts that precede these encounters:

- How honest should I be?
- How can I get my message clearly understood?
- What happens if parents get annoyed?
- How supportive will parents be?

Many students wrongly assume that such events are excuses for parents and teachers to collude and undermine their progress. A well-run and purposeful meeting is about exchanging information in order to develop and improve pupils' performance. Our subject area tells us that preparation and clear objectives are the secret to good meetings, so as business studies teachers it is imperative that we practise what we teach!

Good teachers start by writing a brief synopsis on students including key points on behaviour, academic achievement and future targets. If possible use grade books and examples of work to reinforce praise or disappointment. Aim to make sure these notes reflect any preceding correspondences, as mixed messages can be confusing.

We would also suggest following a few golden rules:

- Start on a positive note. There is always at least one redeeming feature about any student.
- Lead into criticisms with why they adversely affect learning, and where possible give tangible examples, e.g. 'Talking distracts Johnny from completing notes vital to his exam success.'
- Have a clear plan on how any unacceptable behaviour should be dealt with and ask parents how they feel they can contribute to its success.
- Avoid preconceptions about parents, particularly those of disruptive pupils. Parents who take the time to attend meetings are usually interested in their children's progress and are willing to help. Likewise most parents respect honest and constructive criticisms. An open discussion should lead to greater insight into what influences pupils' behaviour; and while defining these may not excuse bad behaviour or underachievement, it can be helpful in formulating the correct strategy for improvement.
- Finally, be on time and don't waffle. Parents have time constraints and could become anxious if kept waiting. A queue caused by your vagueness will make you very unpopular...especially in the staff-room.

Despite trepidation, our experience of meeting parents has been extremely positive. They are vital components in the continued success of able students and to improving performance in underachievers. They should not be undervalued and therefore merit the preparation that is so vital to their success.

Summary

Looking back on the journey from PGCE to NQT, what have we learnt?

What is most evident is that a well-managed and properly structured PGCE is an excellent introduction to teaching. The combination of school placements and campus-based learning provides a solid foundation on which to build a rewarding career.

Many discuss the theory–practice gap, and in any school there will be die-hard cynics that take pleasure in undermining 'the ivory-tower academics that teach theory which is not relevant to teaching at the chalkface'. In our opinion this narrow-minded belief is unfounded, and what is taught on a good PGCE is as valuable as the experience gained in a classroom.

Obviously, in one year it is impossible to cover every nuance of a profession which continually evolves. Educating children presents unparalleled opportunities for change so there is no definitive formula. Actually this evolution makes teaching so rewarding and exciting. While acknowledging that we are still learning, we strongly defend the importance of the PGCE as a stepping-stone to the classroom. Any teacher, however experienced, who closes their minds to new ideas, who fails to develop their teaching methods and simply dismisses suggestions on lesson planning, has, in our opinion, stopped being a good teacher. Good teachers are lifelong learners!

Teaching is like no other profession: the scale of emotional and physical demands is unique, and it is beset with a succession of highs and lows. Every NQT's experience will be unique to their school, the pupils they teach and the level of support offered by colleagues. There is no panacea that will encompass every situation encountered in the first few years of teaching. There are, however, some recommendations that will assist the new teacher to manage the demands that will be placed on them.

Make your requirements clear at an early stage

As this is your chosen career you must take responsibility for ensuring that it gets off to the best start. During a PGCE a lot of support is forthcoming; however, despite best intentions many schools fail to offer NQTs exactly what they need. If this is the case then make your feelings known and clearly define your concerns.

Make the learning experience relevant

Economics and business studies offer unprecedented opportunities to use current affairs to reinforce learning. Tapping into pupils' enthusiasm is easier using examples which are relevant to their lives. As an NQT do not be afraid to experiment, to challenge staid and uncreative teaching practices, and aim to build up a set of resources that stimulate learning.

Be organised

Develop systems for organising paperwork and allocating time effectively when planning is crucial. Ideas that have proved useful in this first year include:

- Colour-coded files
- Clearly labelled sectionalised folders
- Dedicated drawers in filing cabinets
- Organised computer files/folders.

At first glance these suggestions appear simplistic and condescending. However, the first time you experience panic over the loss of an important resource or correspondence will only serve to underline their importance. Not being organised will undoubtedly affect the quality of your teaching, so be warned!

Do not be afraid to seek advice from colleagues

Established teachers have breadth of experience but still encounter situations where there are no precedents. Do not feel that seeking advice is a sign of failure. Taking time to provide the best answers gains respect from colleagues and pupils. A good teacher is one that cares and is respected. Any new teachers that undervalue the advice available from their colleagues are in danger of alienating themselves when they are most likely to need the greatest help.

Do not shy away from difficult tasks

Confronting difficult tasks with pupils and parents is delicate and challenges even the most confident teacher. The correct procedures to follow will depend upon your school, your relationship with students, their parents and the particular circumstances involved. Persistent underachievement, poor attendance or disruptive behaviour cannot be tolerated. It is vital as an NQT to impress your authority. Remember – it is your classroom and your responsibility to manage it.

References

Bubb, S. (2002) *TES* Friday Magazine, 6 September.
Cowley, S. (2001) *Getting the Buggers to Behave*. London: Continuum.
DfES www.dfes.gov.uk
Marland, M. and Rogers, R. (1997) *The Art of the Tutor*. London: David Fulton Publishers.

CHAPTER 17

Being a school mentor

Brian Sanderson and Ian Abbott

Introduction

Most Postgraduate Certificate in Education (PGCE) secondary courses in business and economics are a partnership between higher education institutions and local schools. The higher education institutions are responsible for recruitment, assessment and course organisation. The PGCE is usually split into two parts with trainee teachers spending approximately one-third of their time at the higher education institution and the rest in partnership schools. Partnership schools receive a payment from the higher education institution for accepting trainee teachers. In some cases this is paid directly to the department, but in other schools it is retained centrally.

The training of secondary school teachers in England is heavily regulated by the Teacher Training Agency (TTA) and subject to a rigorous inspection regime by Ofsted. The TTA allocates student numbers to participating institutions and undertakes the management of the system. Common standards have also been introduced by the TTA and all trainee teachers have to successfully pass the standards to achieve qualified teacher status (QTS). The standards fall into three main categories: Professional values and practice, Knowledge and understanding, and Teaching (TTA 2003). The structure of PGCE courses, in recent years, has also been radically changed, with a far greater emphasis and time allocation given to school-based work as opposed to work in the higher education institution.

Role of the mentor

Within the school there will usually be two key members of staff who work with trainee teachers. First, the professional mentor who co-ordinates the trainee teacher's work in the school and arranges a programme of experience which allows opportunities to explore whole-school issues, such as classroom management, school management and working with parents.

The second member of the school teaching staff is the subject mentor, who has a more focused and specific responsibility. They will play a leading role in working with a trainee on a day-to-day and, in some cases, lesson-to-lesson basis. In many respects the subject mentor is the most important person in a trainee's professional training. He or she is the main contact in school/college and, most importantly, the main provider of training. It is easy to regard a mentor's role as a primarily administrative one (sorting out timetables, providing information about pupils, etc.) or as a prop for the trainee during some difficult and challenging times. Of course, a mentor's role is both these things at times, but it is important not to lose sight of the mentor's training responsibilities.

A well-organised mentor and supportive mentor makes life much easier for the trainee teacher. However, a mentor who takes an active involvement in the development of a trainee's competence has a much more profound, long-term impact, not just on the trainee, but on the thousands of pupils whom she or he will subsequently teach. The role is pivotal to a successful PGCE year for the individual trainee teacher.

The precise role of the subject mentor will vary in different schools, but a summary of the main tasks includes:

1   Attending subject mentor training and mentor meetings – it is vital that there is a constant two-way communication between the higher education institution and the school so that any problems can be quickly resolved.

2   Liaison with higher education subject tutor. This link ensures that the training taking place initially at the university is complemented and supported by the school. Sometimes it is claimed that theory is covered in the higher education part of the training and put into practice at school, but in reality it will be a mixture of the two. Mentors will deliver some theory, and practical issues will be a feature of higher education-based sessions.

3   Arranging trainees' induction into the department and access to appropriate departmental resources.

4   Assessment of trainees' needs through the use of a course entry profile or of a first professional placement profile, in consultation with the trainee and the subject tutor.

5   Arranging the trainee's teaching timetable. The subject mentor will try to provide a balanced timetable giving the trainee a variety of age groups, abilities and courses; for example, a mixture of vocational and academic (naturally this will very much depend upon the size of the business and economics department).

6   Organising other training opportunities, for example involvement in young enterprise or school visits.

7   Briefing other members of the department who will share responsibility for training. The subject mentor will have received training, but this needs to be cascaded to other teachers so that the trainee is treated consistently and fairly, also to ensure that QTS standards are correctly assessed.

8   Conducting a weekly mentor meeting with the trainee. This is an opportunity for both the tutor and trainees to discuss progress so far and to tackle any problems that may have arisen. If a positive relationship has been established it can prove to be a very useful tool for development.

9   Arranging a programme of observation of trainees' teaching; this should include a programme of regular full-lesson observations with written and oral feedback. In the first placement it may well be that the subject mentor 'team teaches' with the trainee or remains in the classroom for support. After some informal feedback and advice the trainee will need to be regularly formally observed, perhaps once per week. This will help to formulate the final report in terms of progress against QTS standards.

10   Monitoring trainees' planning, documentation and record-keeping. This will probably happen as a regular part of the weekly mentor meeting.

11   Providing feedback to trainees on all aspects of professional performance. Obviously subject teaching is a very important part of this, but there are many other aspects that a trainee will need to be involved in, such as lunch/break duties, parents' evenings, extra-curricular activities, etc. The subject mentor should ensure that the trainee becomes fully involved in all areas of school life.

12   Setting and monitoring targets. It is quite likely that the trainee will have been set some specific targets to help them develop; for example, to improve subject knowledge to be able to teach A2 Finance. The mentor will be able to provide guidance and support (but not teach them!).

13   Maintaining a training record.

14   Organising assessment of the trainee's work against the standards for Qualified Teacher Status. Reports back to the higher education institution will be based on progress against the QTS standards.

There are also less tangible functions to add to this list:

- To be *positive* and *encouraging*. As previously mentioned the subject mentor will have a pivotal role in the overall development of the trainee teacher. The subject mentor needs to be sensitive in providing support and feedback. If the mentor can be constructive when giving criticism and also accentuate the positive, and build on any successes from the lesson, then the trainee will hopefully gain confidence. However, it is important for the trainee to recognise, if necessary, the need for improvement in certain aspects of their teaching style.

- To encourage the trainee to independently evaluate their own practice. The ability to constantly review/evaluate their own performance is one of the most important features of successful classroom teachers – to try to constantly develop as a teacher. By starting a debriefing with the question 'What do you feel were the strengths and weaknesses of the lesson?' gives the opportunity for self-evaluation and reflection. It is important to keep this in balance though; even the best teachers will have lessons that go badly, and there may be extenuating circumstances, like the ICT network crashing. Therefore, it is important to keep it all in perspective.

And perhaps even more importantly:

- To ensure that the trainee becomes an effective teacher of business education.

How does this actually happen in school?

During the trainee's first few days in a school/college, it is likely that there will be some time provided for induction into the business and economics department. This will be in many respects the most important time for the trainee and a chance to find their way around the department. The following list is a suggestion of what might be useful to cover with the trainee during this induction session:

- introducing the trainee to other members of the department, including ancillary staff, and explaining responsibilities within the department;
- giving information about departmental resources including books, worksheets, videos, software, practical resources, test papers, photocopying facilities;
- allocating some work and storage space for the trainee;
- explaining departmental homework policy and assessment practice including internal testing procedures;
- giving information about external exams and syllabuses;
- explaining departmental schemes of work including expected levels of attainment;
- explaining pupil grouping practice;
- giving information on department meetings and in-service training events;
- discussing behaviour policy, rewards and sanctions, and sources of support on discipline;
- explaining departmental provision for Special Educational Needs;
- introducing ICT facilities and the opportunities for independent learning/supported self-study;
- providing information on education–business links.

Planning serial placement

Serial placement is the time spent in the training school prior to the commencement of the full-block placement. Typically this will consist of one or two days for a limited number of weeks. Serial placement is an important time for the trainee to familiarise him- or herself with the business and economics department, some of the classes they will be teaching, available resources, and so on. It is a very busy time and it can be difficult to fit everything in. The school/college professional mentor may organise generic sessions with the trainees, and this could take up as much as one of the two days per week the trainees have in school/college. In terms of departmental input, it is important that the trainee has the opportunity to:

- Observe you and others teach, preferably with a focus agreed in advance.
- Do some *initial* teaching themselves. This might be team-teaching or teaching just part of a lesson. It is extremely valuable, in all placements, if the trainee has taught at least one full lesson by the beginning of block placement. This will hopefully boost their confidence and improve their ability to plan and prepare lessons.
- Plan and prepare for the block placement.
- Carry out the tasks and gather the information set out in the course handbook by the higher education institution. These should be kept to a bare minimum, and ultimately it is the responsibility of the trainee to complete these tasks.
- Develop an understanding of current issues in business education.
- Meet with the subject mentor for a regular mentor meeting.

Providing feedback

Trainees require positive and constructive feedback on how they are performing in all aspects of the placement. For example, are they meeting QTS standards in terms of professional values and practice? However, the main focus of feedback will be based around the lesson observations undertaken by the subject mentor. These will provide the basis for the trainees' continuing development.

The purpose of observation

There are two main purposes of the series of lesson observations undertaken by the subject mentor:

- so that feedback can be provided to the trainee to enable further progress to be made;
- so that the trainee's progress can be monitored, evaluated and recorded.

It is very important that formal observations are agreed in advance with the trainee and that feedback is formally recorded in writing. Copies of the proforma usually need to go to the trainee, the mentor and the higher education institution (in practice, often to the professional mentor who collates them and sends them to the higher education institution at the end of the placement).

Oral feedback

It is vital that trainees receive oral as well as written feedback. This should be done as soon as possible after the lesson, but certainly within 24 hours. If the feedback is not going to happen immediately after the lesson, it is good practice to say a few words to the trainee to reassure them. Otherwise they might worry about the outcome of the lesson for the rest of the day.

The formal feedback needs to take place somewhere quiet and private. It may seem sensible to give the feedback in the staffroom over a cup of coffee, but the trainee may not wish others – and especially other trainee teachers – to hear what is being discussed.

The essential ingredients of an effective feedback session are:

- trainees are given the chance to say what they thought of the lesson and how it had gone;
- an initial focus on strengths – there are always some in any lesson;
- plenty of comments which are linked to the agreed focus;
- other issues are touched on but are not allowed to dominate the feedback (e.g. not always being dominated by classroom management or the behaviour of individual members of the class!);
- feedback ends with a clear list of agreed targets for future development.

A suggested model for the lesson debrief is given in Figure 17.1.

Written feedback

The essential ingredients of good written feedback are:

- It concentrates on an agreed focus, with some mention of other key issues.
- It begins with a summary of the strengths of the lesson.
- It details areas where further improvement is needed, with suggestions for future practice.
- It concludes with agreed targets that are realistic.

Good written feedback should be an analysis of what was observed, rather than a running commentary on the lesson itself, although you might want to illustrate key points with examples from the lesson which has been observed. It is important to remember that this is a significant part of the training process, and the trainee should be able to utilise the written feedback as part of the overall process of self-evaluation and improvement.

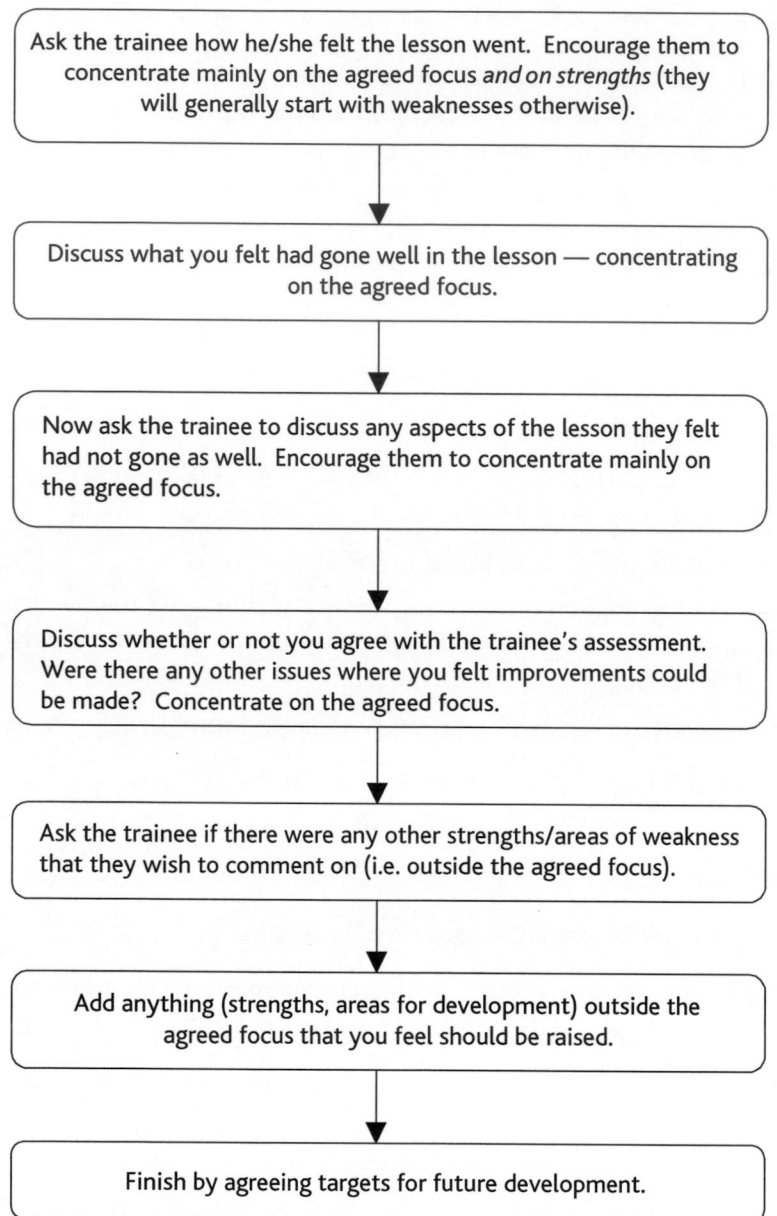

Ask the trainee how he/she felt the lesson went. Encourage them to concentrate mainly on the agreed focus *and on strengths* (they will generally start with weaknesses otherwise).

Discuss what you felt had gone well in the lesson — concentrating on the agreed focus.

Now ask the trainee to discuss any aspects of the lesson they felt had not gone as well. Encourage them to concentrate mainly on the agreed focus.

Discuss whether or not you agree with the trainee's assessment. Were there any other issues where you felt improvements could be made? Concentrate on the agreed focus.

Ask the trainee if there were any other strengths/areas of weakness that they wish to comment on (i.e. outside the agreed focus).

Add anything (strengths, areas for development) outside the agreed focus that you feel should be raised.

Finish by agreeing targets for future development.

Figure 17.1 Model for a lesson debrief

Summary

The subject mentor is usually an experienced member of staff who is willing to spend time training, advising and guiding the next generation of teachers. In many schools the role is undertaken by the head of the business and economics department. However, this is not always the case, and it can be a good staff development tool to encourage other members of the department to take on this role. Often there is much to be gained from involving members of the business and economics department who have recently qualified as teachers in the training process. They can bring a fresh perspective and an awareness of the concerns of trainee teachers.

The majority of a trainee teacher's time is spent in school, and the subject mentor will play a key role in the development of the trainee, particularly on their final placement. The mentor will, hopefully, see the trainee develop teaching skills that will lead to a positive learning environment being established in their lessons. The subject mentor will encourage the trainee to evaluate their classroom practice and suggest alternative strategies and solutions.

It is important for the subject mentor to provide constructive and positive feedback to the trainee. An integral part of this process is the sequence of lesson observations undertaken by the subject mentor. When carrying out lesson observations it is often easy to focus on classroom management, but it is important to remember that all of the standards for QTS have to be assessed. The subject mentor is the key figure in assessing the standards and deciding whether they are being consistently met. The subject mentor will observe more lessons than anyone else in the training programme and should be best placed to make the final decision about whether a trainee should be recommended for qualified teacher status.

Being a subject mentor can be a difficult and time-consuming job, but also extremely worthwhile and rewarding. Trainee teachers bring new ideas, recent subject knowledge and enthusiasm into a school. Increasingly they have recent and relevant business experience. The subject mentor can make a major contribution to the future of the subject area by becoming involved in the training of the next generation of business and economics teachers. It is an opportunity to influence future practice and contribute to the continuing growth and success of business and economics.

References

Teacher Training Agency/DfES (2003) *Qualifying to Teach: Professional Standards for Qualified Teacher Status and Requirements for Initial Teacher Training.* London: Teacher Training Agency.

CHAPTER 18

The role of the advanced skills teacher (AST)

Brian Sanderson

Introduction

The Advanced Skills Teacher scheme was introduced in September 1998 and was designed to reward excellent classroom practitioners and to encourage them to remain in the classroom rather than taking up management roles within the school. The official definition given on www.teachernet.gov.uk states: 'An Advanced Skills Teacher is an excellent teacher who achieves the very highest standards of classroom practice and who is paid to share his or her skills and experience with other teachers.' It offers an alternative career progression route for classroom teachers, and successful applicants are moved onto a separate pay scale with a much higher upper limit than the Main Professional Scale.

At a National AST Co-ordinators' conference in July 2004 David Milliband, Minister for School Standards, said,

> I think that the vision of the teaching force properly trained and supported has got the AST ideal at its heart, because the AST ideal is a simple one: the idea is that our best teachers should be properly rewarded for doing what they do best: teaching. They shouldn't have to leave the classroom in order to develop themselves professionally.

One significant feature of the ASTs' role is that they spend 20 per cent of their time, the equivalent of one day a week, supporting other teachers and developing their skills and experience through the sharing of best practice, ideas and approaches. The work of an AST can be within his or her own institution, and this is known as 'inreach'; but a significant proportion of the role will be with teachers from other institutions, 'outreach'. An example of this could be where a local education authority asked an AST to provide support and guidance to a business education department which had recently received an unsatisfactory Ofsted report.

Although ASTs will have gained their qualification through teaching their subject area, they may also find themselves heavily involved in whole-school initiatives for developing teaching and learning styles as well as developing their own specialist areas. ASTs complement the work of others in raising the standards of teaching and learning across the school.

For example, a 14–19 comprehensive school has appointed seven ASTs from different subject areas, including business studies. The school uses this group of ASTs to implement a number of whole school initiatives. This can take a number of forms including areas as diverse as work on the KS3 strategy and the provision of new vocational courses. In this school the AST group also took on some of the roles that in other schools might be carried out by heads of departments or by the senior management team.

The current situation

By November 2004 the AST initiative had developed in the following way:

- The Government's long-term aim was that there should be 10,000 ASTs, or 3–5 per cent of teachers nationally. The number appointed in November 2004 stood at approximately 4,000.
- There were ASTs in 148 of the 150 LEAs.
- 69 per cent were women and 31 per cent men.
- 63 per cent were in secondary schools, 32 per cent in primary schools and 5 per cent in other schools.
- In practice there were very few business education ASTs. (All ASTs should be registered on the DfES website. By November 2004 there were only nine registered for business and vocational courses, but unofficial estimates indicate that there were around 30.)

As with any new education initiative the future of the AST programme has also become less clear as the funding arrangements for AST posts have recently changed. At the present time funding is only guaranteed until 2006. Currently no decision has been made about funding for 2006 onwards. Given the uncertainty about funding, schools may be reluctant to use their scarce resources to support this initiative.

So what do ASTs do?

ASTs are considered to be subject specialists and use their skills to develop teaching and learning styles/materials within their own schools, but also with teachers in other schools. The following is taken from www.standards.dfes.gov.uk/ast/ and identifies the activities an AST can expect to perform:

- Producing high-quality teaching materials.

- Disseminating materials relating to best practice and educational research.
- Providing 'model' lessons, with staff observing, to a whole class, or a target group of pupils, e.g. gifted and talented (G&T), SEN, EAL.
- Supporting a subject leader with regard to schemes of work, policies or management skills.
- Observing lessons and advising other teachers on classroom organisation, lesson planning and teaching methods.
- Providing support and helping teachers who are experiencing difficulties.
- Participating in the induction and mentoring of newly qualified teachers.
- Leading professional learning groups.
- Supporting professional development.

The role of an AST is different from that of an adviser or inspector. They have been recognised as excellent classroom teachers and they are expected to share these skills with colleagues, whereas an inspector has a more formal agenda, i.e. assessing to Ofsted criteria.

The normal procedure for an AST to become involved with working with another school is through the local education authority; for example, a school has a concern about examination results in business studies and wishes to have the input of an AST from another school. The head teacher or relevant member of senior management will contact the LEA and submit a request for assistance. The LEA has an overview of all the work being undertaken by ASTs (ASTs are required to send an action plan at the start of each academic year with potential projects to be undertaken) and, provided that the AST has outreach time available, will make the initial approach. Once there is agreement the AST makes initial contact with the school and would first meet senior management to establish what kind of support is required.

The role played by the AST is similar to that of the critical friend. When an AST is asked to provide support and guidance, for example, after an unsatisfactory Ofsted report, this will require a sensitive approach and the need to establish a positive working relationship with colleagues.

Who can become an AST?

Once the head teacher and/or an LEA have identified and agreed upon a job description, for example, 'to promote and support the development of vocational qualifications pre- and post-16', then prospective ASTs will need to complete an application form and undergo external assessment to prove they have the required competencies. The candidate will also need to produce a portfolio of evidence to support their application, including testimonials from senior colleagues. The candidate will need to demonstrate that they have the six key qualities and can provide portfolio evidence to highlight each of them.

The six standards are:

1 *Excellent results/outcomes.* For this area the candidate will need to provide statistical data to show that their students had performed 'excellently' in external assessment, for example by comparing individual students' results to YELLIS forecasts – Student 1 YELLIS forecast grade C/D actual result grade A.

2 *Excellent subject and/or specialist knowledge.* Evidence for this will be demonstrated when the potential AST is observed teaching and also by providing evidence of continuing professional development through INSET, courses, etc.

3 *Excellent ability to plan.* Most of this will be in the form of lesson plans and schemes of work.

4 *Excellent ability to teach, manage pupils and maintain discipline.* The portfolio evidence might consist of witness statements and letters of support from senior management, other teachers and, more particularly, parents and students.

5 *Excellent ability to assess and evaluate.* What strategies is the candidate using to assess/monitor the performance of students? How is baseline data being used to track and improve results?

6 *Excellent ability to advise and support other teachers.* The successful candidate is going to need to have the support of colleagues from their own department and school plus any external relationships with other schools, universities, etc.

The head teacher will also complete the above section with their own assessment of the prospective AST.

The final decision about the application will be taken by an external assessor who will usually spend one day at the candidate's school, and typically will:

● Interview the head teacher
● Interview the candidate and review the portfolio of evidence
● Meet with students that the candidate teaches
● Meet parents
● Meet with the candidate's teaching colleagues
● Observe the candidate teaching.

If the assessor is satisfied that all the criteria are successfully met then AST status will be granted.

Ofsted response

An Ofsted report entitled *Advanced Skills Teachers: Appointment, Deployment and Impact* was published in 2001, and among the main findings concluded that:

- ASTs were 'skilled and conscientious teachers who were able to provide effective support for other teachers'.
- The principal duty by far was that of advising other teachers on classroom management and teaching.
- Schools in special measures reported great difficulties in making AST appointments; where an AST had been employed the effect had been 'very considerable'.

A more recent Ofsted survey in 2003 added:

ASTs have significantly improved the quality of teaching and learning in over three-quarters of the schools inspected in the survey.

They were particularly good at encouraging others to do well, and often produced very high quality teaching and learning materials in support of their staff development role...

(Ofsted 2003)

ASTs in action

The AST will have a job description to guide their work, but they will also need to produce an action plan, agreed with the head teacher and LEA, which identifies in more detail what they hope to achieve. In the first year, it is highly likely that much of their time will be on inreach tasks, but by the second year the focus is expected to switch to outreach work. The action plan will also provide a means of monitoring performance. It is quite likely that the action plan will need constant revision, as the role of the AST is likely to be subject to frequent change. If a school within the LEA has been put into special measures, they may decide to use ASTs to help improve standards, and action will have to be revised.

The AST will produce an evaluation of the year's work for his or her line manager and the LEA. It is also vital that whenever an AST is involved with outreach they obtain an evaluation from the agency they are working with. From this evidence the LEA, head teacher and AST can monitor performance and evaluate the effectiveness of their work.

In addition an AST must also keep a work log to show how they have used the time allocated in a proper way, i.e. the one day per week.

Example of AST work in business studies

The following profile illustrates the nature and extent of the work of a business studies AST. The teacher is a practising AST in the West Midlands:

I have been a teacher for ten years. Initially I started as a teacher of business studies before moving on to become head of department at another school. I joined my current school, a large comprehensive, as second in department, in charge of vocational business and the implementation of Curriculum 2000. After three years I was head of department and now combine this role with that of advanced skills teacher. Within the school my focus is 14–19 education, with the emphasis on increasing the number and relevance of vocational programmes. Across the county I am there to help and support business education, primarily at Key Stage 4.

I started the role in April 2004 and have spent the initial months gaining greater knowledge and experience of the different business studies courses on offer. One focus area has been the introduction of Applied GCSE Business, in order to help support other teachers around the county. I have also spoken at the county head teachers' conference about my work in raising Key Stage 4 attainment at my own school.

Currently, I am working closely with two teachers in the county. Both have two years experience and have found themselves as head of department and the only person in the department. There are different aspects to my role. First, I am available for them to share and discuss their ideas with. I can also offer support about the head of department role. I have provided practical advice on how to analyse department results, and advised on and prepared schemes of work and resources for use in their school. I also assist within the classroom, either taking small groups or workshop situations, and I have also assisted in other areas when required, for example, revision sessions or coursework completion sessions.

At both school and county level I am putting together a set of locally based resources to support Applied GCSE Business. Ideally this will involve classroom- and business-based activities. It may also allow collaboration between schools for industry days. The resources will be available for any teacher in the county who wishes to access them.

A longer-term plan is to start a website for local teachers where business teachers can discuss best practice, or share ideas. I would also like to include links to either company or business studies websites to make it quicker and easier for people to access resources.

Summary

The introduction of the Advanced Skills Teacher scheme in 1998 has led to the opportunity for an alternative career path for teachers who want to remain within the classroom. However, the role of ASTs within the education system is still at a developmental stage, and there are some concerns about the future funding of such posts. After 2006 the picture is currently unclear and there may be reluctance on the part of LEAs and schools to continue with the scheme. Feedback from Ofsted on the work being done by ASTs has been positive and recognises the value of their work, particularly in supporting teaching and learning.

The impact of ASTs within business and economics is, on a national basis, very limited, due to the fact that only relatively few appointments have been made since 1998. Business ASTs have been involved in similar work to other subject areas and the main focus has been on the development of new resources, providing support to schools in special measures and the implementation of new vocational courses.

Hopefully more ASTs will be appointed in business and economics in the near future. Given the changes being proposed in the 14–19 curriculum there would appear to be a definite requirement for further support and training. As the role of the LEA continues to be marginalised there is a clear need for the developmental work that can be carried out by ASTs.

References

Ofsted (2001) *Advanced Skills Teachers: Appointment, Deployment and Impact.* London: Ofsted.

Ofsted (2003) *Advanced Skills Teachers: A Survey.* London: Ofsted.

CHAPTER 19

Preparing for inspection

Stuart Langworthy

Introduction

The thought of undergoing inspection conjures up images of preparing file after file of paperwork, tidying up wall displays, doing lesson plans in far more detail than usual and 'dusting down' the model lesson. In these terms it is seen as an event rather than as a part of the ongoing improvement of practice. In fact, my recent experiences of Ofsted have been far more supportive than in the past.

Indeed, I feel like a veteran of inspections given that my school was the first in the county to be placed in special measures, although my department did very well. I was visited for 18 out of 30 lessons in the week and received a thorough 'grilling'. Once placed in special measures we received regular, termly visits from HMI until 18 months later we finally got rid of the 'tag'. During that time, a new head teacher was appointed, there was a large turnover of staff and a focus on improving the quality of teaching and learning. To support the school there was extra funding to help provide the necessary training to improve facilities, in particular ICT, and to attract new staff. In my opinion going into special measures was far better than being labelled 'serious weaknesses' because we received the financial support to help get us out of trouble. Some recent research has suggested that the changes made during special measures are often not sustainable. In my experience, this has not been the case. We have had another huge turnover of staff in the last two years as many have used their experiences to achieve promotion; exam results have shown steady improvement; and the school has recently become the first Business and Enterprise Specialist School in Gloucestershire. I would class this as sustained improvement. So, in the last few years I have experienced my fair share of inspectors. The question is, 'How do you survive and benefit from the dreaded school inspection?'

A survival guide to inspection

- First, there is no substitute for being well prepared. This does not mean hours and hours of work in the six-week lead-up to inspection! It means having things in place – which all good teachers and all good departments should have anyway.

- Schemes of work – these are not *just* written for the benefit of inspectors, but they should inform teaching and provide a framework, *to help both staff and students* who like to know 'where they are'. We plan to put our schemes of work on our school website so that students and parents know where they are.

- Lesson plans – most schools will have a standard lesson plan which it is advisable to complete on loose leaf sheets for the duration of the inspection. These should be copied and be available for the inspector, should they attend your lesson.

- There are some useful publications to help teachers prepare for inspections. Ofsted themselves produce booklets which are downloadable from their website www.ofsted.gov.uk, such as, *Inspecting Business Education 11–16*, with guidance on self-evaluation.

- Inspectors may want to see evidence of lesson planning over a longer timescale. They are very aware that some teachers might try to 'turn it on' for the duration of the inspection. This is why schemes of work and evidence of long-term lesson planning is essential. Without teaching grandmother to suck eggs, a good lesson plan should include:

  Learning objectives – shared with students at the beginning of the lesson and revisited in the plenary;

  Differentiation – including special needs students;

  Variety of tasks and pace;

  Plenary.

- Special Needs – You should be aware of which students are on the special needs register and for what reason. You may be asked to identify these students and to explain what strategies you have in place to help them. Similarly for gifted and talented students.

- Target Setting – inspectors *are* very keen to talk about assessment for learning. Being able to talk about targets for each individual student and tracking their progress against these targets. It goes without saying that they might want to check your mark book to see evidence of your assessment.

- Enrichment – in business studies there are excellent opportunities to enrich classroom teaching. You should bring to the attention of inspectors any extra-curricular activities and clubs, trips and visits, visitors, links with business and other partners, quizzes and competitions, etc.

- Department Meetings – in my experience and that of many of my colleagues, minutes of department meetings have not been asked for. However, it goes without saying that a strong department will meet regularly and record the outcomes of those meetings.

- Evidence of self-evaluation – the best schools and departments are those that monitor their own progress and are aware of their own strengths and weaknesses and have strategies for improvement – this is likely to become even more important.

- The kind of evidence that would be helpful to Ofsted is:

  evidence of monitoring the quality of teaching and learning – lesson observations of all teachers in the department as well as other colleagues in school;

  evidence of monitoring the quantity and quality of homework set and assessment of it;

  evidence of student progress against targets set;

  evidence of exam results against targets set;

  value-added figures – for students against school average, and against target grades;

  surveys of students' views of their business courses, what they find difficult, their preferred learning style and how they feel teaching and learning might be improved.

If a department cannot provide any of the above as part of their own self-evaluation then inspectors are likely to find out for themselves.

- ICT – good business studies teaching makes effective use of ICT — not just students typing up assignments, but use of interactive teaching packages, the internet, interactive whiteboards, etc. There is a huge variety in accommodation for business studies departments – the best-equipped departments have good ICT access – usually within the department.

- Business education department development plan – this sets out the longer-term vision for the subject, identifies targets and performance measures and addresses any key weaknesses identified through the self-evaluation. The plan should take account of resource requirements, including staffing and professional development.

What inspections tell us

The outcome of school and college inspections is made public and gives a good insight into what is looked for. These are not, however, standardised reports but to an extent reflect the style of the lead inspector.

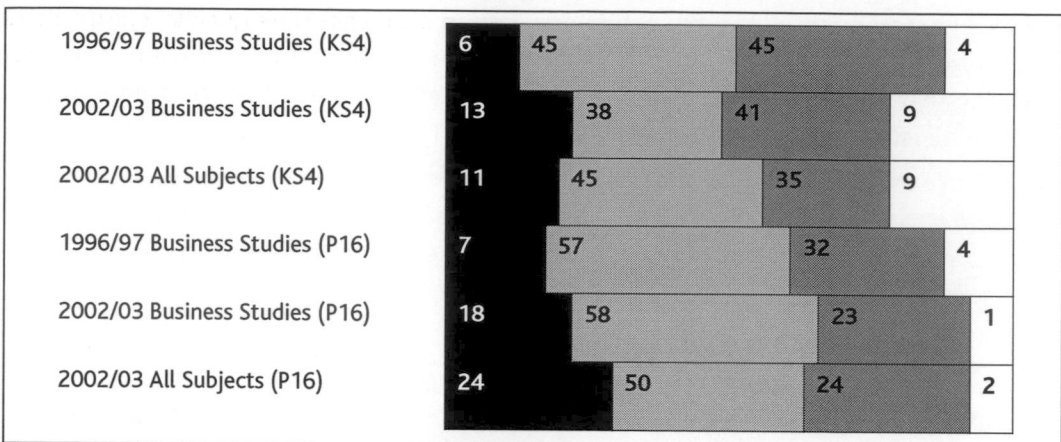

Figure 19.1 How well pupils achieve in secondary schools

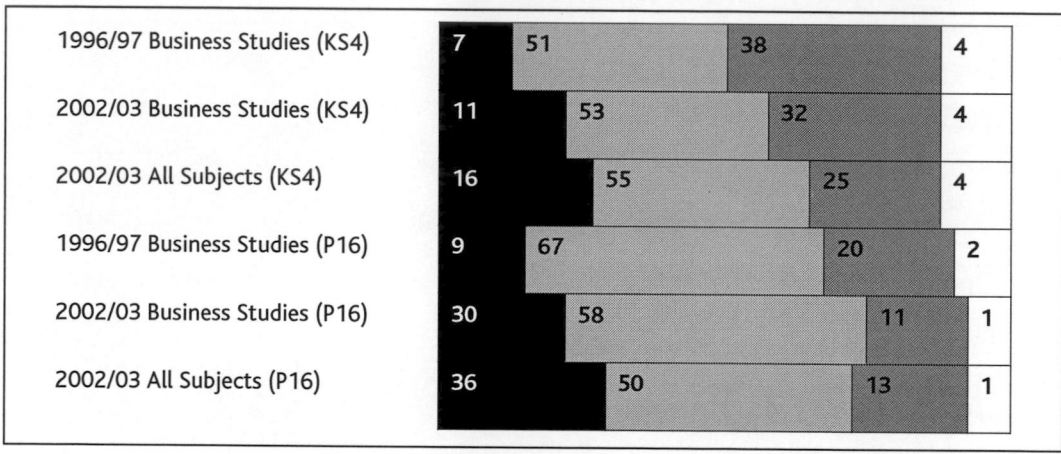

Figure 19.2 Teaching in secondary schools

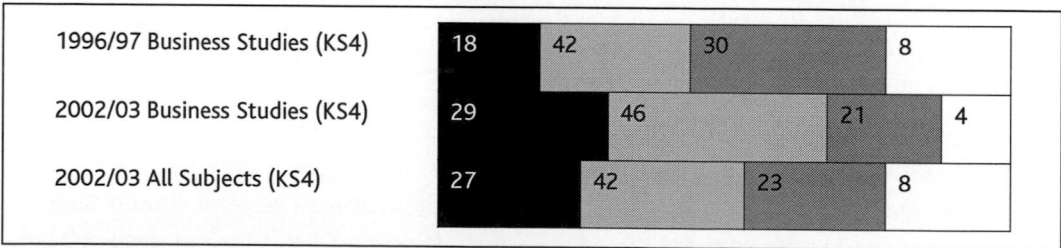

Figure 19.3 Leadership and management in the subject in secondary schools

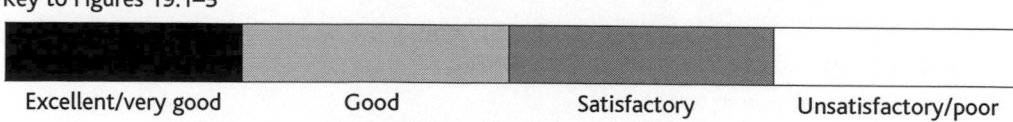

Key to Figures 19.1–3

Excellent/very good   Good   Satisfactory   Unsatisfactory/poor

Findings from inspections (Ofsted, *Annual Report 2004*) are illustrated in Figure 19.1. This graph shows that the proportion of students achieving excellent in business studies has improved at KS4, but also that the proportion of unsatisfactory achievements has increased. Post-16 the situation is better with excellent achievement more than doubling and poor achievement falling.

Figure 19.2 shows that excellent and good teaching at KS4 has improved business studies but it is still just behind the quality of teaching in all subjects. Post-16, the situation is better, with 88 per cent of teaching in 2002/03 being excellent or good, and this figure is higher than 'all subjects'.

Business studies generally makes good use of ICT and new technologies but it is used mainly for presentation, research and data handling rather than modelling. Some departments had developed excellent intranet sites. Other departments used the school website for e-learning and had many resources, schemes of work, and so forth, placed on the internet for students to access. Some schools were making good use of interactive whiteboards. Applied business studies courses were found to be attracting a wide range of ability, and students were generally well motivated. However, there was too much descriptive work and too much data downloaded from the internet. As from 2003 citizenship has been inspected and, naturally, business studies has a large part to play in citizenship at KS4. Business studies departments should be prepared to answer questions about delivery of cross-curricular themes such as citizenship. In particular enterprise learning is bound to have a huge impact on business studies teaching. Many of those things business studies teachers do naturally can be classified as enterprise education. This will be inspected from 2004.

So – what are Ofsted looking for?

The guidelines used by Ofsted to judge teaching and learning are shown in Appendix 1.

The following two examples are Ofsted evaluations of lessons based partly on the criteria for judging lessons, as shown in Appendix 1. Example 1 is based on a GCSE lesson in a school, Example 2 is a post-16 lesson at a sixth-form college. These are actual extracts from Ofsted feedback.

Example 1: Year 11 GCSE BS; mixed-ability class of 28. An introduction to the break-even point, following previous lesson on fixed and variable costs.

After an effective recapitulation of fixed and variable costs through quick fire Q&A, the teacher stated the lesson objectives so that the pupils knew exactly what they were expected to achieve by the end. Her exposition of the break-even point was clear, and her use of specialist terminology precise, reflecting her good subject knowledge. Her explanation was cleverly reinforced by a visually attractive IT (Powerpoint) presentation that gained the full attention of all pupils. The second part of the lesson was an appropriate exercise in which pupils had to identify fixed and variable costs, and pilot costs against revenue to find where a firm would break even. The EAL pupil who did not have full proficiency in English was placed next to two of the abler pupils in case he needed support. By the end of the lesson most pupils had made very good progress in assimilating the concept and applying their understanding to draw accurate break-even charts. This outcome reflected the teacher's high expectations, not least for the slower learners. The only negative feature of the lesson was that the most able pupils finished a little early; they would have benefited from a second or more sophisticated exercise (something the teacher said she would put into her planning on the next occasion she taught this topic).

Example 2: Evidence from a second year GCE A level Business Studies lesson.

A lesson on cashflow statements and balance sheets, using a case study to consolidate earlier learning.

The students are motivated, make careful notes and respond when questioned directly. Their understanding of cashflow and balance sheets is consolidated, in that they apply their understanding accurately to the case study, but there are few extended answers and no spontaneous comment or debate. In the main, the students are happy to be spoon-fed. The teacher provides clear explanations, indicating a secure understanding of the subject area, and she makes good use of the whiteboards to illustrate points. The case study is well chosen as a vehicle to consolidate the students' understanding, and the teacher regularly asks questions about it to test this. However, the quality of the lesson is limited because she does not challenge the students sufficiently to develop the analytical skills needed if they are to attain the higher grades at A level. This is particularly true for a minority of students who are clearly very capable but are not being encouraged to shine. The pace of learning falls away at the end as she dictates notes rather than requiring the students to summarise the main points themselves.

The future

As part of the Government's 'new relationship' with schools, Ofsted has recently announced plans to radically change the way schools are inspected. From September 2005 inspections will be much shorter and focus on the main 'nervous system' of the school. They will not for the most part include the inspection of subjects in detail. The inspections will also give much greater emphasis to school self-evaluation, including that of subjects. Because the new style of inspections will produce little evidence on subjects, Ofsted is proposing implementing a programme of subject surveys to identify good practice and key issues which need addressing. Details of these proposals are still to be confirmed.

Citizenship education and work-related learning (which becomes statutory at Key Stage 4 from September 2004) both have a requirement for all students to develop economic and business understanding. Work-related learning also includes elements of financial literacy and enterprise education. Inspectors will increasingly be seeking evidence that these aspects of the citizenship and work-related learning curriculum are being delivered effectively.

So, the nature of Ofsted inspections is going to change. Gone will be the mad weeks of papering over the cracks and panicking about doing something different or even better than you normally do – we've all done it! Inspections are likely to be less frequent for good schools and more of a 'light touch', possibly every six years. However, for schools where there are problems, inspections may well be every three years and more rigorous. We are also likely to get much less notice – maybe even only a few days. I personally don't think this is a bad thing as it will remove some of the stress associated with the preparation process. However, the National Association of Head Teachers are not convinced. Their General Secretary said he was in favour of shorter, sharper inspections but that the two-day notice was a step too far.

There will be greater emphasis on school self-evaluation and this should be cascaded down into departments. Using a school improvement plan to identify strengths and weaknesses and to set realistic targets for gradual but constant improvement – or as we business studies teachers call it – *Keizan*.

Departmental targets should be set regarding examination results for groups of students. Analysis should be carried out to ensure that students achieve targets. Questions should be asked: If not, why not? Are there any patterns? Do boys do better than girls? Are we stretching the more able? What about the less able? Detailed analysis of results should throw up any areas for development, and new targets should be set. All of this sounds very simple, and good teachers have been doing these things for years.

Individual target-setting and monitoring will be inspected. In a recent inspection at a neighbouring grammar school, the teacher was asked what the target was for each student, how well each was progressing towards achieving their target, and then spoke to the students to ensure that they knew what they had to do to improve. Again, this is good practice and will not come as a great surprise to good teachers.

As part of the drive to improve the quality of teaching and learning, lesson observations will provide good evidence of self-evaluations. By observing each other teach, we can improve our own practice. This does not have to be within departments as we can learn a lot from teachers of other subjects.

Summary

In relation to external quality assessment it is helpful to remember that:

- Inspections will not go away, but they are going to change.

- There is no substitute for being well prepared, but this does not mean only in the six weeks leading up to an inspection.

- Self-evaluation and regular improvement through observations, target-setting, sharing good practice, etc. are the keys to success.

- There is no substitute for good teaching and learning – but this does not mean an isolated lesson.

- There needs to be evidence of continuity of quality in terms of teaching, learning and assessment of learning.

- Inspections are likely to be shorter and more positive as a result and will focus on the self-evaluation carried out by schools and departments.

- Positive and varied enrichment activities will continue to support a positive inspection report.

Appendix

To help you make your judgement about teaching and learning

	Achievement
Very good (2) Difficult ideas or skills taught in an inspiring and highly effective way indicate excellent teaching (1).	All pupils are engrossed in their work and make considerably better progress than might be expected. Achievement is very high. Teaching is stimulating, enthusiastic and consistently challenging, stemming from expert knowledge of the curriculum, how to teach it and how pupils learn. There are excellent relationships in the classroom. Teaching methods are well selected and time is used very productly for independent and collaborative work. Activities and demands are matched sensitively to pupils' needs. Well-directed teaching assistants, and paired or joint teaching, reinforce and strongly support learning. Non-classroom-based Key Stage 4 and sixth-form activities such as private study, research and work placements, develop competencies very effectively.
Good (3)	Most pupils make good progress and achieve well. Teaching methods are imaginative and lead to a high level of interest from most pupils. Individual needs are well catered for, and teaching assistants are well deployed and make a significant contribution. Adults relate well to pupils and expect them to work hard, but the level of challenge is

realistic and pupils are productive. Staff understand the next steps pupils need to take in their learning and they provide a wide range of activities to help them learn. Homework is challenging and extended assignments, for example in the sixth form, effectively extend what is learned in lessons.

Satisfactory (4)	Most pupils' learning and progress are at least satisfactory. Teaching is accurate; teachers have secure understanding of the curriculum and the teaching of key skills. They seek to make work interesting and varied, and they involve pupils productively. Pupils understand what they are expected to do, and tasks have sufficient challenge to keep them working well, independently or co-operatively. The school provides successfully for pupils who do not respond well to school or who have difficulties in learning. Relationships are constructive and there is sensitivity to the needs of individuals and groups. Support staff are adequately managed and soundly contribute to pupils' learning. Homework extends class learning well. Pupils are given scope to make choices and apply their own ideas.

Teaching and/or learning cannot be satisfactory if any of the following characteristics are evident

Unsatisfactory (5)	A significant proportion of pupils make limited progress and underachieve. Teaching is dull and fails to capture pupils' interest and enthusiasm. Activities are mundane and, because of limited tuning to individuals' needs, some pupils get little from them. More effort is exerted on managing behaviour than on learning. Some pupils are easily distracted and lack the motivation to work. Staff have an incomplete understanding of subjects or courses, resulting in patchy coverage. Their sights may be set too low and they may accept pupils' efforts too readily. Support staff provide an extra pair of hands, but little effective support for learning.
Poor (6) Poor behaviour, due to weak teaching with no worthwhile learning outcome, indicates *Very poor (7)* teaching.	Many pupils underachieve and make little or no progress. Teaching lacks challenge and little or no account is taken of what pupils already know. Groups of pupils may not be able to cope, and may disengage or misbehave. Inaccuracies in teaching show insecurity in the subject matter or in understanding how pupils learn. Many pupils are unwilling to work without supervision, and group work is unproductive. Support staff are poorly managed, lack knowledge and skills, and contribute little.

CHAPTER 20

Business and enterprise schools: the lessons so far

Cedric Humphries

Introduction

The Specialist Schools Trust was founded in 1987 to play a lead role in establishing 15 City Technology Colleges and played a key function in obtaining the funding for them. The first schools emphasised technology, mathematics and science. Language Colleges were added in 1995 and Sports and Arts Colleges the next year. The first Business and Enterprise Colleges opened in 2002. The Trust's mission is to 'build a world-class network of innovative, high-performing secondary schools in partnership with business and the wider community'.

Preparing the bid

In September 2003, Higham Lane School, an 11–16 community school of 1,200 students in Nuneaton, Warwickshire, became a Business and Enterprise College, the first such specialist college in the county. Achieving specialist college status was the culmination of months of hard work raising £50k in sponsorship and preparing a four-year development plan.

Higham Lane School has had a broad and balanced curriculum for many years. All students have been encouraged to take a humanities subject, a technology and a modern foreign language course in addition to the core of mathematics, science and English. Business and Enterprise status coincided with the removal of the requirement to follow modern foreign language and technology courses as a result of the disapplication of the National Curriculum. As a result, demand for modern foreign languages has declined. In addition the nature of the intake has changed over recent years with each intake seeing a greater proportion of what might be called 'challenging students'.

Much debate had taken place within school about whether we should go for specialist college status and, if so, which specialism would best suit the school. The debate centred for some departments and parents around the issue of whether all students would be obliged to follow a business studies course, as is the case in some specialist schools.

There was also understandable concern in some departments that they would lose out, or that the overall curriculum experience of pupils would in some way be impoverished. The senior managers of the school made it clear from the start that there was no intention to dilute standards or to exclude any department from developments. In the end it became inevitable that we would join the gold rush and business and enterprise status was chosen because we believed that enterprise learning had application across the whole curriculum, not just in business subjects. Furthermore, the realisation that the work-related curriculum would soon impact heavily on our rather traditional curriculum provided us, in business and enterprise, with a possible change agent.

Raising £50k was never going to be easy. Other schools, also seeking specialist college status, were looking for business sponsorship, and we soon realised what a competitive environment it was. Earlier, we had invited 'Higham Lane 2000', a fundraising team of parents who were business people, to manage the process. We wrote to parents, and our parent teachers association (PTA) also got involved, raising more money in the year than they had ever done. Despite all the efforts of 'Higham Lane 2000' and the PTA, our March deadline for submission of the bid was fast approaching with only £15k raised. Just as panic was setting in, two major sponsors emerged, and with only days to go we reached our target. The lessons were clear: businesses need to be wooed, and they were looking for sustainable partnerships, not 'one-night stands'. Schools need, therefore, to provide a viable business plan and be prepared to argue in business language.

Thankfully, the application process for specialist school status has been simplified. Nowadays, it is online and brief. In September 2002 it was a different matter, with a four-year costed plan being required. A team, involving leaders of the key subjects, business studies, mathematics and ICT, the bursar, the head teacher and myself, began to prepare the plan. The bid document seems to be all about targets, and I am glad that the number of these has been reduced for new submissions. It is very important that targets are challenging but, equally, that they are realistic. Unrealistic targets put immense pressure on the specialist college, and renegotiating them at a later date is not so simple. Another lesson for prospective specialist colleges is to keep monitoring the DfES website, because the format of the bid document is changed frequently and it is essential that the latest version is used. We found rebinding copies of the bid document on the submission day a very stressful activity!

Getting started

The feeling of euphoria within school on hearing that we had been successful in our application was palpable. The head teacher had been informed in advance of us but had been bound to confidentiality until the official publication date. Then it hit us. If achieving specialist college status had been hard work, the worst was yet to come.

One of the hardest things to do was to define exactly what a business and enterprise college is. By its very nature each one is different. In terms of business studies our college increased the proportion of students following an accredited course to thirty per cent. In some colleges there could be a stipulation that every student follows an applied course of some sort. In ours, every student has had a much greater exposure to activities in a business simulation situation but has not been made to follow a business studies course. Work across departments has been reordered to put it into a business context and to develop thinking skills wherever possible. Modules on financial literacy and understanding business are being delivered through our personal, social and health education programme. In this way, existing subject leaders each have a responsibility to embed business concepts into their work. Inevitably, the subject leaders for the three key subjects of business studies, mathematics and information technology have the major role in this area.

Enterprise education is central to the government agenda. Enterprise education is to be an entitlement for all Key Stage 4 students from 2005. To achieve this all students need to be involved in activities that allow them to develop the skills of teamworking, leadership, risk-taking and entrepreneurship. In Higham Lane this is done through a series of business challenges involving whole year groups and also working with primary schools. In addition, smaller numbers of students are involved in specific projects. These can be things such as organising a school production, producing the annual leavers' year book or organising a leavers' ball.

The day-to-day operation of the college is managed by a team directed by me. Time needs to be made available during the day so that team members can make contact with businesses at times that suit them. This does not necessarily fit within the school day or even term! Sometimes, attending meetings conflicts with one's teaching commitments and a balance has to be reached if students' learning is not to be adversely affected. For this reason it was decided to make an additional appointment in business studies to allow me to attend the many meetings arranged by the Specialist Schools Trust, the Education Business Partnership and the many other organisations that can contribute to enterprise education. The first year has been a process of exchanging ideas and good practice among colleagues.

New partners, new challenges

Managing a Business and Enterprise College presents new challenges and requires working with a new range of partners. For example, monitoring of the college development plan is done by a steering group made up of our external partners, including businesses, head teachers from partner primary and secondary schools, community organisation representatives, LEA representatives and, in our case, the Learning and Skills Council. This group meets termly to consider my report of activities in that period, and progress towards targets is recorded and remedial strategies, where necessary, are put in place. The school governors are represented in this group and business and enterprise issues are reported on at the various sub-committees of the governing body and at their full meeting. A yearly report by the governors to parents will be prepared for the annual meeting.

One-third of the college development plan, and the funding, is focused on the community. Specialist school community projects centre on work with local primary, secondary and special schools, with businesses, with FE colleges and the University of Warwick and with statutory and voluntary community groups. With regard to the latter, we focused on not-for-profit enterprise services which would promote social inclusion. These relationships were not easy to establish or sustain. The school has also offered to host businesses in their start-up stage in terms of providing facilities for training and meetings. We are also prepared to assist in the development of websites for fledgling businesses and our business and enterprise status will give businesses an encouragement to take up our offer of support.

One factor that sometimes makes progress so slow is when partners operate in an environment where they are reliant on external funding and often voluntary labour. Partnerships with other schools were a bit easier to manage. The government guidelines stress that there should be partnerships with neighbouring schools so that good practice can be spread and that business education can be available to other institutions. We approached partners not in the spirit of 'This is what we are going to do for you' but by asking, 'How can we help you?' The results have been varied and exciting. We sponsor 'Imagineering clubs' in local primary schools and support them in events such as The National Newspaper Challenge. Local primary pupils have come to our school for a business challenge day, and it has been very interesting to host 120 Year 5 and 6! In the same way we have invited the entire Year 10 from a local secondary school to work with our Year 10 students on enterprise activities. We are also involved in website design for both primary and special schools in the area. Possible projects for transition work in financial literacy and understanding business are in the pipeline.

One benefit of the new status is a much greater emphasis by departments generally on liaising with our partner schools, and in the future we intend to work in a wider number of subject areas. Teachers and students are working in partner primary and secondary schools as well as in further education centres. This is bound to benefit students as there is a much greater awareness of skill levels at each transition stage.

Business challenges to develop enterprise skills for our students did not feature in our bid but have developed as an integral part of what we do. Every year group has had at least one enterprise day and most have had three. Delivering this would have been impossible without our very close links with the Warwickshire Education Business Partnership. This organisation and others such as Business Dynamics, Young Enterprise and the Centre of Vocational Excellence in Logistics, based at North Warwickshire and Hinckley College, have been crucial in planning and running events. In addition, sessions with the Army have been very popular with our students, who acknowledge that their thinking, communication and leadership skills have improved as a result.

The benefits of business and enterprise status

In some ways it seems that support has been more forthcoming now that specialist status has been achieved. Small, medium-sized and international companies are developing real links with the school in a spirit of partnership. Their managers can develop their communication skills and our students benefit from exposure to the real business world. No-one could have predicted that our students would be making presentations in an international company's boardroom a year ago.

Initially, the business and enterprise curriculum was rather imposed on students, but they are, through our school council, beginning to set the agenda. Business and Enterprise status has changed the way in which students are able to express their views about school policy. The level and diversity of consultation not only improves communication, but students, rather like the employees in a well-managed business, can see that their views are respected and that they are able to influence what goes on.

Students make it clear that they believe that they learn best by doing things as opposed to being recipients of teaching. The wide range of activities described above has changed the nature of the education experience. Now that the rush of the first twelve months is over we must consider carefully what has been achieved, emphasise our strengths and address any weaknesses. One important development in this respect is the setting up of a database to map the experience of each individual student. The issue of accreditation is an important one.

At present, accreditation is through the internal certificates that students receive each time they engage in an activity or event. An audit of provision was carried out at the initial bid stage and again at the start of our first year. This process is to be repeated using purpose-designed computer software to give a more accurate picture. It is also possible to obtain external accreditation for many aspects including work experience. The debate continues as to whether or not we will follow this route for our Key Stage 4 students.

An important aspect of becoming a business and enterprise college was the opportunity to network with colleagues across the country in a similar situation. As affiliated members of the Specialist Schools Trust we have been able to attend regional and national conferences both for specialist colleges generally and for business and enterprise colleges in particular. Colleagues in other schools have freely shared their ideas and encouraged us to develop and adapt them for use in our own school. Support from the Trust is excellent. This year there have been bidding support group meetings, and workshops on writing the bid to assist with new submissions. As a specialist college we are able to join a number of pilot projects. We are hoping to become part of a pilot to install a plasma screen in a public area where business news and departmental materials can be showcased to our students and everyone else on our site.

One thing is certain. Every business and enterprise college is different. For us, creating a business ethos within school has become a priority. This is partly achieved through the new way the school is promoting itself and its enterprise culture, but above all it is about the way subject areas are being encouraged to develop learning activities for students. The result is inevitably an improvement in teaching and learning as new resources are developed. All staff have been encouraged to submit bids for projects that they would like to run with students either in lesson time or as extra-curricular activities. In the same way colleagues have been encouraged to accept placements in industry so that their understanding of business is enhanced and they can transmit this to the classroom. The history department, for example, found no problem in developing a case study of Richard Arkwright in the context of the factors of production. The science department has taken a lead in placing work in real business contexts.

Summary

Becoming a business and enterprise college has been a roller-coaster ride. It has highs and lows, all at a terrific pace. The key to our success so far has been the willingness of colleagues throughout school at all levels to become involved. Without the support of them and their ability to go 'the extra mile' nothing would have happened. Inevitably, there are the 'energisers', who seem to have an almost unlimited capacity to suggest new ideas and to develop them for the benefit of students. One must be careful not to exploit them, and ensure that they are allowed the time and space in which to work.

The first six months have been very exciting, not to say nerve-racking, but the school is now a very exciting place to work in and we hope a very stimulating place for our students. One lesson that has been learned is that few things will go as you envisaged. Already, many new ideas have been put forward, and just because they are not in the bid is not a reason to reject them. In our work we must be seen to demonstrate an enterprising approach above everything else. If a good case is made for an enterprising project, whether within school or outside in the community, then we would look to support it.

Our school and the people within it have been transformed by the dynamics of specialist college status. We have no doubt that it was the right decision and are confident that we are building an education that will benefit immensely our students in the years to come and enhance their prospects and preparedness in the world of work.

PART 4

Business Education Resource Guide

GCSE Business Studies

A good range of students' books and teachers' support packs is available to cover the GCSE Business Studies specification. Most are endorsed by one of the GCSE examination boards, are attractively produced in colour and will appeal to students in the age-range. As the GCSE Business Studies specification must cover the same nationally agreed criteria, all of the books are, in theory, suitable for students on any GCSE Business Studies course. In practice, it is probably preferable to use resources designed to match the specification of the exam board being used, as the options, coursework and practice exam questions are based on that board's examination.

Business Studies for OCR GCSE
Peter Kennerdell, Alan Williams and Mike Schofield
Hodder Arnold
Student's book: 0-3407-9052-0 ▪ £14.99 ▪ 2001 ▪ 282pp
Teacher's book: 0-3408-0432-7 ▪ £40.99 ▪ 2001 ▪ 256pp

This book provides excellent coverage of the GCSE Business Studies specification. While written to support the OCR Full and Short Course Linear specifications, significant amounts are relevant to those of the other awarding bodies.

The book caters for the full range of ability from A* to G. Visual material such as charts, pictures, diagrams, etc. will help to make material specifically aimed at the upper end of the ability range more accessible to less able candidates.

There are eight sections in the book. The first seven start with an introductory activity aimed at giving an overview of the units in the section. Each of the seven units follows the same basic pattern with subject content being supported by student activities. Those that provide opportunities for candidates to acquire evidence that can be included in their key skills portfolios are signposted. Exam practice questions, advice on how to answer questions, key terms and examination summary tips are also included in the units.

Section 8 provides coursework guidance that includes, among other things, advice on how assignments are marked and a chart showing how coursework can help with each key skill. In addition to a full index, the top edges of the pages are colour-coded, section by section, to enable students to quickly find their way around the book.

The authors are all experienced teachers and GCSE Business Studies examiners and have been involved in developing GCSE specifications. They have covered all the elements of the revised specification including the options and key skills. The book is well written and is illustrated in full colour. It represents good value for money, especially for those teaching students on OCR GCSE Business Studies courses.

The Teacher's Book is also good value for money as it includes the answers and mark schemes for specimen exam questions; photocopiable worksheets containing additional exercises, tasks, extension activities and solutions. Advice is provided on coursework and case study alternatives of the assessment regime with full guidance for teaching this specification. Additionally there are unit tests, linked to sections of the Student's Book, which can be used to monitor the progress of students against their target GCSE grades. The Teacher's Book enables teachers to make the most of their time and would be invaluable to those teaching this specification for the first time.

GCSE Business Studies Pass Plus for OCR
Peter Kennerdell, Alan Williams and Mike Schofield
Hodder Arnold
0-3408-7302-7 ▪ £6.99 ▪ 2003 ▪ 144pp

This useful revision aid is targeted at OCR students and provides them with a clear, short revision course. It can be used in the classroom and for homework, helping to consolidate the knowledge accumulated over the course and stressing the importance of applying knowledge when answering questions.

Examiners' comments to clarify what is expected of students are included, together with other indispensable items, such as sample answers to demonstrate practical application and exam-style questions and activities to prepare students for the real exam.

GCSE Business Studies A for AQA
Arthur Jenkins, David Hamman, Barry Heywood and Martin Foster
Hodder Arnold
Student's book: 0-3407-7268-9 ▪ £14.99 ▪ 2001 ▪ 282pp
Teacher's book: 0-3408-0183-2 ▪ £49.99 ▪ 2001 ▪ 224pp

This textbook has been written to meet the AQA GCSE in Business Studies Specification A. This could be a bit off-putting if your students are using a different examining board, but, in fact, don't be, as the book should be suitable for all GCSE Business specifications.

The book is divided into units (some of which are subdivided) that more or less follow the same order of topics set out in the AQA(A) specification. The units start with the relevant Key Terms, e.g. 'Business' in the first unit about why business is needed. The underlying theory is then clearly and fully presented. Explanations are followed by activities to aid knowledge and understanding. The activities take the form of Q & A, case studies, ICT activities and examination hints.

Although the book follows the order of topics in the AQA(A) specification, the authors point out that teachers should feel free to cover the topics in the way that suits their particular teaching style. They also point out that the units are not intended to be individual lessons and that the amount of time devoted to a particular unit is a matter for the individual teacher.

GCSE Business Studies A for AQA also provides guidance and support for the pre-issued case studies elements which AQA use as the basis for its examination paper, and advice is given to students on how they can make the most of coursework. Finally a section is included that outlines the type of subject matter that might be covered in the option part of AQA's specification.

The book is fully illustrated in colour and uses appropriate diagrams to aid understanding. There are photographs that, although not necessarily an aid to students' understanding, help to break up the theory. A comprehensive index is provided.

The Teacher's Book includes the answers to all activities in the Student's Book. In addition, guidance is given on delivering the course, including methodologies and teaching strategies. The authors provide some useful additional photocopiable worksheets and exercises together with suggestions of extension activities for more able students with possible strategies for teaching less able students. The Teacher's Book should save teachers a considerable amount of time and be particularly useful to those new to teaching GCSE Business Studies.

GCSE Business Studies Pass Plus for AQA
Peter Kennerdell, Alan Williams and Mike Schofield
Hodder Arnold
0-3408-7674-3 ■ £6.99 ■ 2003 ■ 144pp

This revision aid is targeted at AQA students and can be used in the classroom or for homework. It provides teachers and students with a clear, short revision course that helps to consolidate the knowledge accumulated over the two-year course and to emphasise the importance of applying knowledge when answering questions. The contents of the book are very similar to the revision guide tailored to the OCR specification and it is an invaluable aid to teachers as well as their students taking AQA GCSE Business Studies.

AQA GCSE Business Studies B, 2nd edn
Neil Denby and Peter Thomas
Hodder Arnold
Student's book: 0-340-80116-6 ▪ £14.99 ▪ 2001 ▪ 240pp
Teacher's book: 0-340-80121-2 ▪ £49.99 ▪ 2001 ▪ 224pp

Written by a team of experienced teachers, examiners and authors, the textbook and Teacher's Book are linked to the AQA GCSE Business Studies Specification B. Features in the Student's Book include activities and practice exam questions, highlighting of key skills and incorporation of citizenship and work-related learning.

The Teacher's Book offers the answers to all the activities and questions in the Student's Book together with 50 photocopiable activities, schemes of work and sample exam questions. The guidance on teaching and assessing the exam will be of particular use to teachers teaching AQA GCSE Business Studies specification B.

GCSE Business Studies for Edexcel
Sue Alpin, Ged O'Hara, Jane Cooper and Fiona Petrucke
Hodder Arnold
Student's book: 0-340-81656-2 ▪ £14.99 ▪ 2004 ▪ 288pp
Teacher's Resource CD-ROM: 0-340-81657-0 ▪ £44.99 + VAT ▪ 2004

These brand new resources have been specifically written in an accessible style by a team of examiners for students and teachers of the Edexcel Business Studies GCSE specification.

The textbook is attractively produced and makes full use of colour. In addition to the necessary theory, each chapter is full of key terms, activities and interactive exercises to help students get to grips with all they need to be successful. In addition there are plenty of exam practice questions and tips to help students apply what they have learnt in an exam. A final section gives advice on coursework and assessment, as well as suggesting action plans for study.

The CD-ROM will save teachers masses of time and effort. It is produced in a flexible format that makes it easy to find the right information so that lessons can be prepared quickly and easily. Answers to all the questions and exercises in the Student's Book are, as you would expect, provided.

What makes the CD-ROM invaluable to teachers (especially those new to the subject) is the teaching guidance and advice on successfully delivering the specification and its focus on assessment, coursework, exam preparation and suggested schemes of work.

GCSE Business Studies for ICAA/CCEA

Diane Wallace and Stephanie Wallace

Heinemann Educational

Student's book: 0-4354-5016-6 ■ £16.99 ■ 2001 ■ 208pp

Teacher's Resource Pack: 0-4354-5015-8 ■ £60.00 + VAT ■ 2002 ■ 225pp

This book is endorsed by ICAA for the CCEA/CAA Business Studies specification. It was written to exactly match the specification but also provides all the information and knowledge required for other GCSE Business Studies courses.

There are five units of work, all of which are divided into sections. Each section is kept fairly short but includes all of the necessary theory. Up-to-date case studies, e.g. easyJet.com, are provided to help students apply the theory. Other features include questions to test students' understanding and to reinforce learning, key points at the end of topics to help them when revising for examinations and examination questions, including extension, that are similar to those found on any GCSE examination paper.

The book is clearly written and produced in full colour, each topic being printed on a different background shade. Lots of cartoons are used to illustrate points being made, many of which are amusing. A variety of photographs are reproduced that will add value to the book from the students' points of view, although I do not think they need to see photographs of the outside of two McDonald's, sites with which I am sure they are all very familiar!

The photocopiable Teacher's Resource File with a CD-ROM provides support to teachers and should save hours of preparation time. It contains homework sheets, coursework assignments, sample papers, etc. Files on the CD-ROM can be customised to meet the needs of students and there are electronic files to help them use ICT in their activities.

GCSE Business Studies, 3rd edn

David Butler and John Hardy

Oxford University Press

0-1983-2835-4 ■ £16.99 ■ 2001 ■ 264pp

The third edition of this popular textbook was revised by John Hardy to meet the requirements of the 2001 GCSE Business Studies specification and recent developments in the business world.

The book is divided into sections and units. The first section provides a brief introduction to basic business ideas through a small firm. This theme is continued in the second and third sections. Many ideas are then developed in relation to the large firm, where a number of new concepts are also included. The final section deals with wider issues and looks at the relationship between the state and business activity, and the final unit provides examinations guidance that aims to help students understand what is being asked and the best way to answer.

The aims and objectives of every unit are clearly set out at the beginning and lots of exercises and case studies are provided throughout. At the end of units, there are summaries of key words and ideas, test questions, extension questions and suggestions for coursework.

The book is targeted at average ability students who will like the colourful presentation of text and illustrations. Some sections are marked as 'extension' sections that, together with the extension questions, should help more able students to obtain the highest possible grades. This is a well-written text without too much jargon. It is student-friendly, has a good index and could be a useful resource for post-16 students taking other business qualifications.

GCSE Business Studies

Chris Nuttall

Cambridge University Press

0-5210-0364-4 ■ £13.50 ■ 2001 ■ 318pp

This is written to cover the Edexcel specification and has been divided into sections that closely follow the order of the specification. The book is endorsed by Edexcel, but can, of course, be used with students on any other GCSE Business Studies course.

The book does not assume any prior knowledge of business and uses real ones that will be familiar to students (e.g. McDonald's) as an aid to understanding the theory. The author uses an enquiry-based, active approach to the subject and provides useful advice to students on developing their study skills and tackling their coursework.

There are eight sections, each of which is divided into units of work. These start with their learning outcomes and feature case studies that are set in a real-world or realistic setting, to support the text. Also featured in the units are activities, many of which will support the development of key skills, key terms and unit summaries. A useful, fully comprehensive index is provided.

Although suitable for younger students, I think the style of this book would appeal more to mature GCSE students than some of the other GCSE Business Studies textbooks reviewed. The book is produced in full colour, but instead of having colour-shaded pages it uses colour to distinguish regular features in each of the units throughout. Charts, graphs, diagrams, etc. are meaningful and relate to the theory. Photographs are used sparingly, are in full colour and include a good one of the Spice Girls!

GCSE Business Studies for AQA

Alain Anderton

Causeway Press

1-9027-9629-2 ■ £14.99 ■ 2004 ■ 240pp

Designed for students, teachers and lecturers following AQA GCSE Business Studies Specification A. In full colour. 112 units that match the specification. Contains background information, activities and extended case studies.

GCSE Business Studies for AQA: Teachers' Guide
Alain Anderton
Causeway Press
1-9027-9630-6 ▪ £39.99 ▪ 2004 ▪ 176pp

Contains answers and mark schemes to questions in the student book, plus guidance on coverage of key skills Levels 1 and 2. Useful website addresses are provided.

GCSE Business Studies, 2nd edn
Alain Anderton
Causeway Press
1-8739-2984-6 ▪ £14.99 ▪ 2004 ▪ 240pp

Suitable for the specifications of all the awarding bodies. Arranged in units and sections that focus on decision-making, each unit beginning with a summary of business decisions to be dealt with in the unit. Varied activities, case studies, a dictionary of business terms and a checklist set of questions are included.

GCSE Business Studies: Teachers' Guide, 2nd edn
Alain Anderton
Causeway Press
1-8739-2985-4 ▪ £39.99 ▪ 2004 ▪ 176pp

Contains answers to all questions in the student book and differentiated examination questions and mark schemes.

Business Studies Now! for GCSE, 2nd edn
Karen Borrington and Peter Stimpson
John Murray/Hodder & Stoughton
0-7195-7266-5 ▪ £14.99 ▪ 2002 ▪ 432pp
CD-ROM: 0-7195-7267-3 ▪ £72.50 + VAT ▪ 2002

Covers all the components of the GCSE Business Studies and GCSE Applied Business specifications. No prior knowledge of the subject is assumed. The accompanying CD-ROM provides additional material, including relevant case studies and exam practice.

GCSE A–Z Business Studies Handbook, 2nd edn
Arthur Jenkins
Hodder Arnold
0-3408-5042-6 ▪ £7.99 ▪ 2002 ▪ 288pp

Contains definitions of key terms and concepts; revision lists tailored to different exam board requirements; and lists of examiners' terms to help students understand what is asked of them in exams.

Business Studies GCSE AQA 3/33
National Extension College
1-8430-8085-0 ▪ £78.00 ▪ 2001 ▪ 468pp

This comes in the form of an A4 ring binder and offers a complete course including a study guide, assignment guide, glossary and index.

GCSE Applied Business

A selection of up-to-date resources is available to support the GCSE Applied Business Double Award. Choice of the most appropriate depends upon the students, the teacher's experience and the awarding body used.

The books reviewed below cover the specification of the Qualifications and Curriculum Authority (QCA), common to the three national awarding bodies, but the Carysforth and Neild text (see below) is produced in three versions to cater for differences in methods of assessment so that students do not have to bother with assessment information that is not relevant to them.

GCSE Applied Business for Edexcel
Carol Carysforth and Mike Neild
Heinemann Educational
0-4354-4720-3 ▪ £15.99 ▪ 2002 ▪ 423pp

GCSE Applied Business for OCR
Carol Carysforth and Mike Neild
Heinemann Educational
0-4354-4746-7 ▪ £15.99 ▪ 2002

GCSE Applied Business for AQA
Carol Carysforth and Mike Neild
Heinemann Educational
0-4354-4690-8 ▪ £15.99 ▪ 2002

The books cover all of the knowledge requirements of the GCSE Applied Business Double Award and are divided into three colour-coded units to match those of the specification. The authors use a student-friendly approach and wherever possible relate the theory to students' own experiences. At the beginning of the units there are introductions that give students broad outlines of what they will learn from them. The units are then divided into appropriate chapters, each of which includes an 'Overview' of the contents, regular 'Spot checks' to check understanding and 'Snapshots' – interesting and up-to-date examples of real businesses. 'Fact files' are also included with the aim of helping students to understand important points and 'What can go wrong?' identifies potential problems businesses may encounter.

The books provide numerous activities including problems for students to think and talk about, tasks to do individually or in groups, case studies and integrated activities that provide opportunities for students to apply their knowledge to the real world. All case studies and chapter review practice questions provide differentiated colour-coded questions.

One of the most interesting and novel features of the Carysforth and Neild books is that students gain access to StudentZone, a website created by Richer Sounds. The site links to the topics in appropriate units/chapters and provides students with most of the information they will need for their portfolio investigations. By linking the theory to a trendy national chain of retail stores selling hi-fis, DVDs and mini-disk players, the authors have cleverly demonstrated that what is taught in the classroom is actually practised in business.

To provide everything needed to deliver a GCSE Applied Business course, an accompanying teacher resource file is available:

GCSE Applied Business: Teacher Resource File
Carol Carysforth and Mike Neild
Heinemann Educational
0-4354-7100-7 ▪ £60.00 ▪ 2003

The Teacher Resource File (TRF), with its accompanying CD-ROM, was designed by Carysforth and Neild to support the student textbooks, save teachers' time and help them to confidently deliver a GCSE Applied Business course. It is packed with information, advice and tips for teachers as well as activities and worksheets to consolidate and extend students' learning across the ability range. In addition to all of the resources in the TRF, the CD-ROM contains the keys to all of the activities and case studies in the student book together with Powerpoint presentations and full teaching notes for all the main topics. Help specific to the use of the CD-ROM can be found online.

The well-designed textbook, availability of a website specially created to support it and the teacher's resource file provide everything teachers need to meet the specification and assessment demands of the GCSE Applied Business Double Award in an enjoyable, up-to-date way. The textbook is especially suitable for students who have no previous business experience or are less able, and new teachers will find that using the TRF is invaluable during their first year of teaching GCSE Applied Business.

GCSE Applied Business
Michael Fardon, Chris Nuttall and John Prokopiw
Osborne Books
1-8729-6232-7 ▪ £14.95 ▪ 2002 ▪ 352pp

This is another excellent resource for the GCSE Applied Business Double Award. Rather than being written to support the specification of one awarding body the authors chose to cover the QCA specification that is common to the three awarding bodies.

Like the Heinemann book reviewed above, it is a practical book for a practical course, the design and content of which is driven, in the main, by the opinions of focus groups of teachers and students who wanted a book that was less cluttered and 'busy'. The result is a well-designed resource that makes use of colour throughout. Arguably the text is more suited to more able students.

This book is also divided into three sections to match the units of the examination and is then further divided into chapters. Each of the chapters starts with a case study that sets the scene and introduces the subject together with 'A point to think about'. Additional features include unit-based case studies, activities to aid and test students' understanding of concepts covered and 'Nutshell summaries' and 'Key terms' at the end of every chapter. Highlighted definitions, marginal notes and 'Points to think about' plus the use of coloured photographs and illustrations give added value to this comprehensive learning resource.

Following the index there is a useful 'Website directory' to help students locate background information, human resources information and consumer protection issues. An *Applied Business Tutor Pack* that contains answers, practice tests and guides for the finance unit, is available free with bulk orders of the textbook.

Applied Business for GCSE
Malcolm Surridge
Collins Education
0-0071-3808-3 ▪ £16.50 ▪ 2002 ▪ 224pp

Applied Business for GCSE: Teacher's Resource Pack
Malcolm Surridge
Collins Education
0-0071-3809-1 ▪ £44.99 ▪ 2002 ▪ 136pp

These offer comprehensive support to teachers new to delivering vocational subjects in an easy-to-follow, three-unit structure that mirrors awarding body specifications.

GCSE Applied Business
Dave Hall, Rob Jones, Carlo Raffo and Dave Gray
Causeway Press
1-9027-9662-4 ▪ £14.99 ▪ 2003 ▪ 256pp

GCSE Applied Business: Portfolio Book
Rob Jones, Carlo Raffo and Dave Gray
Causeway Press
1-9027-9663-2 ▪ £6.99 ▪ 2003 ▪ 72pp

GCSE Applied Business: Teachers' Guide
Dave Hall, Rob Jones, Carlo Raffo and Dave Gray
Causeway Press
1-9027-9664-0 ▪ £39.99 ▪ 2004 ▪ 156pp

Purchasers of GCSE Applied Business Teachers' Guide can download interactive spreadsheets, graphs, business documents and case studies free of charge.

GCSE in Applied Business
Neil Denby and Peter Thomas
Hodder Arnold
0-3408-5741-2 ▪ £14.99 ▪ 2002 ▪ 240pp

GCSE in Applied Business: Teacher's Resource CD-ROM
Neil Denby and Peter Thomas
Hodder Arnold
0-3408-1273-7 ▪ £52.86 ▪ 2004

Applied Business GCSE
Richard Barrett
Nelson Thornes
0-7487-5745-7 ▪ £14.95 ▪ 2002 ▪ 208pp

Applied Business GCSE: Teacher Support Pack (AQA)
Richard Barrett
Nelson Thornes
0-7487-6834-3 ▪ £40.00 ▪ 2003 ▪ 216pp

Applied Business GCSE: Teacher Support Pack (OCR)
Richard Barrett
Nelson Thornes
0-7487-6833-5 ▪ £40.00 ▪ 2003 ▪ 216pp

Applied Business GCSE (Edexcel)
Richard Barrett
Nelson Thornes
0-7487-7073-9 ▪ £14.95 ▪ 2002 ▪ 208pp

Applied Business GCSE: Teacher Support Pack (Edexcel)
Richard Barrett
Nelson Thornes
0-7487-5746-5 ▪ £40.00 ▪ 2003 ▪ 224pp

Business Interactive: The Complete Resource for Business Studies
Interactive Learning Limited
CD-ROM ▪ £800 + VAT each / Package of 3 units £2,250 + VAT

This is an excellent but expensive package that has been developed to support delivery of the Applied GCSE Double Award in Business. The resource materials were designed using the generic QCA specification and the package is, therefore, suitable for use with the specifications of OCR, AQA and Edexcel. The emphasis of this multimedia package is on interactive learning where students learn by 'doing'.

Business Interactive was developed by teachers in close partnership with businesses and has been successfully piloted and evaluated in schools. It covers all aspects of the Applied GCSE in Business specification and can be used in a number of ways. It can be used to enhance the delivery of the course by business teachers, supplementing what they have already delivered and helping students to develop a variety of skills, including research, evaluation of business and making presentations.

The package includes video clips with scripted case studies that help to bring difficult business concepts to life. Text is kept to a minimum. Tasks allow for differentiation with beginner and expert levels or extended web-based research tasks. Frequent testing zones monitor student progress and record assessment centrally for teachers to access.

As the package is designed to allow students to work independently it does not necessarily need to be operated by business specialists. When they are not available, students can be supervised by classroom assistants. Finally, although I do not recommend it, the resource could be used for unsupervised independent learning during allotted lesson time or even at home. My reasons for doubting its effectiveness in the latter circumstances is that, because it is so easy and enjoyable to use, many students could well ignore the authors' advice of taking notes and collecting information in their folders as they work through the package, and would end up by not having a real understanding of the subject and/or not having a complete folder of the topics they have covered.

Business Interactive has been designed for use on a standard PC with a CD drive running Windows 95 onwards (Windows 98 onwards needed for database support). The materials can easily be installed to run across a network. Audio facilities (headphones or speakers) are required. Internet access is desirable but not essential to support the web-based research activities. Full installation and setup instructions are provided in hard copy and the website can be used to find the answer to any technical queries purchasers of the pack may have.

The student version of the package consists of three CD-ROMS, each of which covers one of the three units of the specification. At the time of writing, Unit 4 – Marketing and Production – is currently under development. This will fill any gaps between the specifications of the Applied GCSE Business and GCSE Business Studies and will be launched in February 2005. The price of Unit 4 will be discounted to customers who have already purchased the software.

In addition to the three CD-ROMS, the complete package provides a teacher support pack, fully interactive quick start tutorial, full helpdesk support and advice at no extra cost plus additional free resources on the website. Finally, although it is not necessary to have access to the internet, this will obviously be beneficial to support the web-based research activities.

AVCE Business

The current AVCE Business award will be replaced in September 2005 by new Applied Business A level specifications from AQA, OCR and Edexcel. At the time of writing, no resources covering the new specifications are available.

The following resources were designed to cover the current AVCE specification and have proved very popular with teachers and students.

AVCE Advanced Business
Dave Needham and Rob Dransfield
Heinemann Educational
Student book: 0-4354-5316-5 ▪ £19.99 ▪ 2000 ▪ 674pp
Tutor's file: 0 4354-5317-3 ▪ £75.00 ▪ 2001 ▪ 240pp

These resources offer teachers and students a complete package that covers all the compulsory units of the AVCE specification. The chapters in the Student Book match the unit specifications and include many activities to help students build their portfolios. Students have the opportunity of looking at how real organisations plan and manage their businesses in the face of current threats and opportunities.

The Tutor Resource File is photocopiable and provides teachers with many ideas for prompting and extending discussions in class. It also suggests approaches to the case studies and tasks in the Student Book plus plenty of material to help students through their assessments.

Advanced Business
Michael Fardon *et al.*
Osborne Books
1-8729-6204-1 ▪ £17.95 ▪ 2000 ▪ 640pp

This textbook was written by a team of experienced vocational authors and covers the six compulsory units of the AVCE course. It is a student-friendly text with numerous case studies and activities for building up portfolio evidence.

A *Tutor Pack* with practice external assessments is also available free with bulk orders of the textbook.

CHAPTER 24

BTEC National Qualifications

National certificates and diplomas have a long history. They were initially developed to bridge the gap between traditional A levels and vocational qualifications. There is now an upsurge of interest in them and both BTEC and OCR have had a range of National Awards, Certificates and Diplomas, across a range of subject areas, credited by the Qualifications and Curriculum Authority. The following resources, published for the first time in 2004, cover the new 2003 specifications.

> **BTEC First Business**
> Carol Carysforth and Mike Neild
> Heinemann Educational
> 0-4354-0138-6 ▪ £16.99 ▪ 2004 ▪ 284pp

This excellent resource, which has been endorsed by Edexcel, covers the three core units and three of the six specialist units of the BTEC First Diploma in Business. This student-friendly book is produced in full colour, making it attractive and easy to use.

The content is organised to match the BTEC specification. Each unit starts with an introduction that summarises its contents and explains its assessment and ends with a 'Section Review' that poses questions to test students' learning and understanding. The book includes several features that will ensure they do in fact learn and understand:

- 'Business briefs' – clear and concise explanations of key concepts that aim to help students remember them and use them in assignments.

- 'Business matters' – case studies that show students how the business theory actually works in business.

- 'Talking points' – activities which present two sides of an argument that encourage students to think and debate.

- 'Over to you!' – activities that are carefully matched to the assignment requirements of the course to help students achieve their assessment.

Students who are lucky enough to use this book are given special access to StudentZone, a part of the Richer Sounds website. StudentZone enables students to investigate the way a successful British business operates. The site is divided into two parts: one for students taking the BTEC First Diploma in Business and the other for students taking GCSE Applied Business (see review above of Carysforth and Neild's book of the same name). The information in StudentZone is updated every summer so that it is kept fully up to date.

BTEC First in Business: Teacher's Resource File and CD-ROM
Carol Carysforth and Mike Neild
Heinemann Educational
0-4354-0135-1 ■ £89.00 ■ 2004

Details are available on the Heinemann website www.heinemann.co.uk.

The *Teacher's Resource File and CD-ROM* has been designed to support teachers' delivery of the course and provides material they can customise to match their own students' needs. It contains a wealth of photocopiable material, answer sheets, assessment guidance and extra activities, plus the three specialist units which are not included in the Student Book.

The Student Book and *Teacher's Resource File and CD-ROM* together provide everything needed to successfully deliver the 2003 BTEC First Diploma in an effective and interesting way.

BTEC National Business
Rob Dransfield, Catherine Richards, David Dooley and Philip Guy
Heinemann Educational
0-4354-5535-4 ■ £19.99 ■ 2004 ■ 512pp

This resource, which has also been endorsed by Edexcel, was designed to provide students with all the information they need to follow a BTEC National Certificate general pathway. The ten chapters of the book cover the six core units and four of the specialist units, each chapter representing one of the units and using the same headings as the specification.

The book, perhaps reflecting the anticipated older age range of users, has not been produced in colour, but it effectively uses black-and-white illustrations, graphs, photographs and boxed features to break up the theory. These include:

● 'Thinking point activities' – included in each unit to help students broaden their knowledge and improve their abilities in business.
● 'Practice point activities' – practical tasks for students to develop their skills and practise the concepts covered.

- 'Case studies' and 'Real lives' – enable students to keep up to date and aware of what is happening in the business world. These are followed by questions or points to consider, to help students gain a wider understanding of modern business life.

- 'Outcome activities' – relate directly to the unit performance criteria and are included at the end of each unit.

- 'Key terms' – within the text important terms are show in **bold type**. They are listed in alphabetical order at the end of each unit and are included in the Glossary.

- 'End-of-unit tests' – which are probably better completed before the 'Outcome activities' so that students' understanding can be checked.

- 'Resources' – at the end of each unit there is an excellent feature that lists texts, magazines, journal articles and websites which may be used for further research, especially by students aiming for merit or distinction.

This is a fully comprehensive resource that will provide students with everything they need to achieve a BTEC National Business qualification. Teachers can get details from the Heinemann website of a supporting photocopiable Tutor Resource file that provides help with running the course and extra case studies and texts.

A level Economics

The British Economy Survey

A well-established resource, published twice yearly by Longmans and obtainable both in book form and on CD-ROM. It is a source of applied articles covering current issues and supplements a basic text. It is also an excellent support to teachers hoping to keep up to date with a manageable amount of reading. The Survey is typically in 14 sections, examples being government economic policy, the public sector, public finance, the UK and the world economy, marketing and accounting and finance.

The text is often demanding for A level students, but a useful challenge for able students and excellent background for essays and coursework. The questions at the end of each section are thought-provoking. The CD-ROM contains the texts of journals for the previous six years, an excellent archive of materials for students' investigative work and teachers preparing lessons.

AS/A Level Economics Resource Packs

Published by Phillip Allen Updates, strong plastic binder, price £59.95 plus postage and packing. These are intended to supplement textbooks with interesting activities and questions designed to check knowledge, and encourage skills such as data comprehension and analysis. Sample pages are on the publisher's website. Each pack contains 12 planned lessons covering the major topics of all the specifications. For example, the pack on development economics includes sections on world poverty, theories of development, population growth and development, trade, tourism, international finance, etc. Students are provided with information sheets and worksheets with a variety of questions, some using data, with practical examples and encouraging the application of theoretical principles.

For those teachers who prefer to devote lesson time to active learning, discussion and development of thinking and writing skills rather than delivery of content, an attractive feature is that the information sheets provide students with a set of basic notes, relatively brief and useful for revision. Students answer on the worksheets, which then perform a similar function. Suggested answers are provided. The worksheets are good for homework, or classwork, and excellent for setting work when a teacher is absent. They are not quite as innovative as the literature claims but do add variety to teaching. The recently added A2 packs on the labour market and international economics are a welcome edition. They include more challenging theory and longer texts. Students undertaking the worksheets will, therefore, find themselves doing some useful background reading almost without realising. Topic coverage is extensive; teachers may find it impossible to use all the material within the time constraints. Other titles are: *Markets and Market Failure* (AS), *The National Economy and its Management* (AS/A2), *Development Economics* (AS) and *Microeconomics* (A2). The authors are experienced teachers and examiners.

The UK Economy Explained: A Practical Guide to the Performance of the UK Economy and Current Policy Issues for A Level Economics and Business Studies Students

This resource is sponsored by HSBC Bank. It is in the form of a CD-ROM of statistical data and text, covering a wide range of business and economic information. The statistical data can be easily manipulated, graphs are provided and are easily printed off. It is, therefore, a useful addition to a textbook. It also provides good textual summaries which are accessible to most A2 students and to AS students with support.

There are 15 named files, ranging from an overview, through macro- and micro-economics and the company sector to labour and global markets. In these, background, current issues and policy are concisely explained. Hence students could use this as a set of notes, to carry out research, to study data, or for revision. Teachers can easily produce investigative tasks or a variety of worksheets. Ideally, this resource will be updated regularly.

www.jusbiz.org

The 'Just Business' website exists to provide information and activities about global and ethical issues. Sadly it is no longer operating and adding to the materials available, but sections of the site are still accessible. The tone of the site is fairly committed. However, this in no way diminishes its usefulness for essay preparation, coursework, and as a source of discussion materials. Particularly useful features include:

- An articles page with a glossary function
- Links to related sites, including 'The Real Price of Cotton Links'
- Ideal for teaching globalisation, trade issues, international aid and debt and world poverty.

Competitions and other activities

The best competitions can give an added interest and edge to the students' experience.

Target 2.0

Annual competition run by the Bank of England and also sponsored by *The Times*. Participants are invited to 'become a policy-maker and determine interest rates'. Students in teams of four (one per school) take the role of the Monetary Policy Committee, examining a range of relevant indicators and presenting their analysis and recommendation to Bank personnel. They are supported by a large pack of information and advice about making the presentation. In fact this is an exercise which could be undertaken by any AS or A2 economics group at an appropriate level in the classroom, though given an added reality for those competing. It is certainly worth entering a team for the experience, probably A2 students, and teaching can be tweaked to cover the relevant theory to meet competition timings. Those doing pure economics are probably at a distinct advantage. The competition has three stages: local, regional and national (at the Bank itself). The bank invests a considerable amount in venues, catering and manpower; top economists make up the judging panel. The competition is heavily populated by the independent sector, and to win, teams will have to be well rehearsed and competent; the questions are probing and presentations well structured. This is great practice for those aspiring to Oxbridge but would be impressive to add to most UCAS personal statements. Also good for anyone entering the Advanced Extension Award. The teacher can use the information in many ways, putting as much effort into it as appropriate – or leave it to the students. Great prizes – if a bit nerve-racking (for students and their tutors).

ProShare Student Investor

www.proshare.innovation.gov.uk

1   The ProShare Portfolio Challenge

This is an annual competition, described by its sponsors as 'The largest investment competition in the UK in which teams invest online an imaginary £100,000 portfolio in UK and international shares'. It can give a real-world experience and offer the chance to develop key skills, such as working with others.

2   The ProShare Forecast Challenge

Students predict company share prices online based on company information provided.

3   ProShare

Students write an essay of 1,500–2,000 words, based on research and analysis of company data.

All are open to 14–18-year-olds, with excellent prizes. While students will enjoy the competition challenge, teachers will find the sponsored support materials useful in a variety of situations, for instance in teaching a personal finance module in General Studies, to support part of the teaching of Business Studies, as part of the Citizenship curriculum and to support a school investment club.

Books to support the study of A level economics

Books published by Anforme

A range of titles; to date, the publishers have been commendably good at keeping their titles updated. £6.95, or £5.95 when ten or more are ordered.

Each is circa 90 pages, i.e. journal-sized, A4 format. The text is printed on glossy paper with coloured graphs, diagrams and photographs.

Economic Development
Peter Cramp
Anforme
0-9075-2973-9 ▪ £6.95 ▪ 2003 ▪ 96pp

Covers: an introduction to economic development, theories and strategies, population and environment and international trade and finance.

Labour Markets
Peter Cramp
Anforme
0-9075-2960-7 ▪ 2001

Covers: labour supply and demand, differentials, trade unions, government intervention, unemployment, flexibility, ageing population, inequality and poverty and policy issues. Particularly useful at A2 level because of the theoretical analysis of labour markets.

Understanding the European Union
Stephen Romer
Anforme
0-9075-2971-2 ▪ £6.95 ▪ 2002

Covers: origins and institutions, internal market, competition policy, monetary union, CAP, trade, enlargement, unemployment in EU. Excellent additional reading for papers with European content, such as AQA Paper 4 (at time of writing).

Industrial Economics
Robert Nutter and Peter Cramp
Anforme
0-9075-2969-0 ▪ £6.95 ▪ 2002

Covers: entrepreneurs, growth of firms, aims of firms, market structures, privatisation, competition policy, government policy and competitiveness. Intended to support Unit 4 Edexcel or Unit 5 AQA.

All the aforementioned would be well placed in any departmental or school library. Students find them relatively accessible and of a suitable (not too large) size. They are also useful to teachers new to the specifications. Good value for money.

Heinemann Studies in Economics and Business

A very well-established series of texts on individual topics to give more detailed coverage than is possible in a general textbook; groundbreaking when introduced. A5 format, approximately 100 pages, editor Susan Grant, price £7.25. Probably additional texts for library purposes, though class sets on topics for specific papers would be useful, for instance *Transport Economics*, *The European Union*, *Economics of Leisure and Housing*. Most of these are not differentiated into AS and A2. The series is regularly updated, some books being on their fourth edition, for instance one of the most useful, *Supply Side Economics*, or second edition, as for *Environmental Economics*.

Features of the series:

- Small, student-friendly size
- Short chapters
- Key terms defined
- Suggested wider reading
- Suggested essays
- Chapters end with data response questions from previous A level examination, some pre-Curriculum 2000 – no suggested answers or comment on how to answer, but this is not a study skill aid or a textbook
- Clear diagrams
- Detail not found in standard textbooks
- Range of data.

Useful for student reading lists, wider reading for able students, Oxbridge applicants preparing for interview, Advanced Extension Award students, research for essays, etc.

The series is not quite uniform in quality, though all of the books in the series would be worth a place in the school or departmental library at least. Some assume a degree of knowledge before reading and are likely to be more useful for A2. A must for teachers preparing lessons.

CHAPTER 26

A level Business Studies

Common characteristics of A Level Business Studies textbooks:

- Divided into relatively short units
- Key terms
- Summary or review
- Exam and study advice
- Case studies and other questions.

Business Studies
Ian Marcuse *et al.*
Hodder Arnold
0-3408-1110-2 ▪ £19.99 ▪ 2003 ▪ 646pp

This is probably regarded as one of the standard textbooks for this course. The book is certainly a heavyweight and intended to be applicable to all AS and A2 specifications in core content. There is an accompanying *Business Studies Teacher's Book* costing £46.99, which is fully photocopiable and provides teachers with worksheets and answers to all the questions and activities in the Student's Book. *Business Studies* is made up of 95 self-contained units which are organised into six subject topics. All the units are self-contained, allowing teachers to cover the material in the order they wish, or two teachers to work simultaneously; the materials are also cross-referenced. Each unit starts with a definition of the topic area, for example 'Marketing objectives' or 'Types of production', includes a box with key terms and ends with an evaluation. In addition, 'In business' boxes include recent examples of real-life companies in activities relating to the theory.

One of the book's very great strengths is its 'Issues for analysis' sections which encourage students to question theory and evaluate the processes about which they have read; this is excellent for helping students to pick up marks for analysis and evaluation.

There is a workbook of review questions, data responses and essays; the workbook is divided into AS and A level sections, though the book is not. Teachers wishing to have this distinction made explicit might prefer *Business Studies for AS* and its accompanying teacher's book. *Business Studies* follows the current trend in including advice to students on exam and study technique; the most valuable section here describes how exam papers are marked. Finally, there is a detailed 13-page index.

This is a very detailed textbook, relatively easy to read, but with lots of text on each page and certainly not inappropriate for first-year undergraduates. The questions are quite demanding from the start. As such, many A Level students will need support in using this text early in AS. Students may also be put off by the book's sheer size; carrying it is not likely to be popular. However, it will come into its own at A2 level and as a home resource for students undertaking homework or coursework.

Business Studies, 2nd edn
Dave Hall, Rob Jones, and Carlo Raffo
Causeway Press
1-8739-2990-0 ▪ £19.99 ▪ 2004 ▪ 776pp

Another text guaranteed to develop arm muscles, one of its great strengths is the detail of its coverage in 106 units. It includes sections not likely to be seen in all textbooks, such as 'Population and business'. The second edition was rewritten to suit AS/A level and claims suitability for all specifications including AVCE and Scottish Higher Grade. There is a logic in the way it starts, dealing with 'What is business activity?' and 'Setting up in business'. This may help candidates new to the subject at sixth-form level.

Despite large numbers of boxes with diagrams, etc., it looks more textbookish than some others. On the other hand, it provides review questions throughout the units in the form of excellent mini-case studies with review questions and a longer case study at the end of each unit. This text would suit most candidates up to undergraduate level, though its size might be daunting. It does not distinguish between AS and A2 content or questions though teachers are not bound to teach in the order of the units. The unit on 'Collecting, presenting and interpreting data' is very good and comes just before the unit on 'Business decision-making', which deals with how the data is used.

Other features: detailed index and two units relating to 'Study skills' (mind maps, for instance, and key skills) and 'Assessment' (broken down into sections on projects, essay-writing, report-writing, levels of response, pre-seen case studies, etc.). There is an accompanying *Teachers' Guide* book with answers to all the activities.

Business Studies
Michael Barratt and Andy Mottershead
Longman
0-5824-0547-5 ▪ £19.99 ▪ 2000 ▪ 746pp

Organised into six sections and 63 units, detailed index and a section entitled 'Synoptic case study', which is the ongoing story of Ramsbotham Brewery in four episodes. This text has been specifically written to match all the requirements of the AS/A level specifications and does not differentiate questions. The book begins with a section explaining 'Business activity', followed by 'Setting up in business'. Each unit begins with learning objectives and a 'Context box' relating the topic to current business practice and using names students will recognise as exemplars. The text is clearly structured with frequent questions throughout units, often in the form of short case studies. There is an element of evaluation to help students handle longer answers; examples would be 'Is profit a dirty word?' and 'The problems of technology'. In addition some sections must help student revision; for instance, for each method of production, there follows a list of 'main characteristics'. There are key terms and summary points. The pages have an uncluttered feel and clear diagrams. Unit 13, on the presentation of data, is very useful, particularly for coursework.

The outstanding feature of this book is its case studies; each unit ends with a 'Mini case study' and a 'Maxi case study', both giving practice in exam-type questions. The maxi cases are intended to provide more demanding assessment. An additional feature (on pink pages) is the 'Friday afternoon' review section – 100 marks' worth of recall questions and even more data response. The *Teachers' Guide*, £38.50, contains answers to all student activities. A supporting website is planned. This text also contains material which would be useful for candidates sitting the new Advanced Extension Award in Business Studies.

AS Business Studies

Richard Thompson and Denry Machin
Collins Educational
0-0071-5120-9 ▪ £15.50 ▪ 2004 ▪ 304pp

This text is both colourful and more manageable in the two terms available for AS. Its size and general look will make it attractive to students. It is suitable for all AS specifications and begins with a message of advice to students from three examiners. Its accessibility recognises the wider range of students who now undertake A levels and that some of these will take their Business Studies no further than AS. The integrated approach is emphasised by the fact that the first section deals with the nature of business, business ownership and strategy; hence encouraging students to think in an integrated way as soon as possible.

Features: 'Summary' section at the end of each unit, comprising key terms, summary questions, mainly recall, and an exam practice data response/case – these are all short, but then so are the AS questions. Best feature: a 'Getting the grade' section after each topic summarises exam advice in one page in context.

AS Business Studies

Malcolm Surridge and Andrew Gillespie

Hodder Arnold

0-3408-8541-6 ▪ £13.99 ▪ 2004 ▪ 284pp

Covers the Business Studies specifications material of all the major exam boards. It claims to provide a clear insight into the knowledge and skills required to achieve the highest grades in the new examinations, and a number of the book's features are designed to encourage a thinking approach. There are seven chapters, six relating to the main sections of the specifications and an introductory chapter offering advice on examination skills, an insight into how to use marking schemes to advantage and a 'What is business' section. The text is comprehensive and accessible to the whole ability range.

Features: learning objectives, business in focus, with up-to-date examples of business activity, people in business introducing some of the better-known entrepreneurs, points to ponder to engage students in independent thinking, key current issues in business, examiners' advice in boxes distributed throughout the text, maths moments giving advice on how to carry out relevant calculations – if these did not exist, teachers would have to invent them for weaker candidates. There are progress questions, some requiring simple recall, others in a separate section called 'Analytical and evaluative questions' which draws students' attention to the skills to demonstrate in exams, frequent short case studies and longer cases at chapter ends. It does not look as exciting as some other books and, given the number of features, the pages can look busy.

Best aspects: student-friendly size and focus on how to obtain high grades in exams. The A2 book is similar in format with the same strong points. The introduction explains the difference between AS and A2 with specific reference to the requirements of the main exam boards. There is a section on answering questions mainly requiring higher-order skills, emphasising an integrated approach in writing essays and reports. There is a teacher's book with answers to accompany each text.

Books specific to one board:

AS Level Business Studies for AQA

Alain Anderton

Causeway Press

1-9027-9600-4 ▪ £13.99 ▪ 2003 ▪ 304pp

Those who have used Mr Anderton's GCSE textbooks will recognise the same popular format. The book is very colourful, written in six colour-coded sections matching the AS specifications, subdivided into 64 short units, including one on business data which would continue to be useful for A2 candidates. There is an index.

Features: the use of colour will make this an attractive text. Exam skills are emphasised in an opening case study to each unit with knowledge, application, analysis and evaluation explicitly labelled. There are key-terms boxes and checklist questions to check knowledge and understanding.

Best aspects: student-friendly size and format, comprehensive coverage, good external influences unit.

Business Studies AS: The Complete Companion: AQA Specification
Jenny Wales and Neil Reaich
Nelson Thornes
0-7487-7667-2 ▪ £14.95 ▪ 2004 ▪ 272pp

Business Studies AS: The Complete Companion: OCR Specification
Jenny Wales and Neil Reaich
Nelson Thornes
0-7487-7533-1 ▪ £15.95 ▪ 2004 ▪ 272pp

The AQA book is organised in three modules, the OCR version in two parts. In each case, they match the specifications very closely. There is a 'How to use this book' section so that students make the most of the books' format. Each book has end-of-unit and end-of-module assessments based on case studies, the latter with model answers. The OCR version begins with a 'What does business do?' section which would, in fact, be useful for all students.

Features: Each two-page section begins with a starstudy, a short case study to illustrate what the theory means, text labels/icons which indicate sections linking theory and the real world, 'In the know' boxes to provide knowledge and theory, key terms, 'Next steps' boxes which invite students to extend the theory to other situations they know, and critical-thinking questions to encourage analysis and evaluation. The assessment questions have helpful hints indicated by a 'help' icon. Both books offer specific exam advice, some in speech bubbles in the context of case studies.

Best aspects: These texts should be accessible even to less able students; the pages seem to carry less content despite covering the specifications, and colour has been used to maximum effect. These students will also find the suggested answers and help sections useful.

AQA – AS Business Studies
John Wolinski and Gwen Coates
Philip Allan Updates
0-8600-3753-3 ▪ £15.95 ▪ 2004 ▪ 443pp

Format is three modules, subdivided into 51 chapters, index and special section relating to the pre-released case study. This really looks more like a traditional textbook, and the larger number of pages is an indication of depth of coverage. The introduction gives advice on assessment, study skills and exam advice. There are practice exercises with suggested timings and case studies. At the end of each section (e.g. marketing, or accounting and finance) there are longer integrated case studies which provide exam practice and assessment opportunities.

Features: Key terms are signed throughout the text. 'Examiner's voice' boxes offer snippets of advice to gain maximum marks and avoid pitfalls. 'Fact file' boxes give topical examples from the world of business, 'Did you know?' boxes comment on how concepts are applied in real businesses and 'What do you think?' sections offer challenges where there is a range of possible solutions or outcomes.

Best aspects: detail of coverage, range of case studies, exam advice. Good section on the problems of using elasticity (many students do have considerable difficulty here, so it is best to acknowledge this and deal with it).

Business Review AS/A-Level Resource Packs

Published by Phillip Allan Updates in a strong plastic binder, £69.95 plus postage and packing. Written by experienced teachers and examiners. Their claim is to be 'high quality teaching resources covering the main specification areas indicated in the QCA subject criteria for AS and Advanced level examinations' and by and large they succeed in this. There is some unevenness in the levels of difficulty of different exercises, though this is addressed in those packs which are subdivided into AS and A2 sections. The topics are covered by planned lessons, photocopiable information and worksheets.

As with the economics packs, these form a convenient set of notes for students. The exercises draw heavily on material from the *Business Review* magazine. Titles, so far, are *Marketing*; *Accounting and Finance*; *People*; *Objectives and Strategy*; *External Environment*; and *Operations Management*. Sample pages are on the publisher's website. They have already been revised and it is to be hoped that this is an ongoing process. For those daunted by the thought of teaching accounting for the first time, the relevant pack is a godsend, with good explanation and exercises. Teachers might find it useful to put some of these as templates on spreadsheets. Answers are provided. Both sets of packs come with a full money-back guarantee if the purchaser is dissatisfied.

Topical Cases (for A level Business Studies)

This material is obtainable through A–Z Business Training. It can be delivered electronically or by mail on disk. In fact the title does the author a disservice, since it contains lesson suggestions, student competitions and exam tips. Its very great strength is the topicality of the content, written very soon after companies or events are in the news; examples of this would be cases on Virgin, Enron, Meridien Hotels and My Travel.

The cases are graded for AS and A2 and come complete with marking schemes. However, since they tend to be topic-based, they can prove useful for assessing student knowledge on particular topics and are excellent for formative assessment. Particularly recommended for those teaching the AQA Business Studies A level Specification.

The Times 100

This resource began life as a file of case studies, mainly of relevance for A level Business Studies students (though the author has adapted several for vocational courses or GCSE). They are highly informative, detailed and topical (updated each year). They cover the whole of A level and other equivalent qualifications which are cross-referenced for qualification, skill and topic. They were produced in a file, provided free to schools, printed on high quality light card, with suggested activities, excellent colour and graphics which tended to lose in the photocopying. They are now provided in hard copy and online at www.tt100.biz, with information divided as suitable for 14–16 and 16–19 years, and with worksheets as well as cases. There is a teacher zone where lesson plans can be downloaded (related to age and topic), a useful search facility, and macroflash interactive revision pages, marked immediately, with opportunity to try again. One useful section is the detailed information on companies, which includes not only financial data but the economic environment and stakeholders. The topic of company ethics is covered, but of course, much of the information is given from a company perspective; nonetheless a useful insight and definitely worth using occasionally – it would be impossible to find the time to attempt even half of the material. Good background for coursework; wider reading for the new Business Studies Advanced Extension Award; downloadable homework – to make just a very few suggestions.

The Business Review, The Economics Review and Economics Today

For many years now, teachers and students have benefited from the support of excellent journals the *Business Review* and *Economics Review* (published by Philip Allan Updates). They have been joined more recently by *Economics Today* (published by Economics Today Ltd). They are available by subscription, approximately £17.95 for an institutional copy which makes further copies available at approximately £8.95–£9.95, four copies throughout the year. Leaflets of information are distributed to schools. All are topical and well adjusted to the needs of A level students, making excellent use of colour illustration and graphics, and all departments should have copies in their library or for classroom reference. Many schools ask students to subscribe. The articles are excellent, written by examiners and practising teachers. Examples of the content:

Business Review:

- Recommended websites
- Articles on topics in the A level courses

- Examiner comment on recent questions
- Data to analyse
- Brainteasers and revision quizzes

Both economics journals have a mixture of features (on currently important issues) and regular columns. They combine articles on aspects of theory (but always with reference to current examples) with examination advice and analysis of recent data. Often articles are followed by questions for further discussion.

Good to use for:

- The basis of a reference library;
- Preparation for lessons where, for instance, students pre-read content for a lesson emphasising skills or early in an AS course when some students have done GCSE and others have not;
- Wider reading for students, including for Advanced Extension Award students;
- Research for essays (part of the suggested sources);
- Updating textbook coverage;
- Updating teachers;
- Providing the basis of an archive over time (now available on CD-ROM).

The fact that the articles are of a manageable length for most students is a boon.

Students should be encouraged to keep their copies, which become more and more useful as they progress through their course.

Websites

There is an endless list of sites which can be used, but this section refers mainly to those which are dedicated (or have sections dedicated) to the teaching of economics and business studies.

www.bized.ac.uk

This is one of the most important sites for teachers in this area, developed at Bristol University. It has sections suitable for HE, FE, or A level teaching and is constantly being improved and updated. A weekly update is provided during term, delivered by email. Navigation is easy and there is a search facility. Some of the features which make this a must are:

- An 'In the news' section, with topical issues related to business and economic theory;
- Lesson plans which include presentations, arranged according to course (AS, AVCE, etc.) and topic;

- Other activities, some of which are interactive;

- Links to other sites, again organised by topic;

- Company information, in the form of profiles of 37 companies (at the time of writing);

- An archive section;

- Data, links to data sources and help in dealing with data;

- 'Virtual worlds' – one of the best-known features – including a learning arcade;

- A cross-referencing facility with drop-down menus indicating resources related to pages.

There is a variety of levels of difficulty, so there is a need to check the suitability of material and accessibility for pupils. However, this site is a huge asset for teachers in this area.

www.tutor2u.net

A second 'must use' online learning resource. This too grows almost daily. Most of the site is free to use; some materials have to be purchased on CD or by subscription. It has a very different feel from biz/ed, more geared up to the needs of individual exam board specifications and making a feature out of online discussions and student participation. There are specialist packs, for instance for the AQA pre-seen case study. Subjects covered are A level economics, listed under AS and A2; business studies, listed under accounting and finance; marketing, people and organisations and government and politics.

Further features include:

- Interactive quizzes

- Extensive revision notes

- Discussion boards

- Advice for students

- Materials for GCSE economics, rare these days

- A current accounts section which enables visitors to view a selection of recent articles with links to other sections

- Online shop

- *EconoMax* magazine

Recent additions to the offer are the *GCSE Business Studies Powerbundle*, a suite of resources comprising presentations, study notes and Q & As and AQA unit guides and the *European Economics Toolkit*, in virtual textbook format.

There are Powerpoint presentations, some of which need to be purchased. These need careful use – they are summaries of topics supported by wide-ranging data which the teacher would need to research ahead of use. The Business Café is a service available by subscription, providing one-page summaries of recent business news stories, written to incorporate analysis and using terms relevant to exam specifications. This has to be highly recommended as a site for students to use with teacher advice. It is popular in the weeks leading up to the exam season.

www.bbc.co.uk/schools/gcsebitesize

This is a suite of resources, known mainly as a revision aid, though it has potential for wider use. It is useful for GCSE Business Studies, whatever the awarding body, but economics is sadly missing from GCSE, and AS Guru covers neither. There is a *GCSE Bitesize* revision book and a 'Check and test'. The book is good value at £2.00. There is also an accompanying video. Each topic in the book has a double-page spread with good use of colour, particularly to highlight key terms. Other features worth noting:

- A topic checker allowing students to self-assess their knowledge of topics;
- Short answer questions making this resource accessible to most pupils;
- Exam advice;
- Answers to the questions.

The website has interactive quizzes and SOS teacher allowing pupils to send questions if stuck with homework or revision. It is colourful and looks lively. One interesting section which teachers might usefully incorporate into their teaching early in the course relates to motivation tips, mind maps and teach yourself skills such as essay-writing. Students find the site helpful and can use it alone or as part of school-based revision.

CHAPTER 27

Revision materials

There is currently something of an industry in providing materials to help students revise. There is a danger inherent in revision materials in that they provide scope for students to believe they can coast in the knowledge that a sum of money expended at the appropriate eleventh hour will provide all the notes they have not taken: in some sense a replacement for the course. At GCSE, a revision guide is almost considered *de rigueur* in the author's school. Parents give further weight to this trend. On the plus side, if excellent notes exist, teachers can concentrate their efforts on skill development, discussions and active learning. In addition, the best revision tools now combine notes with exercises, self-evaluation, exam tips, etc. Added to the journals and online advice, a veritable avalanche.

Among the most popular are:

Student Unit Guides
Published by Philip Allan Updates, price £5.95. Students like these because they are tied closely to particular units of specific awarding bodies. In Business Studies, OCR (Units 1, 2, 3 and A2 Unit 2880) and AQA (Units 1, 2, 3, 4, 5W, 6) are covered, in Economics, OCR (Units 1, 3 and A2 Unit 2888), AQA (Units 1, 2, 3, 5, 6) and Edexcel (Units 2, 4, 6). The books are small (maximum 85 pages) but pack in content guidance and key terms, sample questions and answers with examiner comment. There is suggested analysis and evaluation for each topic which can make them useful for formative assessment activities. The notes are excellent material for 'the night before'. There are also books of exam revision notes, price £9.95.

The 'Soak it Up' Series. AS Business Studies in a Week (also A2)
Published by Letts, £7.99, written by Steve Dalton. These consist of a timed revision programme of 'intensive one-week courses', 'designed to give you the best results in the shortest time'.

The AS book has 14 units, plus exam practice questions and answers (essential). The units are structured to fill 4 pages, starting with 'How much do you know?' questions, with answers at the foot of the page, 'Learn the key facts', which strips the topic to its essentials, and a 'Have you improved?' timed test with tips (answers at the back of the book). Unfortunately the questions do not have marks attached, so there is no practice in allocating time, but students enjoy the appealing simplicity of approach, and attractive layout, and for those who need to revise the very basics (heaven forbid) this is good value.

Business Studies for AS Revision Guide
Andrew Hammond and Marie Brewer
Hodder Arnold
0-3408-1106-4 ▪ £8.99 ▪ 2004 ▪ 144pp

This is particularly directed towards the AQA award, though much of the content could relate to other boards. All the authors are experienced examiners. This is a much weightier book. As the cover points out, it does not promise miracles in a week. It is a 'serious book for students who want to know what and how to revise'.

The book is divided into 53 sections, following the AS specifications, and each beginning with a number of questions – What?, Which?, How?, etc. There are boxes giving exam insights, student howlers (common mistakes which are corrected at the back), themes for evaluation and test-yourself boxes. The layout is less racy than other revision books, reflecting the authors' objectives. A particularly useful section contains the unit revision checklists to help students highlight their areas of weakness. There is also advice on exam skills, the meaning of terms such as application and analysis, and answers. Teachers may find the advice on the pre-issue case study well worth studying. Given the breadth of content, the book is excellent value.

Business Studies Update: The Student Guide to Business
Gary Cook
Hidcote Press

Published annually, this book is priced £3.50, but discounts are available for large orders. Essentially, these are booklets (48 pages, A5 size) which give a rundown of the most important events/issues over the previous year. The topics, therefore, may vary, but examples would be:

- Business finance
- Human resources
- Technology
- Manufacturing and service sectors
- Human resources red tape and regulation

- Shareholder power
- International markets
- Inflation
- Unemployment
- The balance of payments

The text is excellent for teachers, with minimal time to keep up to date with changes, including details of recent legislation and trends, for example in business investment. There are useful graphs and tables of statistical information. The books have the merit of being short and could be used in class in the period running up to the examination. Useful for Advanced Extension Award candidates or those going for interview.

Flash Revise Cards

Published by Philip Allan Updates, £5.95 per box of cards. The boxes are slightly larger than a box of playing cards; the cards have questions on one side, definitions of key terms and answers on the other, and many students like this rather different format. There are six boxes for A level Business Studies, each one based on one unit of the AQA GCE specifications. Good for individual revision and most students can afford them. A small number of sets would make a useful classroom resource or provide the questions for economics/business versions of quizzes, *The Weakest Link*, *Blockbusters* (for those of us old enough to remember), *Who wants to be a millionaire?* As such, they could be used by candidates for all specifications.

Foundations of Wealth

Written by Antony Jay (The Production Tree Limited), ten videos, on average lasting ten minutes, price £99.99. This series was first produced to great acclaim in the 1980s with the objective of increasing economic literacy. The programmes present economic principles through documentary material and animation and are recommended by Professor Milton Friedman, no less. The videos have been updated (changed accents and slightly different outfits and characterisation and more contemporary documentary sections). They ask how some communities became developed, and the answers to this question form the topics of the videos: division of labour, producing an economic surplus, specialisation, capital formation, supply and demand, money, trade, etc.

The aim of the series is to make these abstractions come visibly to life through a series of cartoon mini-films. Each section reiterates the learning points of the previous one. Each video has an accompanying worksheet, supplied on disk for networking. The videos are basic and could be used to introduce pupils of Year 9 or younger to economics, for instance as part of a citizenship course. Some, especially the second video, numbers 6–10, are useful for early lessons in GCSE, particularly those on the development of markets in which complex ideas are explained well in accessible language. There is considerable emphasis in the first video on specialisation and division of labour, probably in more detail than one would want for GCSE. There is a certain charming 'naffness' about them now, which pupils often like. The author has had more than one upper-sixth economics class asking to see the *Foundations of Wealth* videos as a treat for their final lesson – the one where the sheep eats her skirt! They do make some early concepts both fun and very clear and link them directly to our standard of living. Teachers should think carefully about their specific students, but as a whole-school resource, this is valuable. If economics and business teachers don't use it, someone else will.

BBC Video Workpacks

Available from Holdsworth Associates, 42 Boxworth End, Swavesey, Cambridge CB4 5RA (tel. 01954 232789). This resource consists of 14 packs based on the 'Back to the Floor' series. Each pack is £29.45 and comes in a plastic box file containing a copy of the video, and a set of photocopiable activity sheets. The activities are also on a CD-ROM which can be networked for easy access by students. The packs vary as to level of difficulty and appropriateness for exam specifications. Hence, careful selection is needed, but the activity sheets can be very useful. One of the best aspects are the Powerpoint presentations which students have to complete from headings or questions already on the slides. Comparing the resulting mini-presentations is a useful stimulus to discussion. By way of an example, number 6, *Sausage Wars* has the following sections: 'Understanding the market', 'Forming a limited company', 'Shareholders', 'Consumer laws', 'Small business and the Law', 'Business ethics', 'Closing down a business', 'How can good businesses fail?' 'SWOT analysis'. There are suggested answers for each section. By selecting materials, the programmes can be made relevant for A level, AVCE and GCSE classes. They might also form part of general studies or citizenship courses with older pupils. Good activities, making for easy lesson preparation.

Resource packs

Most packs consist of photocopiable materials for students and other support for teachers.

Anforme photocopiable resources packs

Written by teachers, writers and examiners in the field of A Level Economics, published by Anforme Limited, www.economics.ac, price either £30 or £35, depending upon the pack. These can be divided into groups according to their name:

- *10 Top Topics* in

    Development Economics

    Business Economics

    International Trade and Globalisation

Each of these contains 10 topics, units or cases. Most include a summary of the main points, some include supplementary data and all include questions for discussion. Includes suggested answers.

- *Current Issues* in

    Macroeconomics

    Microeconomics

Again, 10 topics/issues, each explained using A level language and concepts with a summary of key points and questions for discussion.

- *10 Case Studies* – in *Economics*

These look almost exactly like the *Current Issues* and *Top Topics* packs.

All of the above make useful additions to a basic textbook. The readings tend to be longer than an average case study and could be used to set work to extend more able candidates, as the basis of group presentations to class, research material for essays, preparatory reading, or for homework. They have the very great merit, therefore, of encouraging students to undertake wider reading in a form convenient to themselves. They are not organised or selected as to their applicability to AS or A2, so teachers will have to check content and questions for relevance to their specifications and to ensure that their candidates (particularly AS) can cope.

As with all resources which seek to provide or use current examples, they are subject to dating. One way round this is to ask students to do the updating as an exercise, or to compare actual with predicted outcomes.

Basic Economics and More Basic Economics

These are based on the 'Back to Basic' series in *Economics Today* which give a detailed explanation of a particular concept in economics, often with current examples. Useful reading to reinforce material studies in class.

Easy Mark Economics Exercises for AS Level

29 sections each dealing with a different topic, using a variety of questions and suggested answers.